The Secret Life of
Families

BANTAM BOOKS

New York · Toronto
London · Sydney
Auckland

The
SECRET LIFE
of
FAMILIES

*Truth-Telling, Privacy,
and Reconciliation in
a Tell-All Society*

Evan Imber-Black,
Ph.D.

THE SECRET LIFE OF FAMILIES
A Bantam Book / March 1998

Excerpt on p. 54 © Copyright National Public Radio, Inc. 1994. The news commentary by NPR's Edward Ball was originally broadcast on NPR's "Weekend Edition®, Saturday" on March 26, 1994 and is used with the permission of National Public Radio, Inc. Any unauthorized duplication is strictly prohibited.

Excerpt on p. 124 reprinted by permission of the publishers and the Trustees of Amherst College from THE POEMS OF EMILY DICKINSON, Thomas H. Johnson, ed., Cambridge, Mass.: The Belknap Press of Harvard University Press, Copyright © 1951, 1955, 1979, 1983 by the President and Fellows of Harvard College.

Book design by Susan Yuran.

Library of Congress Cataloging-in-Publication Data

Imber-Black, Evan.
The secret life of families : truth-telling, privacy, and reconciliation in a tell-all society / Evan Imber-Black.
p.   cm.
Includes bibliographical references and index.
ISBN 0-553-10094-7
I. Family psychotherapy.   2. Confidential communications—
Family therapists.   3. Communication in the family.
4. Family—Mental health.   5. Secrecy—Psychological aspects.
6. Shame.   7. Reconciliation.   I. Title.
RC488.5.I45   1998
616.89'156—dc21   97-35287   CIP

Published simultaneously in the United States and Canada

Bantam Books are published by Bantam Books, a division of Bantam Doubleday Dell Publishing Group, Inc. Its trademark, consisting of the words "Bantam Books" and the portrayal of a rooster, is Registered in U.S. Patent and Trademark Office and in other countries. Marca Registrada.
Bantam Books, 1540 Broadway, New York, New York 10036.

Printed in the United States of America
BVG/10   9   8   7   6   5   4   3   2   1

WITH LOVE TO MY GRANDDAUGHTER,
JOSEPHINE CHARITY BLACK,
FOR ALL THE SWEET SECRETS
OF YOUR TOMORROWS

CONTENTS

ACKNOWLEDGMENTS

So many caring and openhearted people helped me to bring forth this book. I want to thank Judith Stone, who served as "midwife" to my proposal. Our spirited conversations in coffee shops around New York, coupled with her thoughtful ideas and early editing, led me in the right direction. Thanks to Elizabeth Stone for our talks about secrets and the book proposal. And I thank Katy Butler, who collaborated with me on the 1993 article "Ghosts in the Therapy Room," beginning my wish to translate my scholarly work on secrets for a lay readership.

My dear friend and colleague Janine Roberts supported this project through careful reading of and mindful responses to the proposal and the manuscript, and through her constant availability.

This book builds upon the academic book *Secrets in Families and Family Therapy*, which I edited in 1993. An outstanding group of colleagues contributed to that book and to my current thinking about secrets. I want to thank Marilyn Mason, Rosmarie Welter-Enderlin, Peggy Papp, Ann Hartman, Judith A. Schaffer, Ronny Diamond, Lorraine Wright, Jane Nagy, Jo-Ann Krestan, Claudia Bepko, Laura Roberto Forman, Dusty Miller, Gus Kaufman, Gary L. Sanders, Joan Laird, Sally Ann Roth, Alan Cooklin, Gill Gorell Barnes, Nancy Boyd-Franklin, Lascelles W. Black, Kathy Weingarten, and Janine Roberts for their early collaboration with me, opening the topic of secrets in the family therapy field.

This book took its original shape under the thoughtful guidance of my agent, Beth Vesel. Her enthusiasm for my ideas and her strong belief in the need for this book were an anchor throughout the process.

Toni Burbank was all I could possibly wish for as my editor. At our initial meeting she offered me her excitement about this work. Her probing questions, at once firm and gentle, helped me to clarify and expand my thoughts. In her outstanding editing, she addressed the lives of the people in these pages with care and compassion. I also want to thank Toni's assistant, Robin Michaelson, for attending to the many details connected to organizing this manuscript.

My loving friend Rosmarie Welter-Enderlin spent hours and hours reading the manuscript, sending me incisive comments, and helping me to reach more deeply into the meaning of secrets. Our transatlantic Sunday afternoon telephone talks, our train rides from one European city to the next, and the meals we cooked together in our kitchens in New York and Switzerland were all occasions to talk about secrets, professional and personal.

I have been blessed with a professional partnership and special friendship with Peggy Papp at the Ackerman Institute for the Family. When we began our work, I wanted to do a clinical project on secrets. Peggy astutely observed that we might have trouble getting families to come to a project called "Family Secrets." Nonetheless, as we have worked together every Wednesday afternoon for the past seven years, we've seen many families struggling either to open secrets or to deal with the emotional aftermath once a secret is revealed. Our mutual consultations with each other, both in the therapy room and behind the one-way mirror, along with our many nights at the theater, have contributed powerfully to my ideas about secrets.

So many dear friends showered me with their interest in this project and their abiding support of my work. My deep appreciation goes to Pat Colucci, Ellen Landau, Gary Sanders, Betty Carter, Olga Silverstein, Vicki Dickerson, and Paul Browde.

During much of the writing of this book, I was the director of Family and Group Studies and director of the Urban Institute for Families and Family Therapy Training at the Albert Einstein College of Medicine in the Bronx, New York. I was fortunate to have a loyal faculty whose belief in me and encouragement of my work made it a joy to do. I especially thank Maddy Abrams, Johnine Cummings, Judy Cobb, Barbara Iwler, Anne Shollar, Myrna Hernandez, Eliana Korin, and Linda Torres. I also thank Seth Aronson for sharing his ideas on children and HIV/AIDS.

There are not enough words of praise and appreciation for Marie Mele, my secretary, confidant, recipe swapper, and caring family friend for the past decade. Marie kept track of every task related to preparing this manuscript, never let me walk out of the office with the only copy of a chapter, and helped me deal with the mysterious and continual freezing of my computer every time I worked on chapter 4. Her loving humor and bountiful hugs kept me going.

During the writing of this book I had many conversations with my mother, Dena Imber, about secrets. Some were funny, some were painful, most were moving, and all connected me to her and her eighty-four years of life. I thank her for her generous conversation and her unflagging support of my work.

For a quarter of a century, scores of individuals and families have opened their lives to me. Their stories and their courageous journeys, written here in highly disguised forms, have profoundly shaped the therapist and the writer that I am. I thank them all, with respect and humility.

This book was given the breath of life by my loving family. My son, Jason Black, my daughter-in-law, Frances Schroeder, my sweet granddaughter, Josephine Charity Black, my daughter, Jennifer Coppersmith, and my soon-to-be son-in-law, David Bukai, all give me constant love, support, and care. My special thanks to Jason for his technical help, thereby preventing my murdering the computer, and for his willing spur-of-the moment Internet searches.

And finally, I give my love and appreciation to my husband, Lascelles W. Black, for all our learning to hold each other's secrets tenderly; our long talks connecting secrets with racism; his careful thinking about skin color secrets; his inspiring work with people with AIDS and their crucial secrets; his commitment to compassion and justice, which always encourages me; his vision that I could write this book; and his generosity, which has made it possible for me to do so.

PREFACE

In early 1997 a secret broke open on the American national scene—our new secretary of state, Madeline Albright, discovered that she was born to Jewish parents who converted to Catholicism during World War II. Her Czechoslovakian Jewish grandparents died in concentration camps during the Holocaust. And Albright herself was raised with no knowledge of her Jewish legacy. Interest in Madeline Albright's story was intense. For a few weeks my telephone rang almost daily with reporters wanting to know my views on her secret. "How could this be?" they asked me. "How could she not have known?" "Why wasn't she curious about her own grandparents?" "She's a historian of Central Europe—surely she knew and just kept it hidden." Harsh and critical judgments abounded, but my own thoughts were quite different. It made perfect sense to me that Madeline Albright not only did not know as a child that her parents were Jewish, but also showed no interest in her grandparents' personal history *and* chose to become a historian of that very part of the world that held her family's secret. I started to imagine her family. Her parents must have created a seamless story, complete with reminiscences of childhood Christmas celebrations. The only mention of her grandparents was that they died during the war. Like so many children I've worked with in family therapy, Madeline Albright lived with a powerful paradox, absorbing the family "rule" not to ask, to live in the present, and to believe her loving parents, while at the same time feeling a compelling pull toward the past, toward history, toward Central Europe. The exquisite combination of her family injunctions and her career choice would make her a historian with personal blinders. And because she chose a public life, when her family's secret finally opened, it was quickly claimed by a nation hungry for other people's secrets.

I've been a family therapist for twenty-five years. From the beginning, I've been privileged to guide, to walk alongside, to intervene, and to serve as a witness for people struggling with secrets. As a young therapist, I sought direction from leaders in my field: Should I help families open secrets? Were there some secrets that should never open? What if I met with an individual who told me a secret and then insisted that I hold the secret from his family? I found surprisingly few answers. The professional literature was sparse where secrets were concerned, prompting me to think that secrets were a secret in the family therapy field. The literature that existed was polarized and absolute: "never open secrets" or "always open secrets." I was told by my mentors never to keep a secret with one member of a family, and never to let family members call me individually between sessions, because someone might tell me a secret. While one supervisor told me always to be direct about secrets, another told me always to be indirect about secrets. I was taught to make little speeches at the start of any new therapy: "Please don't tell me any secrets, because if you do, I'll have to insist that these be shared with the whole family." It didn't take me long to realize that this rap prompted people to hide important issues in therapy, the very place where silenced voices should be heard. I began to think that secrets, which generated so much heat but very little light in my profession, deserved my very careful attention. And so began my two-decade-long search to enable thoughtful and effective responses to the relationship kaleidoscope spun by secrets.

I quickly became dissatisfied with family therapy models that taught me simply to focus on what went on inside a family, as if families did not exist in complex ecologies that impact their daily lives. The families I knew who were coping with secrets brought with them rich and often painful histories from their own families of origin; stories of migration, war, sexism, and racism; tangled webs of relationships with institutions—work, schools, hospitals, churches, and synagogues; and an embeddedness in a wider culture that shaped their beliefs about secrecy and openness.

During my own search to discover ways to work well with the incredible range of secrets that took up temporary residence in my consulting room, I watched as the meaning of secrets changed in our society. Secrets have existed throughout time, but today's families face special dilemmas about secrecy, privacy, silence, and openness. We live in a culture whose messages about secrecy are confounding. We're told the stigma attached to alcoholism, drug addiction, adoption, mental illness, cancer, or divorce is gone. But is it? The families I see still struggle with decisions of how and when to tell children that their mother has a drinking problem, that their father's been downsized, that a brother has manic-depressive illness. And while the heavy social disgrace previously driving certain secrets, such as divorce, may have melted away, new secrets have taken their place. I meet now with individuals, couples, and families in turmoil about whether to tell a grandmother that her grandson has AIDS or when to tell a child that her biological father was a sperm donor.

We're told in a daily diet of talk shows to "let it all hang out," only to discover that mimicking what we see on *Sally*, *Geraldo*, or *Montel* can get us into serious trouble in our own intimate relationships. Prescriptive self-help literature and a proliferation of twelve-step programs remind us that "we're only as sick as our secrets," promoting total openness while ignoring the complicated consequences to our relationships when we follow such advice. In the spring of 1997 a new cable television venture, the Recovery Network, began to broadcast twenty-four-hour-a-day, seven-day-a-week secret-telling by "addicts" of every imaginable stripe, adding to an already overloaded context of voyeurism and pseudo-openness.

As the cultural trend toward one-size-fits-all rules where secrets are concerned has grown louder and more pervasive, my own experience with families has moved me increasingly toward a position I call "it all depends." In a quarter of a century, I have never met two families whose experiences with secrets are exactly alike. I've grown to respect and even welcome the messy complexity adhering to every secret.

In 1993 I edited an academic book, *Secrets in Families and Family Therapy*. I invited twenty-three authors to explore the topic of secrets from many perspectives, including the historical context that gives life to any particular secret and pattern of secret-keeping; the many systems in a family's life that influence decisions about secrecy and openness; the ways in which family communication, relationships, emotions, identity, and issues of trust and reliability are affected by secrets; distinctions between secrecy and privacy; how secrets affect well-being; and how each therapist worked with the individual and relational aftermath when a secret is opened. The range of responses was stunning, underscoring my belief that every secret is like a member of a family, reflecting familiar patterns handed down generation after generation, while simultaneously embodying its own unique soul.

I decided to write this book in order to offer readers a way to think about the secrets in their own lives and to revisit decisions they may have made about secrecy and openness with a new lens, a lens that shifts from the wide angle of our culture to the close-up snapshot of our next family dinner. I've written this book in order to make explicit the usually implicit or largely unnoticed connections among societal values; cultural meanings; institutional pressures; family-of-origin themes, beliefs, and patterns; and each of our specific daily attempts to come to terms with secrecy and openness with the people we love and cherish.

I've organized this book in a fashion that is similar to the way I think about secrets. Every person I've known who decides to wrestle with a particular secret faces a special set of circumstances that they've never experienced. The outcome is always uncertain. At the same time, this struggle is a part of the universal human experience. Common dilemmas, important distinctions between secrecy and privacy, and categories that I've found useful in thinking about secrets open this book.

Making a secret, keeping a secret, opening a secret—all shape and alter our most important relationships. When I first meet an individual, a couple, or a family struggling with a secret, we begin by looking at the impact of the secret on their lives. I turn in chapter 2 to a discussion of the ways secrets sculpt our close relationships with our parents, siblings, spouses, children, and dear friends.

When I encounter any secret, I work with my clients to explore the wider context of their experience and the decisions they face. Together we look at societal beliefs about secrets, particularly as these are promulgated in the popular media. We examine the influences from their ethnicity, race, religion, gender, and social class. We explore the history lived by their family—war, migration, economic changes. We think about ways that institutions have impacted secrets in their lives—medical secrets, adoption, mental illness, infertility, sexual abuse, death. In chapters 3, 4, and 5 I've written about the deep and far-reaching consequences of these larger systems on the secrets in our lives.

Crucial decisions about concealment and revelation follow in chapter 6, coming only after we've considered all of the levels that contribute to any secret.

Secrets are born, live, grow, change, harden, or dissolve inside individuals, in couples, between parents and children, and among adult siblings and aging parents. Seeing the family as a dynamic organism with critical life-cycle changes organizes my thinking and actions about every secret. Secrets may be created or shattered at key moments in a family's development—a wedding, the birth of a child, a death. Alternatively, they may be made or opened at times that alter a family's expectable path—an illness, a rape, an addiction, a suicide. Couples make and break commitments, children are born and grow, adolescents explore the boundaries of life in and outside the family, young adults leave home, parents age, and family members die as the cycle repeats and repeats. In the midst of all of this, secrets change us and our relationships in unpredictable ways. The second half of the book, including chapters 7 through 11, is organized to give perspective on how secrets my clients and I have encountered dramatically alter life at various points in the family life cycle.

Questions that my clients and I have struggled with frame this book: "When do I have the right to keep a secret? Who has a responsibility to open a secret? How do I know the time is right to maintain a secret or open it? How do I make it safe for myself and others? What are my obligations to the people I love where secrets are concerned?" In my work, I've found no pat answers to these questions. In the past quarter-century, sometimes with doubt and sometimes with humility, I've learned from people who decide that it is not the time to open a painful secret, that to do so would risk more than might be gained. I've witnessed—sometimes with terror and more often with joy, and always with deep respect—families making the courageous journey from secrecy to openness. Their stories are the life force of this book. I offer this book with my hope that it will enable readers to embrace the complexities of secrets, and in so doing bring forth their own informed judgments, ethical positions, and imagined futures as they meet the secrets in their own lives.

AUTHOR'S NOTE

Ironically, I suppose, a book about secrets must itself harbor a number of secrets. The names, identifying characteristics, and other details of the case studies presented in this book have been changed to protect the privacy and preserve the confidences of individuals and their families. In very few instances, information from two or more cases have been combined to form composites, which further serve to disguise identities. Readers who believe they recognize any of the people described in these case studies will inevitably be mistaken.

Part
I

~

*Secrets in a
Talk Show
Age*

Chapter

I

Living the
Dilemmas

➤

Secrecy is as indispensable to human beings as fire, and as greatly feared. Both enhance and protect life, yet both can stifle, lay waste, spread out of all control. Both can be used to guard intimacy or to invade it, to nurture or to consume. And each can be turned against itself: barriers of secrecy are set up to guard against secret plots and surreptitious prying, just as fire is used to fight fire.

—*Sisela Bok*

TOUCH A FAMILY DEEPLY and you will likely find a secret. We may keep secrets from our spouses, our siblings, our parents, our children, our best friends. Or we may create secrets with these very same people. There are secrets an entire family keeps from the outside world, longing for protection and fearing stigmatization: that a daughter was born five months after a wedding; that a mother's month-long "vacation" was a stay at a drug rehabilitation center; that a father's humiliating job loss was simply his choice to "change his lifestyle"; or that a supposedly English grandfather was a light-skinned black man from the West Indies. There are secrets from children, driven by an illusory hope that they can be protected from pain: that a father is really a stepfather, or that a mother is in prison and not "traveling." There are secrets everyone knows, such as Dad's alcoholism, that prevent a family from reaching beyond its own rigidly defended borders for needed help. And there are secrets, such as AIDS or homosexuality, kept out of the realistic fear of losing family support, a job, an apartment, a school placement, or a friendship. There are secrets the powerless keep from the powerful in order to gain safety, and secrets by which the tyrannical coerce the disenfranchised.

A secret may be silently and unknowingly passed from generation to generation, like a booby-trapped heirloom. A young girl becomes pregnant before marriage and is thrown out of her family home. Ten years later, she discovers that her mother had been pregnant with her before her parents married and was made to leave her family in a break that never healed. A young girl pulls out her hair and is excoriated by her mother for her "self-destructive" behavior. Kept from the child is the secret of her own grandmother's death by heroin overdose, a death her mother valiantly and frantically tried to prevent, a death she speaks of as "self-destructive."

Or a secret may be made tomorrow morning and quickly grab hold like an uninvited weed in the garden, sending thorny branches into every corner of a family's life.

Clearly, no secret stands in isolation. In my work with people who are wrestling to make decisions about secrets—"Do I tell? Do I keep silent? If I tell, whom do I tell?"—it's become apparent to me that every conceivable secret lives in a complicated web of family and social history, past and current relationships, powerful emotions, intense beliefs, attributed meanings, and an imagined future.

While no two sources, instances, or contexts of secrecy are exactly alike, the complications and ambiguities engendered by secrets stir us to declare absolutes—"always tell" or "never tell." Over the years my clients, my trainees, and journalists have pressed me for one-size-fits-all rules to cope with secrets: "Should spouses tell each other everything? At what age should our children hear our family secrets? Are all secrets bad for my relationships?" Popular self-help literature of the last two decades has added to our misguided belief that we can find one answer that fits every situation. The longer I've worked with families and their secrets, the more convinced I've become that we need to eschew such unsatisfying oversimplification and stretch our capacity to inhabit the complexities posed by secrets.

LIVING OUTSIDE A SECRET

Gisela Kroch was thirty-eight when I met her. Recently divorced from her American husband, with whom she had lived in Austria, she described a life at once preoccupied and bewildered by her single-minded desire to "be American."

"Ever since I was a young child, I wanted to live in the United States. I had no interest in anything to do with Austria, in the village where I was born in 1948, or even in the history of my family. As soon as I could, I learned English, and spent my teen years reading American literature and listening to American music. As a little child, my fascination with the United States was met by stony silence from my mother and anger from my father. My requests for English storybooks went unmet. As a teen, I began to proclaim that I would one day leave and go live in America. My parents and I would fight endlessly about this, furthering my resolve to go. My brother told me I was ridiculous. Always I felt his closeness to my parents, especially to my father, in contrast to my own sense of distance, my lack of belonging. I had few friends. I spent a lot of my time watching American movies, reading American magazines, thinking about American fashions."

Gisela grew up wanting some connection with her mother and aware of a certain sadness that never seemed to disappear from her mother's eyes. "I truly began to enjoy the anger I could provoke in both of my parents when I would go on and on about America. In my family, it was either anger or silence. I hated the silence. I never understood it until very recently."

About a month before I met Gisela, she had gone to visit her parents' home. As she walked in the door, she heard her mother and father yelling at each other. Unaware of her presence, her parents shouted out the mystery that had oriented Gisela's choices in life and had shaped her identity. Transfixed, Gisela listened as her parents tore at each other over unspoken events from four decades earlier.

During World War II, Gisela's father had been taken prisoner by the American army and lived for two years in a prisoner-of-war camp in the United States. At the end of the war, while her father was still missing, Gisela's mother had a brief and surreptitious affair with an American soldier. Gisela's brother, then twelve, caught his mother with her lover and revealed her secret to his father when he returned home. Two years later, as her parents struggled to remake their marriage, Gisela was born into a family marked by obvious but unspoken pain. The story was never told in her presence. Indeed, care was taken to maintain the silence.

"For years I watched my mother being tormented by my father's cruel words. He criticized everything she did, and I so wanted her to stand up to him. Only now do I see that she must have thought she deserved how he treated her. Whose feelings was I voicing every time I spoke of wanting to live in America? How did I manage to choose an American husband who happened to be visiting Austria?"

Gisela lived outside of a central family secret until just before I met her. No doubt sensing an unspoken mystery, she organized her entire life in response to all that had gone underground in her family. She became the repository for all of the family's anxiety stemming from what happened during the war. And while World War II may have ended, Allied and Axis battles raged on in this family's confusing and bitter relationships. Swirls of furtive anger, guilt, betrayal, and sadness congealed in a child's fantasies of a distant land, in an adolescent's provocative exclamations, in a young woman's impulsive marital choice. With a poignancy common to those who discover that their central decisions in life have been made with a lack of crucial information, Gisela told me, "Now I have to rethink my entire life."

LIVING INSIDE A SECRET

Living outside a central family secret can shape identity and behavior, generate feelings of self-doubt, distance, and suspicion, and contribute to key decisions that are made without sufficient information. Living inside a secret may propagate a strange mixture of responsibility, power, anxiety, protectiveness, shame, burden, and fear. Much depends on how you came to live inside a secret. Are you the initiator of a secret? Are you the recipient of someone else's confidence? Are you keeping a secret freely, by coercion, or with some complicated blend of keeping a trust in one relationship while feeling simultaneously guilty for doing so in another relationship?

The complexity of living inside a secret can be heard in many voices:

- "Which is more important," Seymour asked me in our first therapy session, "that I'm lying every day to my daughter or that I'm insulating her from the pain of knowing that my wife is dying?" Seymour came to see me when his daughter, Janice, was eleven and his wife, Esther, was in the terminal stages of bone cancer. "She knows that Mommy has a 'back problem' and needs to stay in bed. Everyone I talk to says she'll find out soon enough. I don't know what to do." Here, love and protection were knotted up with fear and deception. As we talked I realized it would be my job to help Seymour question and expand his own definition of what it means to help a child feel safe in the midst of frightening and tragic loss. Living outside this palpable secret, Janice had begun to wake up several times a night to "check on Mommy." Living inside the secret, Seymour realized he was holding his daughter at arm's length at the very time that he needed to comfort her.

- "I'm the only one in the family who knows that my mother still abuses her tranquilizers," Karen said.

"Everyone else believes that she's recovered. Frankly, it gives me a certain power in relationship to her. She knows I know, and it backs her off me in ways that I like. I'd rather just keep it that way." Karen had chosen to use secret knowledge of her mother's drug addiction to gain a sense of advantage in a painful relationship, feeling it was the best she could get. Only as we talked further did she begin to think about how this also affected her relationships with everyone else in her family, promoting distance, feelings of being cut off, and resentment between her and her two brothers. Karen's predicament does not yield to simplistic solutions. "If I open my mother's secret, I guess I need to be prepared to change a lot of things in my relationship with her. I think I'd feel more responsible and more vulnerable. If I don't open it, my relationship with my brothers stays superficial and remote."

· "I hate family gatherings. I don't want to go to one more Thanksgiving where I have to be polite and cordial to my uncle," Cathy told me. Cathy's uncle lived upstairs from her widowed mother's apartment. He had sexually abused her all during the early part of her adolescence. "Opening this would blow apart my whole family. My mother needs my aunt. My uncle relies on my staying loyal to my mother—that's how he knew he could get away with this. He can't hurt me anymore, but it just eats at me that he stays protected by my devotion to my mother." As she went on to describe to me her belief that living was a series of damned-if-you-do-and-damned-if-you-don't choices, it became clear that Cathy's sense of being trapped by this secret permeated all of her relationships and paralyzed her sense of herself in life.

· "He thinks keeping the secret of being gay from his parents is just his decision, but it affects me, too." Cal and Jim had come for couples' therapy. Cal was open about his homosexuality to his family, friends, and co-workers. Jim had told almost no one. "This secret makes me feel he's ashamed of our relationship. We spend every holiday apart. I worked hard to be open and here I am, living *his* secret life!" Jim just slowly shook his head while Cal spoke. "I'm sorry my decision not to tell has become his burden, but I know my parents. I keep feeling as though I have to choose between losing Cal and losing them."

Over the years, many of my clients and I have struggled to respond to the complex questions that dog life inside a secret. While the answers have differed in every instance, reminding me each time that secrets never yield to easy formulas, the questions arise in every careful conversation: "Whose responsibility is it to open a secret, especially if the content of the secret is about another person? When is it okay to break a promise I may have made to keep a secret? If I open one secret, does that mean I have to open others? How do I determine whom to tell? Do I know best what another person should know? When does keeping a secret slip over the line from protection to arrogance? And how do I weigh the seeming certainty of silence against the unpredictability of speaking the previously unspeakable?"

WHEN SECRETS AFFECT OUR RELATIONSHIP TO SELF AND OTHERS

Secrets are born, draw breath, stay alive, explode, or resolve in our most meaningful relationships. They shape, allow, and constrain possibilities to connect both within and outside the family. They are kept or opened by nations, cultures, institutions, families, and individuals. The decision to create and keep a secret has deep and complicated roots. While it is simple to say that we keep secret the things we are ashamed of and the things we fear we cannot face, the complex issues that we need to address reside in both the genesis and dissolution of such shame and fear. Intimidation by others may drive and underpin our silences. The fear of losing a spouse, a dear friend, a job, or one's own sense of self may lead us to nail the closet door shut. Or we may keep secrets to protect the people we love, and then find ourselves mired in a confusing morass of protection and deception that erodes the very relationships we were hoping to preserve. And sometimes we keep secrets to protect ourselves or to secure power, and in so doing betray spouses, parents, siblings, children, or friends.

Any given secret can serve to paralyze our sense of self and our position vis-à-vis others. Flexibility in response to problems, the capacity to change our relation to others, and our own ability to expand and grow over time often disappear when we feel trapped in a web of secrecy.

While the creation or dissolution of a secret can occur at any moment, many secrets get made or opened at periods of intense relationship change, such as marriage, divorce, the birth of a child, leaving home, or death. A secret constructed at such key developmental points can stop the natural unfolding process. Relationships that would ordinarily change and grow become frozen in time, as the presence of a secret locks people in place. A secret opened at the instant of other core changes—before a wedding or just after a death—can provoke upheaval in family relationships, producing confusion rather than clarity.

WHEN WORDS ARE MISSING, ACTIONS TAKE THEIR PLACE

Elana Sokel, ten years old, looked sad and frightened while her mother angrily described to me how the police had brought her home two nights earlier after a shopkeeper had caught her trying to steal a scarf. "This is the third time this year—they're going to take you away if you don't stop this," her mother shouted, while Elana cringed and remained silent. "I don't understand—she's always been the best of my children until this year." What could be happening in the life of this little girl and in her family to explain her behavior to her bewildered mother? I wondered. The youngest of three, Elana had indeed been a good and popular student. But for several months now, she had come home alone every day and had stopped playing with her friends, who used to be at her house constantly. Her most recent report card described a little girl increasingly in trouble. Elana just shook her head and remained mute when I asked her what she thought was happening. Later that afternoon I met with her mother alone.

"My husband is in prison for embezzlement. Elana doesn't know. My sons and I have told her he's working overseas. He calls her once a week. When he was first arrested, she was only eight years old. I hid the newspaper stories and just hoped no one in the neighborhood would say anything. Mostly she doesn't ask about him, so I don't think it's on her mind too much. Lately she asks why I won't buy her certain toys. It doesn't make sense for me to tell her we can't afford them. She doesn't know there's no money coming in. Now that she's getting into so much trouble, I feel even more strongly that I shouldn't tell her about her dad. I just hope no one finds out about her shoplifting—people are going to think this runs in our family." The shame that enveloped her words filled the room. No doubt Elana was tasting this shame every day with her breakfast cereal before she left the house and yet was mystified by its source.

Behavior like Elana's at first seems very mysterious and un-explainable. Why would a delightful little girl begin to shoplift? Only when we hear about the secret that is being kept from her about her father's criminal behavior and incarceration does her behavior begin to make sense.

Not knowing the content of the secret, Elana no doubt experienced her family's anxiety every time her father called from prison. Like many children, she sensed when she was being lied to by her family. The family's rapid economic decline was at once obvious and hidden. Living on the borders of a painful puzzle, Elana kept dramatizing the family secret of criminal behavior.

I have seen in my work that many otherwise unexplainable behaviors are often ways to comment metaphorically on the unmentionable. A small child's refusal to speak outside the home, a homosexual teen's intractable seizures that prevent him from going into the outside world, or an adult woman's severe stomach pains that occur only before social functions that involve her husband's secret lover all may be signals that secrets are known at an unspeakable level.

I've seen many families who are so ashamed of alcoholism, drug addiction, eating disorders, mental illness, or criminal activity that they refuse to acknowledge what's happening right in their midst. Such silence prevents any family from getting help or support.

In Elana's family, her father's criminal behavior provoked great shame for the family. Wanting to protect Elana from this overwhelming sense of mortification, her family kept his incarceration a secret, and then had to support this secret with lies. Thus shame engenders secrecy, which in circular fashion underpins a deepening sense of shame, cutting everyone off from necessary relational and therapeutic resources.

When families have dreadful and incommunicable secrets, one member's behavior can sometimes serve as an effective distraction, providing everyone with a safe, albeit upsetting topic of conversation. When I first met Elana and her mother, it became immediately clear to me that Elana's behavior had become the subject of endless family discussions, guaranteeing that the truly crucial topics of her father's embezzlement, his imprisonment, and the family's terrible shame would find no space in conversation. As is true in many families where children create enormously upsetting diversions from core family secrets, Elana's family fixed on her behavior as further proof that the secret should remain buried.

When behavior is truly a distraction for the unspeakable, therapist after therapist may be brought in, each attempting to intervene at the wrong level, mistakenly addressing such signals at the biological, behavioral, intrapsychic, or interpersonal level, while completely missing the unimaginable maze of secrecy in which such actions are embedded.

When I first spoke to Elana's mother, I was immediately struck by how anxious she seemed. Constantly guarding against the disclosure of a secret provokes anxiety. At any moment, what is to remain hidden may emerge. Simultaneously, those kept out of a secret experience tension in family or therapeutic relationships. The anxiety bound up in guarding a secret spills over onto those who do not know. Thus we had no easy give-and-take in our initial conversation. Rather, I experienced a powerful need on her part to guide our conversation, lest I ask about something I was not supposed to know.

TYPES OF SECRETS

I've found that I need to draw distinctions among types of secrets. Paradoxically, the very same actions used to create secrets that engender pain can be used to create secrets that enable joy. Behavior that shapes destructive secrets is similar to behavior that enhances individual, family, and cultural development. Enforced silence, selective telling, covert talking, and whispered confidences all can be used to plan a surprise party or to shield a pedophile. In my work with secrets, I've needed to differentiate them by purpose, duration, and outcome.

SWEET SECRETS

These are time-limited and made for the purpose of fun and surprise, such as gifts, parties, or unexpected visits. Sweet secrets can shift relationships temporarily and create new bonds. A little girl is brought into a sweet secret with her father to surprise her mother with a new kitten, and momentarily she feels quite adult. Teen siblings who normally fight with each other get together to do something for their parents' anniversary. When sweet secrets open, they often enable a new and positive view of a person or a relationship.

Sweet secrets can protect and expand our sense of self. A

baby's very first game of peekaboo is about discovering the delights of temporary concealment. The hiding places of young children, the locked diaries of teens, and the unspoken hopes and dreams we carry in our hearts are the sweet secrets that crisscross our lives.

ESSENTIAL SECRETS

Many secrets promote necessary boundaries that define a relationship. Such secrets are essential to well-being. Your family may have its own private language, including special and endearing words that promote and maintain closeness. An essential secret between spouses creates intimacy, a sense of knowing another person that is unique. In my work with couples, I've often heard about secrets of vulnerability, pillow-talk secrets regarding fears and insecurities. Through their very telling, these secrets enhance closeness and connection while differentiating a couple from children, parents, and friends with the sense that "this is only between us." I've been struck that when essential secrets emerge in therapy, they are a sign of growing trust, of fences coming down. I've listened while a husband for the very first time tells his wife of sixteen years that the reason he backs off from their children and leaves all of the disciplining to her is that he was beaten by his own father. I've watched the transformation of an angry, distant lesbian couple as one woman tells the other about her mother's frequent and hidden suicide attempts that held her hostage as a child. I've seen tenderness replace hostility when a husband finally tells his wife that he's been diagnosed with diabetes, at last explaining his recent inability to sustain an erection and his refusal to make love.

Essential secrets are part of our relationship "contracts," and breaking them can be an act of treachery and betrayal. In Edward Albee's play *Who's Afraid of Virginia Woolf* we watch with horror as George and Martha shatter one essential secret after another. In therapy, I've witnessed a wife embarrass her husband, telling me of a business failure she had promised never to mention. I've listened as a woman wept more over her broken secrets that her husband cavalierly told his lover than over the sexual infidelity of an affair.

In contrast to sweet secrets, which are temporary and are created to benefit another person, essential secrets are long-lasting and are made to enhance the development of self, relationships, and communities.

As adolescents, most of us kept secrets from our parents. Thoughts and beliefs that differed from those of our family went underground. We secretly tried out behavior that facilitated our tentative steps toward adulthood and eventually leaving home. Such secrets shaped our friendships and imparted a needed sense of separateness from family. And likely, a decade or two later, sitting around the dining room table, we shared such secrets with our parents, who laughed and breathed a sigh of relief at not having known our secrets at the time.

Many rite-of-passage rituals have aspects that require secrecy, differentiating participants from others by virtue of their new and special knowledge. Teens are told the secrets of adulthood and enjoined from telling these to younger children. It is this secret information that marks their entry into a new phase of life. Similarly, religions may have secret practices, known only to those who belong. Membership in the group is defined by knowing the secrets.

Finally, those who are oppressed may create essential secrets, often regarding protection or escape. Thus African-Americans held in slavery encoded escape plans in the words of spirituals, such as "Wade in the Water," signaling a meeting down by the river. Today, shelters for battered women keep their locations a secret in order to provide essential protection for their occupants.

TOXIC SECRETS

Toxic secrets poison our relationships with each other. A toxic secret may have been formed three generations ago or last month. In either case, key family stories remain untold and unavailable. These are the secrets that take a powerful toll on relationships, disorient our identity, and disable our lives. They handicap our capacity to make clear choices, use resources effectively, and participate in authentic relationships. Maintaining such secrets often has chronic negative effects on problem solving, conversational repertoire, perceptions, and emotional well-being. Even when no one is in immediate physical or emotional danger, toxic secrets nonetheless sap energy, promote anxiety, burden those who know, and mystify those who don't know.

Living inside a toxic secret amplifies our doubts about other people's responses to us. If I'm keeping a secret from my best friend, can I truly trust her friendship? Would she still care about me if she knew what I was harboring? A woman tells me, "If my husband knew I had an abortion before I met him, he would be disgusted with me. But since I can't tell him, I also can't believe his love for me." An adolescent hangs his head and says to me, "I'm a fraud. My parents are always telling everyone how great I am. If they knew how much cheating I've done at school, they'd be through with me, for sure."

Living outside a toxic secret clouds our vision. Sensing a secret but lacking confirmation, we start to doubt our own perceptions. What are we seeing when we are told we are not seeing what we think we see? When ten-year-old Lucas Gordon came to see me with his mother and father, he refused to speak in the meeting. He curled up on the couch between his parents. For two months Lucas had been refusing to come to the dinner table, the only time of day when both of his parents were together. When his mother told me that she and her husband got along well, Lucas pulled his jacket over his head. Only when Lucas briefly left the room did his father tell me that he and his wife were planning to get a divorce but that Lucas "didn't know."

Since the keeping of toxic secrets does not often create acute crises, such secrets tend to linger, easily promoting a sense of confusion regarding who, when, or whether to tell. How, for instance, do you determine that the secret of your brother's suicide, a secret kept from your children when they were small, should be opened to them now that they are young adults?

Living with a toxic secret can feel like living in a pressure cooker. The need to tell the secret can build and build until it explodes in an unplanned and hurtful way. Or the secret can leak out through seemingly inadvertent clues that force someone else to discover it.

In the popular 1996 film *Secrets and Lies*, a mother has kept a secret from her daughter: She has another daughter, whom she gave up for adoption. She's never planned to tell her daughter, now twenty, about this first child. The mother, Cynthia, is white. Unbeknownst to her, the child she gave up, Hortense, is black. When Hortense reappears in her life, Cynthia, lonely and largely estranged from the daughter she raised, begins to forge a close and meaningful relationship with her. Rather than think through how to tell her daughter in a careful way, Cynthia brings Hortense to her child's twenty-first birthday party and opens the secret impulsively and recklessly, with no thought given to the consequences.

In my work as a family therapist, I've often been confronted with situations where toxic secrets appear to have been opened carelessly, leaving profound relationship fallout in their wake. Upon closer examination, this seeming carelessness turns out to be anxiety that could no longer be contained. It's become clear to me that toxic secrets opened recklessly take longer to resolve than those opened in a carefully planned manner.

If you are the keeper of a toxic secret, you have time for careful deliberation about and preparation for its revelation. Such preparation, in my experience, usually lowers anxiety, allowing thought before action. Be aware that opening toxic secrets often throws a family into necessary disequilibrium; it will likely take quite a while for individual and family identity to coalesce and for relationships to heal and be reshaped.

DANGEROUS SECRETS

I sat behind the one-way mirror one day in 1984 watching a world-famous therapist conduct an interview with a mother, a father, and a sixteen-year-old daughter. The daughter became more and more agitated as the interview went on, but the therapist pressed ahead, asking questions about family relationships. As I listened, it seemed clear that the daughter was giving as many hints as she could, without coming straight out and saying it, that her father was sexually abusing her. The mother began to sob. She knew what was happening to her daughter but until this moment had chosen to protect her husband. As she began to reveal the secret, her husband leaped from his seat and pulled out the cord for the microphone and video camera. A dangerous secret had opened, profoundly altering this family's relationships to one another and to the outside world. As with the opening of any dangerous secret, this one would require an immediate shift to deal first and foremost with the daughter's safety.

There are secrets that put people in immediate physical jeopardy or such severe emotional turmoil that their capacity to function is threatened—for example, physical and sexual abuse of children, wife battering, incapacitating alcoholism or drug abuse, and plans to commit suicide or harm another person. In many public jurisdictions, the discovery of dangerous secrets requires action. For instance, if I learn that a client is planning to harm another person, I'm legally required to break the normal ethical bounds of confidentiality under what is called "the duty to warn." Adults in responsible positions with children must report instances of suspected child abuse.

In contrast to toxic secrets, which allow time to carefully consider the impact of continued secrecy or openness on a network of relationships, dangerous secrets often require swift and immediate action to safeguard life. If you are pondering what to do about your knowledge of a suicide in your family a generation ago, time is on your side. You can reflect about who should know and about what is to be gained and lost in telling. You can think through how opening this secret might change family relationships or alter myths and beliefs about the person who killed himself. But if your niece's best friend confides in you that she is planning to kill herself, the luxury of reflection is not available to you. Rather, you have to act swiftly in order to protect her, even though such action may violate her confidence.

Intimidation, fear, power over others, and powerlessness are usually intertwined in dangerous secrets. Often the powerless person in a dangerous secret lives in a context of profound physical and emotional threat and feels that greater harm will result if he or she opens the secret. The person with power to cause harm and demand silence in dangerous secrets frequently invokes "privacy"—"What goes on in our house is no one else's business"— thereby blurring important distinctions between secrecy and privacy.

HEALTHY PRIVACY OR UNHEALTHY SECRECY?

In my work with families, I've found that distinguishing between secrecy and privacy is both critical and slippery. A couple comes to me contemplating pregnancy through egg donation. They ask me, "If we have a child this way and never tell her, are we keeping a secret from her, or is this our own private business?" In another couple, a husband insists to me that it is his right to keep a special bank account secret from his wife. "It's private," he tells me. When I ask him if his wife might do the same, he tells me that would mean she was keeping a secret from him. A woman makes a will leaving all of her money to her children from her first marriage and doesn't tell her new husband. Is this her private business or a troublesome secret from him?

What a wife-beating husband or a sexually abusive stepfather calls privacy is actually secrecy. A person with AIDS may be accused of keeping a secret from neighbors when actually she is acting out of a right to privacy. When that same woman refuses to tell her sexual partner that she is HIV positive, maintaining privacy rapidly shifts to keeping a dangerous secret. A husband may define his extramarital affair as private, while his wife may be living her life sensing a toxic secret, making decisions in the absence of this critical information. A biological mother who gives up her child for adoption may consider her wish not to be known or contacted by this child part of her right to privacy. The government may even codify such privacy into law. Yet an adult adoptee may regard the very same information as an essential secret about his life that no one has a right to keep from him. An adolescent may think her sexual life is private, while her parents may believe she is improperly keeping a secret. Making a claim that something is private may be inappropriately self-serving or appropriately protective.

The definitions of what is secret and what is private change across time, cultures, and sociopolitical circumstances, depending on what a given culture or a particular family stigmatizes and values. For instance, the sexual relationship of a married, heterosexual couple is considered private in our culture, while the sexual relationship of a homosexual couple must often be kept secret, since it isn't protected by law and is certainly subject to prejudices that violate privacy. The dilemma of what is private and what is secret plays out in the unsettled legal and moral debate over a teenager's right to make her own decision regarding abortion and the demand for parental notification or consent.

Secrecy and privacy sometimes coexist in a circular and paradoxical relationship with each other. When an action that limits privacy is taken on one level of the many overlapping social systems in which we live, we may respond at another level by making a secret. When arenas of personal privacy are rezoned by legislation, courts, insurance companies, or hospitals, for instance, then individuals and families may respond with secret-keeping. Persons with AIDS often live with the carefully guarded secret of their illness. Their right to privacy is frequently threatened by proposed legislation. Such threats intensify secret-keeping. During the struggle to gain the right to legalized abortion, a struggle that turns on a woman's right to privacy regarding her own body, many women had to go public with the previously long-held secret of their abortions in order to rally pro-choice support.[1]

FAMILY RULES

Every family makes its own rules about what is secret and what is private. Take a moment to reflect on your own experiences, both in the family that you come from and in your current relationships.

· How did your family of origin define what was private?

- Did you know how much money your parents earned?
- What family matters were you forbidden to mention outside the family?
- Was it assumed that everything that went on inside your family was to be kept private from the outside world?
- Were there differences in what adults or children could keep private? For instance, if you couldn't enter your parents' room, could they enter yours? As you were growing up, did any of this change?
- Were there differences in what men and women could keep private?
- Were some family members afforded more privacy than others?
- Did physical space such as bedrooms or drawers mark zones of privacy? For whom?
- How do you define privacy and secrecy in your adult life?

Toxic and dangerous secrets most often make us feel shame, while truly private matters do not. Hiding and concealment are central to secret-keeping, but not to privacy. In my work I've found it useful to consider whether withholding information impacts another person's life choices, decision-making capacity, and well-being. When it does, then it is secrecy rather than privacy that holds sway. If a husband believes he and his wife are working on their marriage in therapy, yet all the time she's having an extramarital affair, she's keeping a secret. If a woman knows that many of her female relatives died of breast cancer and keeps this from her twenty-five-year-old son, she may be acting out of privacy. Keeping this same information from her twenty-six-year-old daughter, whose health may be affected by it, is to keep a secret. What is truly private doesn't impact our physical or emotional health. Keeping toxic or dangerous secrets cuts us off from the resources we need to solve problems. Private matters in your life don't prevent your access to necessary resources. When you're living outside a secret, the lack of information cripples your capacity to make fully informed decisions. When you're living outside someone else's private concern, your life is not directly affected.

Finally, what is secret in our lives may be transformed to what is private. When you open a secret, you usually do so within an intimate circle of family members or dear friends. Seldom do you tell a secret to your whole neighborhood, take an ad out in the paper, or go on a talk show.

OPENING THE DOOR TO COMPLEXITY

Why are secrets so compelling? Perhaps it is because secrets defy simplistic solutions. Despite the claims of pop psychology, secrets seldom wrap up neatly. They require us to experience a sense of splitness. Secrets at once attract us and repel us. The very same secret may be a blanket of protection one day and a bed of nails the next. It may provide warmth and coziness in one relationship, while alienating us from other people with whom we long to feel close.

When I'm asked and agree to keep a secret, I may quickly find myself struggling in a network of relationships where I'm simultaneously reliable and unreliable, trustworthy and untrustworthy, powerful and powerless. Opening a secret involves us in both potential enhancement of relationships and potential loss. Surely, dealing with secrets is the high-wire act in the circus of life.

Chapter

2

The Sculpture of Family Secrets:
How Secrets Shape Relationships

───

In my family, as in many, secrets provided a temporary aura of safety, but eventually they outlived their usefulness and tyrannized those they originally protected. Like tiny film monsters projected on a giant screen, secrets appear to have a power far in excess of their actual content. In my family, . . . it was fear and brooding imagination that made the secrets toxic, that gave them their most damaging legacy. Now, uncovered, the secrets seem far more ordinary, more humanly understandable and benign than the dark shadows they cast over generations of my family.

—*Michele K. Martin*

"OUR FAMILY lived by one rule: The less said, the better," said Molly Bradley. "As children, in order to figure out what was going on, we became high on intuition and very low on words. When I went to other kids' houses to play, the amount of real talking shocked me. In my house, you heard the meaningless noise of nonsensical arguments or you heard silence."

Molly and her siblings were raised in a family with many secrets. Her older brother, Calvin, thirty-seven, her younger sister, thirty-two-year-old Annie, and Molly, who is thirty-five, grew up in the Midwest in the 1960s and early 1970s in a white, middle-class, Anglo-American Methodist family. "We looked like a regular TV family," Molly said. "But it turns out we were far from that."

When Molly called me, she told me that she and Annie had not spoken to Calvin for six years. Her son was about to be confirmed, and Molly felt a deep need to have her whole family together. "Even though Calvin and I were never that close," Molly told me, "I miss him more and more as my own son gets older." As in many families I've known, an important life cycle event was pushing Molly to repair a cutoff relationship. With a lot of trepidation, Molly asked her brother and sister to meet with me.

Our first session was rescheduled three times. As first one and then another sibling called me with reasons to postpone, I began to feel the powerful mutual avoidance that permeated their relationships. Finally, on a late autumn evening, Molly, Annie, and Calvin met with me to begin a journey at once painful and illuminating.

The first secret the sisters recalled was the mystery surrounding their grandmother. "I remember Molly and I would sneak around to see our grandmother, our mother's mother," said Annie. "Our mom never wanted her to come over, but we didn't know why. Our father was silent about everything, and so we never knew what he thought about our grandmother. It was kind of fun to have these secret visits, but sometimes Grandma acted quite strange, and then it was more scary than fun." Calvin never visited, and if he found out that Molly and Annie had been to see their grandmother, he scolded them and threatened to tell their mother. "When he acted like that, it just made Annie and me closer, angry with him, and more determined than ever to see our grandmother," Molly told me. "I was my mother's confidant," Calvin said. "I was the oldest and her only son. It made me feel special to know things my sisters didn't know. She made me promise to keep her secret—that our grandmother had manic-depressive illness."

When the three were young teens, their grandmother committed suicide. Molly and Annie were told that the cause of her death was "hardening of the arteries." Their mother told only Calvin the truth, and he was told never to tell anyone. Molly and Annie sensed there was a mystery about their grandmother's death, but whenever they tried to bring it up, their mother changed the subject.

Two years after their grandmother's death, their mother's sister committed suicide. This too was kept a secret from Molly and Annie. After her funeral, her death was never spoken of in the family. Visiting with other aunts, uncles, and cousins ceased. All photographs of their mother's extended family vanished. Over the next several months, Molly and Annie watched in horrified silence as their mother became severely depressed. By maintaining what were now many secrets, Mrs. Bradley fueled her own deep and unspoken fear of mental illness. Once again Calvin stayed close to his mother. No one was allowed to ask questions or to comment.

"You could feel the shame that pervaded our family," Annie said. "You could taste it in the breakfast coffee. You could hear it in my parents' voices, but never in their words. You could see it in the hunched-over way my brother walked. A lot of my energy went into trying to figure it out."

Annie described an adolescence marked by furious fights with her mother over seemingly small matters. "I was determined to make her speak, but she never would. To me, the yelling was somehow preferable to the silence. In the end, both the silence and the noise amounted to the same thing."

The blowups between Annie and their mother soon became choreographed into another repetitive family dance, with each sibling taking a prescribed place. Molly observed, "It was like somebody had handed us a script to follow. Annie was always asking questions. I took the path of busying myself with activities outside our family. Not knowing things that were going on in the family seemed to bother Annie the most. My mother always responded to her with sarcasm or dismissal. Pretty soon they'd be fighting fiercely over nothing. Calvin would yell at Annie that she was upsetting Mom, that she was making Mom sick and to stop it. I always ended up comforting Annie. Our father was simply missing in action."

Relationships in the Bradley family were shaped by many secrets. Beginning with the secret of their grandmother's mental illness, about which their mother felt enormous shame and fear, making secrets became the family's modus vivendi. Secrets between Calvin and his mother became matched by secrets between Molly and Annie, tightening the family alliances. In her late twenties Molly discovered the secret of her grandmother's manic-depressive illness from a cousin who was a social worker and had figured it out from their grandmother's behavior. Together, they speculated that she had killed herself. Rather than talk to family members who might know the truth, Molly simply told Annie and they kept it to themselves until our therapy.

Changing this pattern felt increasingly impossible to the Bradleys. As with so many families I've known, for them secrets were like concrete. As they harden into place, a family becomes trapped, despite desires to free themselves. When I asked Annie in our second meeting if she had ever considered confiding in Calvin when she was a child, she told me the thought had never occurred to her. *If family members cannot even imagine a different way of interacting, then secrets hold them in their grip.* Since relating in some new and untried manner runs the risk that secrets will emerge, the family's repertoire becomes narrower and more rigid.

This is true whatever the content of the secrets. Secrets are like magnets in family relationships, drawing some members close while repelling others. Repetitive family coalitions, who is "in" and who is "out," closeness and distance, intimacy and estrangement, and rewards and punishments all flow from the presence of secrets. Such patterns, in turn, generate secrets in an ever-widening circle.

In the Bradley family, as in many families where there are secrets, such patterns pervaded areas of family life that had nothing to do with the secrets. As I listened to Annie describe her constant fighting with her mother, I knew I was hearing about a convenient distraction from the genuine pain in the family. As the siblings spoke about their memories, each sadly acknowledged how their needs to connect with each other and with their parents went unmet. None had ever heard their mother's subterranean fears about mental illness. The Bradleys suffered profound losses—two suicides and nonexistent relationships with extended kin. These losses could have been an opportunity to give each other support and love. Instead they went underground and were never openly mourned. For so many years, silences were temporarily relieved by flashes of meaningless anger, serving only to reinforce the ever-narrowing relationship patterns.

As I worked with Molly, Annie, and Calvin to create an atmosphere that made truth telling safe and manageable, their relationships began to shift. After our fourth meeting, the three had dinner together for the first time in many years. After our sixth meeting, Calvin went to Molly's home to talk to her son about the boy's pending confirmation. When they returned for the seventh session, Calvin said he needed to speak about something he had never told his sisters.

"When I was seventeen, I fathered a child, a boy. Our parents and my girlfriend's parents insisted that we put the baby up for adoption. We broke up. I never saw my child. Mother was furious with me, like I had betrayed her. I was told I must never tell the two of you," Calvin said as he wept. As we talked that afternoon I questioned Calvin about the impact of this secret on his life. Not able to unpack what had happened to him at seventeen, Calvin had pulled further and further into himself. He had remained single and stayed away from his nieces and nephews. "Like so many of the secrets in our family," Molly remarked, "this one just chopped us apart. Now I think I understand why you didn't come to my son's christening. You said you had to go out of town for your work. I was so hurt and angry."

I saw the Bradleys for one more session following Molly's son's confirmation. "This was so different from other family events," Annie remarked. "Among the three of us, things felt genuine for the first time. Calvin said a special prayer for Molly's son. Together, we lit a candle for our grandmother. Our parents looked surprised. I guess that's the next piece of work we need to do, to talk to them about what's happened to us. First I need to live with our new relationships for a while."

HOW KNOWING AND NOT KNOWING SECRETS CREATES A FAMILY'S DANCE

Every family I've known has a collection of available relationship patterns. Whenever I participate in a family's complex dance, I experience the push and pull of patterns that result from the rich interplay of what people witnessed and absorbed in their families of origin, their ethnic roots, social class, past and current religious affiliations, alternative possibilities gleaned from watching friends, and the particular requirements of their daily lives. When I see a couple in therapy, I know that I'm entering a complex ecology. Their pas de deux is the result of steps learned before they ever met each other. And whether they are graceful or constantly step on each other's toes, new patterns will emerge. No matter how long I've worked as a therapist, I'm constantly moved by the endless variety of ways people create to be together. On any given day, I might see cooperation, blame, betrayal, collaboration, treachery, and support—and I might see them all in the same hour. When I first get to know people, I usually see repeating patterns that are keeping them immobilized. Like a needle stuck in the groove of an old phonograph record, unsatisfying and frustrating interactions play over and over. Family members are usually pretty good at seeing each other's contributions to a troubling pattern, but seeing one's own part is often like trying to see the back of your neck without a mirror. Our work in family therapy begins as people recognize their own steps in the family dance. When our work goes well, a family's repertoire of patterns expands to provide stability, competency to solve problems, a sense of meaning and mutual caring, and enough variety of strategies to cope with inevitable crises.

Over the years I've been increasingly struck by the ways secrets affect family patterns. When therapy sessions are marked by repeating uncomfortable silences, faltering conversation, veneers of politeness, sudden changes of the subject, constant eye contact between two family members whenever a particular topic is broached, or distracting and nonsensical conflicts, I begin to wonder about secrets.

The creation of any secret between two people in a family makes a *triangle*. This tight twosome is, in reality, at least a threesome, as a secret between two people always excludes another or several others. The ubiquitous affair triangle involves one spouse and a lover, who know a secret, and the other spouse, who remains in the dark. The moment two family members know a secret, regardless of content, and others are unaware or kept out of the secret, a complicated family geometry comes into play. Not only is the issue per se a secret, but the secret-keeping relationship is also hidden.

When Calvin Bradley's mother told him the secret of his grandmother's mental illness and told him not to tell his sisters, a pattern was established that affected family relationships for over thirty years. Each new secret between Calvin and his mother that was kept from Molly and Annie amplified this pattern. As in all families when a parent tells a secret to a child that the child must not share with brothers and sisters, Calvin's relationship with Molly and Annie was marked by distance and mistrust. From the outside, the family relationships looked like two close pairs—Calvin and his mom, and Molly and Annie. In actuality, these pairs were a function of triangles formed by powerful and painful secrets. Any time the closeness of two people is the result of keeping a secret from one or more others, then the operative relationship is a triangle, not a duo. While all families have open triangles shaped by mutual interests—Mom and daughter like to ride horses, while Dad prefers to golf—families with secret triangles lose their elasticity and spontaneity, as only certain relationships are allowed, while others are proscribed. When triangles are underpinned by secrets, attempts by a family member to change a pattern or even express a new opinion are met with swift and vehement reactions.

JUAN'S STORY: SECRETS AND INTERGENERATIONAL TRIANGLES

When Juan Delgado was a seventeen-year-old senior in high school, he began hearing voices telling him to hurt his stepmother.

These voices began on the third anniversary of his beloved grandmother's death. During a brief psychiatric hospitalization, Juan had been diagnosed with schizophrenia, a diagnosis, as we shall see, that was incorrect. Juan was placed on antipsychotic medication, and he along with his father, Carlos, and stepmother, Eliana, were referred for family therapy.[1] The family seemed frightened and bewildered by what was happening to them. Hospital staff had given them mixed messages, telling them on the one hand that Juan had a mental illness that was likely to be chronic, while on the other hand suggesting that family relationships were somehow to blame. Even organizing the therapy was difficult, as Eliana insisted that Juan's half-siblings could not miss school to attend the sessions. From the beginning, family meetings were marked by long silences. The family's discomfort at speaking together was palpable.

As their story slowly unfolded I learned that Juan had come to the United States from Puerto Rico to join his father and stepmother when he was fourteen. His biological mother seemed to have simply "disappeared" many years earlier; his father said he had no idea where she was. Juan insisted that he never thought or wondered about his mother.

Another silence surrounded Juan's migration to New York. It was to be a "summer visit," his father had told him, but in fact his grandmother, with whom he had lived his entire life, was dying of cancer. Neither grandmother nor grandson was told that they would never see each other again. "I didn't know how to tell them. I didn't know what to say," his father remarked sadly.

Like many secrets, this one had its origins in a wish to protect people from pain. And like many secrets that start out that way, the plan for protection backfired. A few months after he arrived in New York, Juan's grandmother died. Juan had grown up hearing his grandmother constantly criticize his stepmother, blaming her for taking his father to New York. Feeling angry and betrayed when his grandmother died, Juan turned his anger on his stepmother, who seemed to be a convenient and familiar target.

Only later in family therapy did Juan discover that his stepmother had endured the wrath of his grandmother for many years.

Juan's inability to form anything but a bitter and angry relationship with his stepmother was embedded in a secret triangle.

At the beginning of the therapy, Eliana was mostly silent. She responded to efforts to involve her by insisting that she was "just a stepmother," that anything that mattered was between her husband and his son. Only after several family meetings in which she was given lots of support for her difficult role as a stepmother of an angry teen did Eliana feel sufficiently comfortable to tell the story of how she entered the family. Carlos and Juan had never before heard Eliana's aching experience, the details of which held many secrets.

During his infancy, Juan's mother mysteriously left the family. When Juan was three, his father left Puerto Rico to work in Costa Rica. Juan remained with his grandmother. Carlos met Eliana in Costa Rica and brought her back to live at his mother's home. Like Juan's mother, Eliana was from a lower social class than Carlos and his family. An intense, subtle, but devastating campaign to ostracize her immediately got under way. Nothing was said to Carlos, who no doubt also chose not to see what was going on. Juan's grandmother refused to allow Eliana even to touch Juan. Each day, while Carlos was at work, Juan's uncle would pick the child up and take him out of the house to keep him away from Eliana.

When Eliana told this painful story, Carlos said with surprise, "You never told me that!" Not wanting to turn Carlos against his own mother, Eliana had kept the bad treatment of her a secret. Even when Eliana gave birth to a daughter, Juan's grandmother remained adamant that Juan was the favorite; Eliana's daughter was of no importance. Still maintaining silence, Eliana simply made plans to take her infant daughter and go to the United States. Ultimately Carlos chose to join her, leaving Juan with his grandmother.

Juan grew up hearing terrible lies about his stepmother and never hearing her side. He was told by his grandmother not to repeat these stories, that these were secrets just between them. When his grandmother died, his loyalty to her, coupled with his lack of information, required that he continue the vendetta. "I just knew my grandmother would hate it that I was living with my stepmother," Juan said tearfully. "Then my stepmother wanted to help me get ready to go to college, and it was coming up on the anniversary of my grandmother's death, and I was just so confused."

After learning Eliana's story of what was done to her, Juan stopped hearing the voices that were telling him to harm his stepmother. Gradually he began to let Eliana into his life, talking over his college plans and letting her know about a girlfriend.

Shortly after the discoveries made in this meeting, Juan went to his father to ask more about his mother. As often happens, when one secret opens in a family, another secret soon yields. Until this moment Juan never knew that his mother lived about an hour away and had tried over the years to see him. Swayed by his extended family's insistence that he keep her away from Juan, Carlos had told her she would upset Juan's life too much if she tried to contact him.

"I met my mother for the first time," Juan said in our next therapy session. "I couldn't believe it—I met an uncle and an aunt and another grandmother. All my life I was embarrassed when people asked me about my mother. I never knew what to say." As Juan got to know his mother, he discovered one last secret: Wanting to raise Juan herself, his grandmother had made his mother's life miserable until she finally fled.

After Juan found out all of the secrets in his family, he needed to do a lot of work in therapy to think through his relationships with his grandmother and his stepmother. His grandmother had loved him very much, perhaps too much. Despite Eliana's enormous pain, she had kept the war with her mother-in-law a secret in order to preserve her husband's and stepson's relationships with the older woman. Juan's place in this ferocious and hidden triangle burst forth when he heard voices directing him to hurt Eliana.

When therapy ended, Juan was preparing to go away to college. He crafted a letter to say a final goodbye to his grandmother. He told her how much he loved her and that he knew she had done her best for him, but told her that it was "unfair in the eyes of God to sin for love, and that it is better for my mental health to see things fairly." He concluded, "Not only are my father and I your sons, but my stepmother is also your daughter."

Like so many families, secrets in the Delgado family enabled some relationships to be quite close, while requiring that others be in perpetual conflict. When relationships in a family seem to be marked by fixed and unyielding patterns of closeness and distance, secrets often underpin that family's geography. For the Delgados, multiple and secret triangles froze family relationships. While Juan's grandmother had taken very good care of him, his unquestioned devotion to her depended on Eliana's silence. By keeping the secret of how she had been vilified, Eliana allowed her husband and stepson to maintain their loyalty to her mother-in-law at her own very great expense. When she finally opened this secret, many relationships had to be reconfigured. Triangles could at last be replaced by one-to-one relationships.

WHERE SECRETS LIVE IN THE FAMILY: THE ISSUE OF LOCATION

When two people in a family make and keep a secret and others are excluded, a triangle is formed. But not all secrets live simply between two people with others excluded. As I work with people I look carefully for where a secret is located. A secret located inside one person that has never been spoken to another is very different from a secret that the whole family knows but keeps from the outside world, even if both secrets are, for instance, about drug abuse. I've found that where a secret is located will define its impact on individuals and relationships, shaping boundaries and coloring identities. The location of a secret, regardless of the content of that secret, contributes to complex interactions that, in turn, feed back on decisions regarding secrecy and openness.

WHEN A SECRET IS KEPT FROM EVERYONE

Imagine a gay adolescent who has never told anyone in or outside the family of his homosexual feelings. As long as the secret remains inside this youngster, relationships between him and others in his family or friendship network become imbued with distance. Over time, this boy's life grows more and more isolated, as he keeps a secret from all of the people he loves, a secret so integral to who he is. He mistrusts responses from others to him, as these are continually filtered by the secret. In an internal dialogue, he tells himself, "If they really knew, they would dislike me, disrespect me, maybe even disown me."

When an important secret is located inside one person, it's not too difficult to appreciate the impact on that individual. Most of us have kept such secrets, at least temporarily. The effects on family relationships are less considered and more difficult to grasp. When this gay teen hears his parents ask with anticipation, "Who are you taking to the prom?" the knot of secrecy is pulled ever tighter, for he becomes increasingly convinced that the secret must be maintained.

Family members often sense when a secret is being kept from them by one member. The parents of this gay teen may create their own fantasies and myths about their son—"Our son is too shy," "Our son is a late bloomer," or, far worse, "Our son is emotionally disturbed." Unless such fantasies can be discussed and either confirmed or denied, family interaction becomes based on illusion.

When family members sense that important information is being withheld from them, they may pursue the content of the secret in ways that ultimately violate privacy. A mother reads her daughter's diary. A husband rifles the contents of his wife's purse. Relationships corrode with suspicion.

Conversely, family members may respond to their sense of a secret being kept by one person with denial and pervasive distance, affecting areas of relating that have nothing to do with the secret. A pattern of mutual and escalating exclusion from one another's lives may be set in motion. Conversations become increasingly superficial, making authentic talk more and more difficult.

WHEN SOME PEOPLE IN THE FAMILY KNOW A SECRET AND NO ONE ELSE KNOWS

When a secret is located among some people in a family while excluding others, I always want to know which people know what. In our tell-all society, many parents express anxiety to me about keeping *any* secrets from their children. However, if the children are young and the content of the secret does not directly affect their lives or is beyond their ability to comprehend, then it's quite appropriate to keep certain secrets from them.

I've worked with parents who become fearful if they sense that their child is keeping *anything* from them. Buying into the cultural belief that good relationships mean no secrets, these parents forget that their own first real awareness of a life separate from their parents sprang from making secrets, usually with their siblings. When children keep a secret from their parents, they're experimenting with the experience of drawing boundaries and realizing what their life is like when they're temporarily independent from their parents' point of view. I often ask parents to think back to the first time they agreed with their brothers and sisters not to tell Mom or Dad. Suddenly they remember the giddy discovery of a world not controlled by adults. Secrets made *within* generations and kept by adults from children or children from adults are very different from secrets that are made across generational lines.

A toxic secret between one parent and a child that excludes the other parent can easily place that child in an untenable loyalty bind. If a child keeps such a secret, he or she is immediately disloyal to the unknowing parent. If the child opens the secret, then his or her loyalty to the teller is sacrificed.

In most households, adults appropriately carry the lion's share of power to decide what is best for their children. As children grow to adulthood, this equation gradually shifts. When children are used as confidants for secrets, especially secrets that directly affect the life of the excluded parent, then the natural hierarchy of information and decision making in a family is turned upside down. The parent who is left out of the loop loses influence and respect. A child gains more power and privilege in family relationships than his or her years would ordinarily allow. Since all of this is embedded in secrets, the issue of who gets to decide what for whom becomes slippery and unavailable for conversation.

The fragile power of a child who shares a parent's secret evaporates when that secret is dangerous. A child who shares a toxic secret with a parent may still have a sense of choice. But children who are intimidated and coerced into silence by a sexually abusing parent lose not only trust in adults, but a sense of their own effectiveness in the world. Threatened with family disintegration or worse if they open the secret, many children sacrifice their own safety and well-being.

The threat such children experience may be covert. Hearing from a parent, "Remember, this is a special secret just between us," said with a tone that implies the jeopardy in telling anyone, can be as effective to silence a child as, "If you tell anyone, it'll be your fault when I have to leave."

As we saw with the Bradleys, relationships among brothers and sisters are powerfully affected when one child is selected to be told a secret by parents. Another client of mine, Leanne Bowers, grew up as an only child until she was fourteen years old. Her mother, Carole, and her father, Jeff, very much wanted to have more children but were unsuccessful. Finally they made a decision to use donor insemination. Leanne knew they were keeping many appointments at a hospital and became quite worried. "I thought one of my parents was ill, and I went on a campaign to find out what was going on," Leanne told me. She overheard their conversation one evening and found out that what they were trying to keep secret was the donor insemination. Since she was a child who had always been encouraged to ask questions, she went to her mother, told her what she had heard, and asked directly for information. At that juncture both Carole and Jeff sat down with their daughter and explained what was happening. Carole was three months pregnant with a baby who would be Leanne's brother, Jon. Carole ended this conversation by telling Leanne that when the baby was born, it was important that he not ever know about the donor insemination.

"I remember my mother said, 'Daddy is your daddy and he will be your baby brother's daddy. That's all that's important,'" Leanne told me. "I felt so confused. My parents had *always* stressed the importance of honesty. Now I was being told to lie about something that felt very big. I watched my father be with Jon in ways that were different from how he was with me—less comfortable—but we could never talk about what that was about. I never knew quite how to relate to Jon. Here I knew this important thing about him that my parents said wasn't important. If it truly wasn't important, I don't think we'd have hidden it all these years."

It is not surprising that Leanne and Jon's relationship was marked by distance. "My parents and grandparents and aunts and uncles all said that Jon and I weren't close because we were so many years apart. That became the family explanation. But I knew better. Jon looked up to me. I was his big sister. He wanted my attention, and I kept pushing him away, ignoring him. Sometimes I was quite mean and then I hated myself for acting that way. I know my parents meant to do the best thing, but this secret just drove us apart," said Leanne.

WHEN A SECRET CROSSES THE FAMILY BOUNDARY

When Jack and Eileen Baker were first married, Eileen's parents gave her several thousand dollars and told her not to tell Jack. They instructed her to keep a separate bank account in order to "buy little treats" and "for an emergency." Eileen's parents had disapproved of her marriage to Jack, saying he was "not suitable," by which they meant that he came from a family with little money and had less education than Eileen. Over the seven years of their marriage before I met them, this financial secret was repeated many times, tying Eileen to her parents in ways that remained mysterious to Jack and preventing the young couple from establishing a clear boundary around their own relationship.

Enduring secrets between one member of a couple and members of that person's family of origin can profoundly affect the couple's relationship with each other. I needed to help Eileen and Jack distinguish secrets about matters that rightly belonged in their couple relationship, such as finances, sexuality, children, or work, from secrets with their parents or siblings that did not affect their intimate partnership. The financial secret between Eileen and her parents contained the hidden message "Jack is incapable of pulling his weight in this marriage." By agreeing to take part in this secret, Eileen confirmed her parents' belief to them and to herself. This is a very different secret than if her sister had told her she was planning to move across the country and requested that she not tell her husband or anyone else until the plans were firmer.

Many times secrets are located between a family member and another person outside of the immediate household. These may be the warm and wonderful sweet secrets shared in friendships, the essential secrets that promote healthy individuation for a teen, the toxic secrets that betray a marriage, or the revelation of a dangerous internal family secret by a person who is desperate to get outside help. Secrets that cross the family household boundary should be judged by their intent and their effects. Clearly, Eileen's parents intended to keep their daughter tied to them financially and to belittle Jack. When I first met Jack and Eileen, they had not been able to negotiate many of the normal tasks of a young marriage—decision making, finances, relationships with in-laws—as these were all tangled up in Eileen's secret with her parents.

Secrets between an individual and his or her extended family that exclude a spouse may be repeating patterns that have spanned generations. Intergenerational secrets among the men or among the women, between parents and a grown child, or between adult siblings may be deeply etched in a family's portrait. If a mother, grandmother, and great-grandmother made secrets that excluded their husbands, it may feel natural for a daughter in a new generation to do likewise. While these secrets may have created a strong bond among the women in a family, I always want to think about how such secrets affected marriages or other intimate partnerships. Were secrets made between generations because of painful realities in marriages, or were secrets made at the expense of committed marriages?

Sometimes making a secret with someone outside one's immediate family can be quite liberating. This is especially so if the family is one with little room for individual thoughts, ideas, and feelings. Temporary secrets across the family boundary can provide needed space to try out new views of one's self. Experimenting with telling a secret to someone outside the family can often be the first step toward opening it inside the family in the future. Rehearsals with a best friend or an excellent therapist can help us to clarify whether or not we want to open a secret inside the family.

MAKING A SECRET WITH A PROFESSIONAL

As a therapist, I'm a professional secret-keeper. I'm often the very first person with whom someone risks telling a long-held secret. A secret never before told is suddenly relocated from inside a person to between that person and me. When clients trust me with their secrets, I'm always aware that my responsibility goes far beyond simply listening.

When clients tell me their secrets, they sometimes ask me about confidentiality. Historically, the healing professions have made confidentiality a touchstone of relationships. The ethics in medicine, law, religion, and mental health all require confidentiality. Without a patient's or client's permission, what is revealed can go no further. Or can it? It's important to remember that in today's culture, confidentiality with a professional helper is relative, not absolute. Insurance and managed-care companies require diagnoses and records for reimbursement, and court decisions have limited the definition of privileged information.

Making secrets with professional helpers is a double-edged

sword. A client's relationship with me or with another therapist, a minister, a priest, or a rabbi can be an excellent arena to explore painful secrets. Such a relationship can help dissolve shame, offer acceptance and empathy, and reduce the power of certain secrets. It can lead to new and necessary resources. At the same time, sharing secrets *only* with professional helpers can sometimes negatively affect marriage and family relationships.

For instance, I've frequently seen couples for marital therapy in which one or both have been in individual therapy for many years. All of their secrets have been told to their respective therapists with little or no thought given to the impact of this enduring confidential relationship on their marriage. Important issues get discussed more and more in therapy and less and less at home. I've worked with many people whose therapists have warned them not to discuss anything that comes up in therapy with anyone else. Rather than therapy being a dress rehearsal for life, it becomes the long-running show. At an extreme, I've known people who not only have shared all of their secrets only with their therapist, but also have been counseled to keep the fact that they are going to therapy a secret from their spouse. Such relationships come to resemble an affair.

Secrets between a client and a professional helper that exclude a committed partner form a triangle. When this triangle is temporary, it may have little consequence. The therapy relationship can provide a safe haven to deal with secrets and to explore whether or not they should be opened to others. When the triangle is long-standing, however, aspects of one's life may become secret in ways that were never intended. When I start a new marital therapy, I always ask about each spouse's experience with individual therapy and the impact of professional secret-keeping on their marriage over time. Sometimes this is the first arena for a husband to tell his wife how threatened or excluded he's felt during her years of individual therapy.

When my clients tell me secrets, we begin a critical journey that always involves our considering whether anyone else should be told. We talk about the future impact on relationships of creating new secrets, this time with me. Only rarely do people want their first and final telling to be with me. More often, I find that people want a receptive and empathic context in which to unpack a secret initially, room to explore the consequences of telling, and the help to do it well.

WHEN EVERYONE IN THE FAMILY KNOWS A SECRET

When Sara Tompkins, thirty-seven, first came to see me, she spoke with great hesitation. In meeting after meeting, she seemed frightened and choked on her words. After several months, she finally said, "If my mother and father and the rest of my family knew I was speaking to you, they would be very angry." She went on to tell me about growing up in a family that was completely organized by her mother's addiction to tranquilizers. "My father is a physician. To this day, he writes her prescriptions. She never got up with us in the morning. When we got home from school, she was usually zonked out on the couch. My brother and I made dinner from the time we were eight and nine. I never brought friends home. No one was supposed to know. The worst part was, we were supposed to act like we didn't know. Once when I was twelve I tried to ask my father what was wrong with my mother. He acted like he didn't hear what I said, and changed the subject. Our family invented 'don't ask, don't tell' long before the government ever thought of it."

As Sara spoke, her voice grew tighter and her breath came in short, anxious gulps. Even though Sara had not lived with her family for fifteen years, this was the first time she had ever broken the strong family rule against speaking to anyone outside the family about their secret.

When a family's secret is an ongoing situation—such as alcoholism, drug addiction, physical abuse, and mental or physical illness—then both internal daily family relationships and interactions with the outside world are profoundly affected.

In families like Sara's, *family members must organize their everyday lives according to the requirements of the secret, while performing the breathtaking feat of pretending not to notice that anything is out of the ordinary.* Young children might stay up very late at night, fearfully waiting for a drug-addicted mother to return, only to be told that she was delayed at work. An adolescent might be expected to skip school in order to care for his physically abused mother, all the while being told that she "fell" and that "Father loves her very much." Conversation is superficial, since what is truly important cannot be discussed. More and more topics become unavailable for dialogue if they even remotely relate to the subject of the secret. Authentic relating is replaced by masks, myths, and illusions. By some sleight of hand, families with disintegrating relationships deem themselves "stable," and fathers who beat their wives and children call their families "traditional." Children who take on adult tasks long before they should are told they are being "responsible."

Children who grow up in a family where everyone knows certain secrets that must remain inside the family at all costs learn that the family unit *always* takes precedence over individual well-being. Family loyalty is valued over personal integrity. The family's capacity to nurture growth and value difference among its members erodes.

Since autonomy and individual development take a backseat to group fidelity, being the family member who challenges secrets that are located within the whole family is extremely difficult. The anticipated catastrophe of being excluded from the family stops many people from even imagining opening a secret.

All families have some secrets from the outside world. Your family, no doubt, has some sweet secrets of shared humor, stories that are told only within the family circle, and aspects of family life defining a unique culture that is separate and distinct from any other. Also, your family has a zone of privacy that demarcates inside from outside. All of this contributes to your family's identity, its sense of itself over time. If, however, a toxic or dangerous secret is located within your entire household, the boundaries between your family and the rest of the world become rigid and impermeable. Friends and relatives are not invited in, and family members' forays out are limited. Children learn to live in a small world, circumscribed by secrets. "No trespassing" and "Don't take family business to the outside" are the operative rules.

These rules make it impossible to ask for assistance or to use needed resources in the outside world. Even problems that do not touch on the secret may go unsolved if solving them requires outside help. I've sat with couples in marital therapy and watched as a husband backs further and further into the corner of the couch while his wife goes on about how he doesn't believe in therapy. Only later do I discover that his father was an alcoholic and his mother warned him repeatedly, "Never tell anyone our troubles." As with Sara, these constraints can remain with people long after they have left home. I've witnessed forty-year-olds challenge their family's requirement of silence for the very first time. Suddenly they feel nine years old, once again experiencing the demands of not knowing what they deeply know.

WHEN YOU DON'T KNOW WHO ELSE KNOWS A SECRET

Many years ago I sat in a family therapy session with Regina and Robert Bellingham, seventy-two and seventy-four, and their two grown sons, Peter, thirty-six, and Keith, thirty-three. Regina and Robert had prepared a long time for this session, during which they planned to tell Peter that he was adopted. With trepidation and tears, Regina told the secret. Peter looked at her and with a mixture of sadness and relief said, "I've known this for years. I found papers when I was eleven. I confided it to Keith when we were teens. He always said I shouldn't say anything. I never knew how to tell you I knew. Since you didn't bring it up, I thought it must be very upsetting to you. I was too afraid to ask you."

In some families, each person knows that everyone knows a secret. In other families it remains unclear who knows and who doesn't know. Secrets may, in fact, be located within the family and known by all, but family members are separated and distant because of a secret about the secret. For a quarter of a century, Mr. and

Mrs. Bellingham and their two sons all knew the same secret. Peter and Keith, of course, knew that their parents knew the secret, but the Bellinghams had no idea that their sons were aware of it. With a wish to protect their parents, the boys kept their knowledge and their secret-keeping relationship a secret.

As with the Bellinghams, discovery of an existing secret may be unplanned and accidental. When we stumble onto a secret, we most often feel confused and even frightened about questioning the secret-keeper(s) directly. The sheer fact that something was kept a secret adds to its emotional weight. Telling another family member may relieve anxiety, but it also makes us vulnerable to that person's point of view about what to do next. The same secret can inadvertently become located in several relationships.

In other families, the location of one secret in several relationships can be the result of deliberate action. One person tells a secret to several others, giving each to believe that they are the only one who knows. Each remains tightly bound to the teller, but out of one another's reach. The relationships that develop are marked by mysterious triangles, jealous alliances, and unfathomable splits. Secret knowlege becomes the currency of manipulation, and family relationships become a marionette show in which the teller pulls the strings.

A secret can move among many relationships in a family when the recipient of a secret breaks his or her word about silence. When a promise to maintain a secret is broken, the promise breaker may insist on a new promise of secrecy: "Don't tell I told you."

Jodi Fein, like many children, had adamantly opposed her father's remarriage. She was an only child and had lived with her widowed father, Aaron, for many years. She and her father's new wife, Susannah, had a testy relationship, not unlike many between stepdaughters and stepmothers early in a remarried family. When Jodi left for college, tensions seemed relieved. But Jodi did poorly in her first semester, and on a trip home she confided to her father that she had a drinking problem. She made him promise not to tell his wife. Aaron's first wife, Jodi's mom, had died years earlier in a car accident. Jodi had never been told about her mom's alcoholism. Aaron was frantic, and within days he told Susannah about Jodi's drinking but insisted that Jodi not know that she knew. Susannah now occupied the unenviable position in family relationships of being both "in" and "out" at the same time. Any ability that Susannah might have had to help Jodi directly was disabled.

The already existing triangle—marked by enduring closeness between Aaron and Jodi, new and fragile intimacy between Aaron and Susannah, and conflict between Jodi and Susannah—now had a heavy dose of lying and deception, guaranteed to create greater distance and prevent reconciliation.

Just as how a secret that is located within an entire family creates unyielding boundaries between the family and the outside world, so not knowing who else knows a secret produces rigid boundaries between individuals and relationships *within* a family. Such fixed limits between family members can handicap problem solving and diminish caring. Susannah, for instance, had many good ideas to help Jodi, but she could not voice them directly because she was not supposed to know what she knew. While she told some of her thoughts to Aaron, he was not able to tell his daughter that these ideas came from her stepmother. Hence, Jodi was never able to experience Susannah's concern for her.

WHEN THE LOCATION OF A SECRET CHANGES

Secrets are dynamic. They move from person to person, from relationship to relationship, and from inside a family to the outside world. The location of any secret, and therefore the relationships shaped by secrets, may shift and change many times before the content of the secret and its personal and interpersonal effects are resolved.

When Anna Perada, thirty-two, came to therapy, she had been keeping a secret for over twenty years.[2] Just before Anna's twelfth birthday, she was sexually abused by a man in her neighborhood. When her parents discovered the abuse, they moved swiftly to keep it a secret. Feeling enormous shame, they turned on

Anna and took away her planned birthday party. None of Anna's brothers, sisters, or friends was told why the party had been canceled. The secret remained located between Anna and her parents but was never spoken of again.

Anna began to relocate her aching secret by first opening it with her therapist. In contemporary culture, the process of relocating a secret in adulthood often begins this way. *Shifting the location of a secret to include a therapist should be considered the beginning of a thoughtful process and not the end.* Anna's therapist first worked with her to reopen the secret with her parents. For years Anna had kept her questions a secret deep inside herself: Why had her parents punished her? Why had they not sought justice on her behalf? Her answers to herself for two decades had been a litany of stigma and self-blame. When her parents revealed their own fear, confusion, and desire to protect her from further pain in their very traditional community, Anna's shame began to melt.

Taking courage from the good outcome with her parents, and with continued support from her therapist, Anna next relocated the secret to include her brothers and sisters. Indeed, they had not known what had happened to Anna, but they vividly remembered the tone of sadness and mysterious humiliation in the family when Anna's birthday party had been canceled. Anna's isolation in her family, stemming from this secret, changed powerfully. When she relocated the secret to include her siblings, they responded with stories about their own lives from which they had excluded Anna for many years.

In a final relocation of the secret, Anna told close friends of hers. Together they decided to have a "twelfth birthday party," marking a celebration of Anna's newfound self-respect and reconnection to family and friends.

Through thoughtful and careful relocation of both the original secret and the hidden thoughts about herself, Anna reversed all that had been closed down in her and her family's life. Her relationship with her parents had grown distant, marked by too many silences. All three knew the secret, but the prohibition on discussing it caused separation among them, not closeness. Her brothers and sisters had grown up in a family where some people knew an important and painful secret and they did not. They were left bewildered by a long period in family life when the family's normal outgoingness and connection to the community was suddenly replaced by unexplained sorrow and disgrace. Boisterous childhood friendships turned to whispers.

In order to release the secret's hold on her, Anna went back to the set of relationships in which it had begun. Recognizing that she had kept her own secrets about the secret, and genuinely seeking to understand her parents' actions, Anna began with questions, not angry confrontation. With her therapist's help, she saw that as an adult she no longer needed anyone's permission to continue relocating the secret until it no longer held any power in her life.

Anna originally came from a family that valued relationships and had deep community ties. A secret derailed that life for many years. A twelfth birthday party at age thirty-two, complete with childhood games, toys, and food, clearly symbolized how careful and courageous relocation of secrets can reconnect us with some of what's best in our families.

THE DEVELOPMENTAL DEEP FREEZE

Imagine what it would be like if your sister made a secret with you on the eve of your wedding and told you that you must not tell your new husband, or if you were pulled into a secret about your parents just when you were making tentative steps into the outside world. Have you ever attended a funeral that was shrouded in silence when the cause of a death of an important family member was kept secret?

If a secret is made at a key point in a family's development, then the natural unfolding of self and relationships may be frozen. Changes that should be happening, the shifting of boundaries that ordinarily would be taking place, and negotiations among family members that ought to be occurring all are suspended when a secret is made at just those times when transformations are most likely.

Every family has stages of development. These occur most vividly when someone enters the family by marriage or other committed adult relationships, birth, or adoption, and when someone leaves the family by leaving home or through separation, divorce, or death. Such entrances and exits require that a family reinvent itself, building on what has gone on before and adding to its repertoire in order to meet the requirements of new relationships. All of these changes involve some loss of a family's prior equilibrium, coupled with the challenge to create something new. These stages are not discrete events, but rather processes that take place over time. For instance, before a young adult actually leaves home, family relationships usually have been gradually shifting through that person's teen years. When that process goes well, complex changes occur in every corner of the family. *When a secret is made in the midst of this life cycle process, what should be changing stops.*

Samuel Wheeler tried to leave home when he was nineteen to go to college. His discovery of a central family secret pulled him back home and short-circuited his young adulthood. When Sam came to see me, he was thirty-four and still struggling with the aftermath.

"I had always been quite close to my mother as a young child. We struggled a lot when I was a teen, but gradually she seemed to accept that I was getting more independent. She and my dad gave me more responsibilities, and I lived up to their expectations. Their marriage never seemed too great to me. It's not that they fought much, but they went their separate ways a lot," Sam told me.

When Sam left home, he moved about three hundred miles away. Early in his first semester, he invited his mother to come to see him. "I was more than a little surprised when she showed up with a close friend of our family, Duncan. She said that she would stay with me in my apartment and that Duncan would stay in a nearby hotel. She gave no explanation for why he had come," said Sam. Each morning for three days Mrs. Wheeler left Sam's apartment at five A.M. and returned to have breakfast at eight o'clock. When Sam finally confronted her and asked what was going on, she told him that she and Duncan were having an affair. The affair was long-standing, and as Sam listened to the details it became apparent that his younger sister in fact had been fathered by Duncan. His mother then said he must never tell his father or his sister. "My mother had kept this secret for years. Why did she have to put it in my face at that moment?" Sam wondered.

Why, indeed? I asked Sam what effects he thought knowing about his mother's love affair and his sister's paternity had. "It stopped my leaving home at that point," Sam said. While very bright, he did poorly his first semester, dropped out, and went back home. "It was crazy, but I felt like I had to keep an eye on things," he remarked. As we talked, it became clear that Sam had returned home to play watchdog for the family's relationships. His sister was fifteen at the time and he was worried that she would discover the secret in some unplanned way that would hurt her. He remained at home until she herself left home. Exemplifying the developmental deep freeze, Sam said, "Knowing these things about my mother's life has kept me from changing my relationship with her and my dad in ways that I would like. She treats me with too much deference, almost like she's scared of me. It keeps us embroiled, but not really close—a lot like when I was a teen, but for different reasons. I wanted to get closer to my dad, but this secret is like a giant rock between us."

Pulling Sam into a secret just at the stage when he and his family were both physically and emotionally moving apart stopped this process. It is unlikely that Sam's mother consciously intended to have Sam come back home or even realized the potential impact of drawing him into her secret at this juncture. Nonetheless, the timing of the secret dovetailed with the timing of central family changes and blocked these.

When secrets are made at the point of entrance to or final exit from a family *and* are about such entrances and exits, their influence on family relationships and well-being is enormous and may cascade down the generations.

When secrets are made about births or deaths, family rituals, which are a key resource in our lives, often disappear. Ordinarily such rituals, including holidays, birthdays, and anniversaries, both announce and facilitate our movement through time. Life cycle passages and changes in our selves and our relationships are made possible with meaningful rituals.[3]

When there are secrets relating to a birth, anxiety will often surround birthday celebrations. If a death cannot be mentioned, holidays become empty and devoid of meaning. Family members are left without an anchor connecting them to the past and without a rudder steering them to the future.

Carl Polanski was fourteen when he was killed in a gang fight just before Thanksgiving. Feeling enormous shame and grief, Mr. and Mrs. Polanski took down all their pictures of Carl. Every reminder that he had ever lived disappeared. Catherine was born two years after her brother died. Her parents and older sister, Jennifer, kept Carl's very existence a secret from Catherine, who grew up in an atmosphere of deep, unexplainable sadness. Since there could be no open grieving to deal with their loss, the family's sorrow remained perpetual.

Because Carl's death went unmentioned and unmourned, normal family rituals went uncelebrated. Since Thanksgiving and Christmas coincided with Carl's death, the family downplayed these, leaving Catherine to wonder why her family was so different from the families of her friends. Carl was killed shortly after his fourteenth birthday, an event he had marked by getting drunk with his friends. As Catherine approached adolescence, her birthday became fraught with anxiety. After a huge fight with her parents just before her fourteenth birthday, they declared there would be no more birthday parties in the family. Rituals that might have made and marked life's passages were unavailable, having disappeared behind a veil of secrecy. There were no visits to the cemetery, and while the family had been religious Catholics, there were no candles lit in memory of Carl.

The secret of Carl's life and death reached a climax when Catherine herself turned fourteen. Watching yet again her mother's yearly mysterious depression just before Thanksgiving, and chafing under her father's hypervigilant attention to her every action, Catherine began to run around with a gang of girls. In what felt to the Polanskis like a nightmarish replay of Carl's life, Catherine spent her birthday getting drunk with friends.

Since birth and death are the quintessential passages in life, secrets regarding birth and death may initiate patterns in a family that result in our most feared outcomes. Concealed dread cannot be discussed and potentially debunked, but it is powerfully experienced in any family's emotional climate. When the family member who's living outside the secret reaches the same age or stage of development as the subject of the secret, family relationships become enveloped in unspeakable tension. Catherine Polanski sensed all that was unmentioned in her family, but she had no way of making sense of it. The closer she came to the age her brother had been at the time of his death, the more anxiety rose in the family. Any tiny variation that she made from her family's wishes was met with swift punishment by her parents in a misguided effort to allay their own terror that she would turn out like Carl. Absent any words between her and her parents to talk about the stage of life she was entering, Catherine went forth with a map where all roads led to the secret life and death of Carl.

Following her birthday binge, Catherine's guidance counselor referred her and her family to me, telling me, "This is a nice girl from a good family—I don't know what's going on, but they need help." I spent the first four meetings trying to stop the family from scapegoating Catherine, all the while sensing their very real panic and wondering what was beneath it. When unacknowledged yet palpable anxiety is sky-high, family members often engage in unrelenting blame of one person. As therapist, it was my job to carefully interrupt the condemnation of Catherine, without in turn blaming family members.

I decided to meet alone with Mr. and Mrs. Polanski. In this meeting, I was able to create a safe and accepting atmosphere to enable them to tell me their story. As they spoke for the first time to an outsider, their enormous and bottled-up grief and shame poured forth. Gently and respectfully I made connections for them between Catherine's current behavior and the secret of Carl's life and death. Very gradually they were able to consider that Catherine needed to know—indeed, had a right to know—about Carl.

I spoke with them about all of the missing rituals in their lives, rituals that might help them to heal. Mrs. Polanski burst into tears, telling her husband for the first time how much she longed to go to the cemetery to visit Carl's grave. He, in turn, had kept his wish to do likewise a secret from his wife.

The remainder of our family therapy involved telling Catherine about her brother and about why they had kept his life and death a secret from her. We looked at old family photographs together. Open grieving led spontaneously to new family rituals. Catherine spent her fifteenth birthday at a rock concert, broke her curfew, and, like all the rest of her friends, was grounded for a week.

REFLECTING ON RELATIONSHIPS SHAPED BY SECRETS IN YOUR FAMILY

You may want to take some time to think about how secrets shape the relationships in your family now.

- Where are secrets located in your family?
- What impact do you think these locations are having on various relationships in your family?
- What enduring triangles are shaped by secrets in your family?
- How does the presence of secrets affect closeness and distance in your family's relationships?
- How do secrets affect the boundary between your household and your family of origin? Between your household and the outside world?
- Do secrets prevent you from using necessary resources to solve problems?
- Have secrets had an impact on the naturally occurring rituals in your family's life?
- How have secrets affected the development of individuals and relationships in your family?

The Bradleys, the Delgados, the Bowerses, the Polanskis, and all the other families I've known with secrets have taught me the endless variations of complex patterns shaped by secrets. However, from the beginning of my work as a family therapist, I was dissatisfied with a point of view suggesting that family problems, particularly those involving secrets, simply hatched inside a family. I cringe when I hear a family called or calling itself "dysfunctional," as if any family's complicated repertoire of responses to life could possibly match a narrow list of universal traits. My search alongside the families I've known for the genesis of any secret in their lives has led us outside the family to their matrix, to which we'll now turn—their history, culture, ethnic origins, race, religion, gender, and social class.

Chapter

3

The Secret Society

—✦—

After my father's death when I was twelve, I had little contact with the Ball family. Years later when I visit Charleston, I come as a New Yorker, a Yankee. Over the years, I've heard a lot about the Balls, but I'd never heard much about the slaves. There were 2,088 people born into slavery on the Ball plantation between 1800 and 1865, plus many others bought at auction. Similar numbers stand from the previous century. I feel compelled to find out more about my family's role during the slave period. To this day, my motives aren't clear to me. But when I look across the rice fields where thousands of people worked, I want to hear their story told alongside my family's tale.

—Edward Ball

HOW PETER BECAME DAVID: A SECRET BORN IN NAZI GERMANY

"Every afternoon when I returned from school in our small German town, my grandmother gave us tea and cakes. My two younger brothers and I were entranced hearing our grandmother tell and retell family stories. But there was always a point when her stories stopped, and I sensed some earlier time was missing. I would ask her for more, and she would deftly change the subject.

Her cooking was not like the cooking in the homes of friends. My parents lit candles in church to pray for dead relatives. She lit candles at home on the anniversaries of people's deaths and could never explain why she did that. Then when I was thirteen I became very interested in Judaism and fought with my parents when I refused to go to church. When I was eighteen I was discussing a financial matter with my great-aunt. She looked straight at me and said, 'That's the Jew in you coming out.' When I tried to pursue what she meant, she said, 'You'd better ask your grandmother.' Only little by little have I been able to piece together my maternal grandparents' secret conversion from Judaism to Catholicism in the 1930s, a matter so hidden that while my mother knows, she has never told my father."

David was born and baptized Peter, in honor of St. Peter. As an adult living in New York City, sorting out the secrets in his family that were intricately connected to Nazism, he reclaimed Judaism and changed his name to David. "As far as my father is concerned, I converted and it's all a mystery to him. I'm not even sure anymore who I'm protecting by keeping this secret."

As I got to know David, many more secrets emerged. His father is an only child, born to a family who trace their landed-gentry lineage to the Middle Ages. His paternal grandfather was born with one leg shorter than the other. Under the Nazi laws, permission to marry would be denied to him unless he agreed to be sterilized. Caught between shame, fear, and determination, he and his young wife-to-be decided that she should get pregnant before they were married. These circumstances of David's father's birth were, of course, kept secret. David discovered it by searching baptismal records and asking a cousin who knew the family's history. David's mother has never heard this story. "Today," David told me with deep sadness, "both of my parents speak very little to each other and drink too much. At family gatherings, we're not supposed to notice the silence."

It would be all too easy to meet David's family and, in today's popular idiom, declare them to be "dysfunctional." Alcoholism, distant relationships, a son who changes his name and then makes a religious conversion and moves across an ocean, and myriad secrets all fit the prevailing notion that internal family relationships wholly explain behavior. David's story, however, illustrates the multiple social and political levels that shape secrets inside any family. The Nazi Nuremberg decrees regarding so-called "racial purity" and physical handicaps powerfully drove David's two sets of grandparents into lives of secrecy and shame. Both families of origin made and kept secrets out of pervasive fear and need for safety. David's parents were each born into secrecy regarding difference from the dominant culture, secrets shaped and driven by pre–World War II Nazi beliefs and laws, secrets so deep that unearthing all of them even sixty years later feels impossible. "I live my life knowing that there are many things I will never fully know," David told me, "and of those things that I do know, I live uncertain over whose job it is to tell other family members, and so I join the silence."

The complex weaving, at the political and cultural level, of the poisonous policies and practices of anti-Semitism and discrimination against handicapped people combined with centuries of class bias resulted in a tapestry of guilt, shame, and strangled voices at the family level.

MULTIPLE, NESTED CONTEXTS OF SECRECY

No family wakes up one morning and says, "Let's make a secret." Searching for the origins of what is concealed and what is revealed leads inevitably beyond the boundaries of any given family into a wider world of history, culture, power, and politics. Too often the details of this larger context are blurred or hidden, adding further layers of the unspoken and the unknown.

While societal definitions of stigma and shame find expression in what we keep secret in our personal and family relationships, connections between any given act of secret-making and the culture from which this act springs are often obscured. When the genesis of any secret is inscrutable, then stigma and self-blame blossom, and decisions about what actions to take remain uninformed. A family that conceals a suicide today is not simply acting in a vacuum. Such secret-making has its origins early in recorded Western history. During the Middle Ages and the rise of the Catholic Church, not only was the body of a person who committed suicide forbidden burial in hallowed ground, but it may well have been thrown over the city wall. Acknowledged suicide was a public humiliation for a family, rather than a solemn occasion for private grief. While this history is hundreds of years old, the potent mixture of historical religious proscription, societal shaming, and personal guilt can still alter a family's version of a death certificate today—a suicide becomes instead a single-car accident.

Early in the AIDS epidemic, African-American community leaders were criticized for promoting secrecy about the prevalence of HIV/AIDS among African-Americans.[1] Everyone wanted to believe that this was a disease that struck only "high-risk groups"—gays, drug addicts, and Haitians. That some gays and some drug addicts might also be African-American was neatly sidestepped. This seeming denial begins to make a different kind of sense when we connect it with the painful historical reality that slaves who became ill on the passage from Africa were treated as worthless cargo and brutally thrown overboard.[2] No doubt this experience left a searing legacy, deeply embedded in the collective mind of a people: Serious illness should be kept secret from those who are in power. It is but a small leap from such secret-keeping at the community level to the quagmire of maintaining such a secret within one's family.

A given family today may wrestle with how much to tell their adopted child about her birth origins. It's unlikely that this same family opens the hidden beliefs of their ethnic group regarding adoption, or considers the ways in which contemporary culture may be in harmony or conflict with those opinions. Yet it's these very beliefs that powerfully weight decisions about what to conceal or reveal.

A woman who keeps her abortion a secret today may have a shadowy memory, just at the edge of her awareness, of a time in the not-so-distant past when women who had abortions ran the risk of prosecution. While reasons to keep an abortion secret today are myriad, this forensic fact and all that it implied about personal guilt, societal and family shaming, lawbreaking, religious rules, and the specter of back-alley abortions hums along beneath the surface.

As I've worked with individuals and families who are struggling to make informed decisions about secrets in their lives, I've found that viewing secrets in their multiple, nested contexts opens possibilities. While decisions about making, keeping, or opening a secret are ultimately an individual responsibility, they are intricately related to these multiple contexts.

Let's look now at some specifics of the broader social, cultural, and political contexts that shape societal injunctions about secrets.

THE HIDDEN THREADS: RACE, ETHNICITY, RELIGION, SOCIAL CLASS, AND GENDER

Confounding and distressing secrets in our lives often contain hidden dimensions involving power imbalances. In my work with both families and institutions, I've often seen people who have power over others assume they have license to conceal information. Those with little or no power, in turn, are intimidated into silence. I've seen women, children, poor people, and minorities use secrecy to redress power inequities or to protect themselves. Power differences at the societal level, such as male over female, white over black, and rich over poor, echo loudly within family relationships, affecting how secrets are handled.

People who are different from the majority culture and who feel threatened or ashamed of their status often make secrets. While power imbalances, divergence from the majority, and threat permeate all levels at which secrets exist, the least examined places for broadening and deepening our choices regarding any particular secret in our lives are the social, cultural, and political levels.

Race, ethnicity, religion, social class, and gender make potent contributions to what is hidden, silenced, or taboo. Historical experiences and the beliefs that spring from them reverberate in our contemporary encounters with secrets. Discovering ways in which people's secrets are connected to these domains often means that long-lasting mysteries will finally yield.

RACE

How has the history of race relations and racism contributed to specific secrets in your life? Secrets shaped by race and racism—pervasive the world over—are a template for all kinds of secrets based on power, difference, and threat.

We need go only four or five generations back to unearth the origins of secrets that vibrate within many African-American families today. Recently I received a wedding invitation with a picture of a bride and groom joyfully jumping over a broom. What did this mean? During slavery, marriages could be forbidden by white masters. Since men, women, and children were abruptly sold away from one another, committed bonds were often discouraged and even illegal. A secret practice called "jumping the broom" developed in order to ritualize a marriage.[3] A tradition originally requiring secrecy began in a context of coercion and fear on the one hand, and bravery and determination on the other. It has been reclaimed in today's context as a celebration of survival.

While forbidden to learn to read and write, African-American women expressed their otherwise unheard stories by sewing quilts that told the secrets of oppression and the struggle for freedom.[4]

"Whose Boy Is He?": Sara's Story

When I first met Sara Williams, she came to see me with her seven-year-old son, Trevor. An African-American single parent living in the Bronx, Sara, thirty-nine, was competent in all areas of her life except with Trevor. His teachers complained that he was disruptive. "I can't get him to listen to me," Sara told me. She was a registered nurse who supervised others, and yet when she spoke to Trevor, she was timid and indecisive. What was going on here?

As I got to know Sara better, she confided in me that she was actually Trevor's grandmother but that he didn't know this. Through her tears, Sara spoke with shame about her daughter, Bernice, who gave birth to Trevor when she was fifteen, replicating Sara's own teen pregnancy. As conflict grew between mother and daughter, Bernice fled, leaving Trevor with his grandmother. "He's mine, but he's not mine," Sara cried. "I live in fear of the school or other authorities finding out and taking him away from me. I don't know if I'll ever tell him." The secret of Trevor's parentage and Sara's informal adoption of him was creating enormous anxiety for Sara, disabling her as an effective parent and contributing to the tension between her and her grandson. At the same time, this informal and secret adoption made a lot of sense to Sara and felt quite familiar to her, both from her family of origin and from her culture.

Just as marriages were forbidden under slavery, so parent-child ties were frequently torn apart. When parents were sold away, young children were cared for by a method of informal adoption. Frequently the biological parentage of these children was kept a secret from them. What began as a secret intended to protect children from the pain of losing their parents continues as a secret in many instances of informal adoption today. When Sara sought advice from relatives or friends, they all told her to keep Trevor's parentage a secret from him, at least until he was grown. Their fears of outside authorities mirrored her own and were a direct link to a time in the history of her people when children and parents could be separated forever with no recourse.

When Sara and I were able to place her current situation within the historical and social context of African-American family relationships, many possibilities opened to her. Through talking to her extended family, including her ninety-two-year-old aunt, she discovered several instances of informal adoption that she had not known about, including some that were not kept a secret from the child. "I see this more as part of a tradition of survival than something I should be ashamed of," Sara concluded. "I want Trevor to know that, too."

When coercive power shapes relationships, sexual exploitation and abuse is rampant. Under slavery, African-American men were used as "breeders" to increase the number of slaves, while African-American women were used as sexual objects by white slave masters.[5] Rapes and other forms of sexual exploitation resulted in babies with lighter skin. Such children were often treated better by the slaveholders. Thus began the painful and paradoxical secret of skin color within African-American families. Lighter skin may bring privilege and opportunity, yet lighter skin is also a reminder of the sexual exploitation of black women. Since lighter skin continues to be valued and favored within white American society, skin color distinctions are often an unspoken dimension in African-American family relationships. Skin color may underpin painful family secrets, including scapegoating family members whose skin color is most different from the rest, "passing for white," living a double life, or cutting oneself off totally from one's family.[6]

The process of keeping secrets from "outsiders" was essential during slavery, as it is for any oppressed group in which life and death may turn on what is hidden or revealed. When a family has a "rule" regarding keeping "family business" strictly within the boundaries of the household, even on matters where it makes little sense to do so, likely there was a time in family and cultural history when such a rule may have been an effective and adaptive response to threatening circumstances.

ETHNICITY

Much of the United States is a nation of immigrants. Whether migration occurred in our own generation or long ago, each of us is related to a people with a set of values, beliefs, and experiences that contribute to who we are today. Key positions and conflicts about secrecy and openness in the families I've worked with often have unnoticed roots in ethnicity.

Until quite recently in the American context, assimilation was the most valued route for immigrants who wanted to be accepted and to thrive. Consequently, many people changed their names, expunged any connection to their ethnic origins, and even resorted to surgery to alter their appearance. Such drastic measures to fit in with the majority culture resulted in long-held family secrets arising from the shame of being different.

Deviations from qualities valued by any ethnic group often lead to secrets. For instance, if you come from a people who value conformity because it enabled survival, then acts of rebellion will likely be kept secret. Every ethnic group has aspects of life in which they take particular pride. For one this may be educational achievement and for another success in work, while for still another it may be having large and connected extended families. Each of these sources of ethnic pride contains the seeds of shame when individuals depart from what is expected. Such shame breeds secrecy.

Relationships between minority ethnic groups and the majority culture may shape profound secrets involving violent and coercive disruptions of family relationships, group identity, and individual well-being. For many decades, Native American children in the United States and Canada were taken from their tribes and placed in government-run boarding schools, based on the perverted belief that their families were incapable of raising them properly and that these children needed "white culture." Only recently have Native American adults revealed the secrets of physical and sexual abuse that went on in these settings. Similarly, Aboriginal children in Australia from 1918 to the 1960s were kidnapped from their families by government workers and given to white families to raise, while their ethnic origins and biological family histories were kept a secret from them.[7]

YOUR ETHNIC GROUP AND SECRETS

Think specifically about how your ethnic group responds to such issues as intermarriage, adoption, child rearing, substance abuse, finances, and family violence.

- How have historical experiences, even many generations ago, contributed to beliefs about secrecy and openness?

- How has war, political terror, or migration contributed to secrets in your ethnic group?
- If your family comprises two or more ethnicities, how has this influenced patterns of secret-keeping?

RELIGION

"No One Knows Me": Anne's Story

Anne McDougal was thirty-one when she came to see me. She felt hopeless and alone, she told me. Brought up in a large, boisterous Irish Catholic family that expected each child to marry and have lots of children, Anne was the one who remained single. She was a teacher in a local elementary school. She did her job well and went home alone each day to her apartment. She had no close friends.

Anne spent most of our first three sessions together weeping, but she could not tell me what was troubling her. I was able to piece together that seven of her eight siblings were married with children and lived nearby. She saw them rarely. Family gatherings were intensely uncomfortable. The impending large church wedding of her youngest sister had prompted her to call me. She described a severe panic attack at her brother's wedding a number of years earlier. She was certain she would have one again at her sister's wedding.

In our fourth meeting, Anne revealed a secret that she had never told another person: "My mother would die and my father would disown me—I've broken everything they hold dear, and everything I hold dear." Anne had had an abortion six years earlier, just before her brother's wedding. She interpreted the panic attack at her brother's wedding as a punishment from God. "I felt so ashamed. Near the end of the ceremony, I fainted. I took attention away from my own brother's wedding mass. I just hated myself and I couldn't tell anyone why." Over time she withdrew from family and friends. "I go to church, but I feel like I have no right to be there. People think they know me, but no one knows me," she said.

Our work together involved close examination of Anne's religious beliefs and what it meant to her to have broken a central tenet of her faith. We spoke about what forgiveness meant in her religion. I worked with Anne to draw distinctions among her many family members, helping her determine to whom she could tell her aching secret. She realized that she was judging herself far more harshly than most of her siblings would. She decided to risk telling her closest sister, and when she received acceptance from her, she told three other siblings. She returned to her church and sought absolution. Gradually she came to see her abortion as a private matter rather than a shameful secret.

Some religions have secret practices known only to the adherents. These are often essential secrets that contribute to a sense of membership and boundaries between the particular religious community and the outside world. Expressed through rituals, liturgy, and styles of worship, such secrets often contain and protect spirtual beliefs.

Religious persecution is fertile ground for secret-making. If you belong to a religious group that has experienced persecution, likely there are secrets going back many generations about conversions or other modes of survival. Very recently, lots of information has emerged about Iberian Jews from Spain, Portugal, and their colonies in Mexico, Peru, and Brazil. Forced to convert or face death during the Inquisition, many such Jews outwardly converted while secretly practicing Judaism.[8] Five hundred years and many generations later, one still finds remnants of Jewish tradition—life cycle celebrations, dietary observances, superstitions—in what are now Catholic descendants of these families. On the other side of this coin, religions that practice persecution keep terrible secrets of their tyranny over others.

All religions include rules for behavior. When religious beliefs prohibit certain actions, such as divorce, contraception, abortion, suicide, sex outside of marriage, religious intermarriage, or homosexuality, many individuals and families respond by maintaining their religious affiliation while keeping the behavior a secret. Although there is nothing inherent in religion per se that promotes secrecy, rigidly held religious beliefs coupled with actual behavior that belies those beliefs often leads to secrets. When secrets spring from violating religious principles, denial, guilt, shame, and pretense run high.

Secrets that are made and kept because they violate religious rules exact a very high price. When beliefs and actions collide, alienation from self and others results. Family relationships become hypocritical; the very existence of a problem is denied. For instance, when Susan Smith was tried for the drowning murder of her young sons, the previously secret and denied fact of her stepfather's sexual abuse of her as a teenager became known. This man, Beverly Russell, was a respected and highly placed member of the Christian Coalition. Smith's own mother and members of the community who knew about the abuse helped to keep it a secret.[9] When the reality of ongoing sexual abuse of a young girl conflicted with the "family values" agenda of the Christian Coalition, the sexual abuse was simply made to "disappear."

The standing of a religious community within the wider community may also contribute to toxic secrets, since members are afraid to bring shame on their religious group in the eyes of outsiders. Wife battering within the Jewish community is as frequent as it is in other communities, yet among Jews it has often been kept a secret.[10] Here, a religious group's fear of stigma and shame vis-à-vis the outside community functions to maintain secrecy and denial within given families, thereby preventing a solution.

YOUR RELIGIOUS BELIEFS AND SECRETS

As you think about your own religious beliefs, consider how these factors may contribute to secrets in your life.

- What are the beliefs of the religion with which you identify that relate to secrecy and openness?
- Are you keeping the secrets of other family members in order to maintain a facade within your religious community?

- Are family members keeping secrets from you because they fear your response to a broken religious precept?

- Are you living a double life, professing religious beliefs while secretly violating them? What effect does this have on your sense of self and your capacity to relate authentically to others?

SOCIAL CLASS

The official myth in the United States proclaims that we are all the same, that we have no social-class distinctions. In fact, social class is an often unspoken dimension that profoundly organizes our lives. While powerfully visible in such domains as educational opportunities, job choices or the lack thereof, housing, neighborhoods, child care, and income, class differences—freely admissible in most other nations of the world—remain largely unmentionable here. Thus, social class creates the kind of secret that everyone knows exists but that no one can acknowledge openly.

In my family therapy practice, I've witnessed many parents who are upset and angry that their child is choosing to marry someone who is "not good enough," but they refuse to specify that "not good enough" means coming from a lower social-class background. One husband complained bitterly to me, "Every Christmas we go to my in-laws' house. They give lavish gifts to everyone except me. I get dime-store items. It's because I come from a working-class family. It's their code way of saying I don't belong. They never say it openly. If I get upset, they laugh and say I have no sense of humor."

Our inability to acknowledge class differences can lead to very peculiar distortions of reality. As one extremely wealthy woman told me, "We weren't supposed to notice that we were rich when I was a child. Our house stood on the top of the hill in our town and was larger than any other house, but my parents insisted that we were just like everyone else. To keep us from thinking we were better than others, they sent us to public school. We arrived each day in a chauffeur-driven limousine!"

YOUR SOCIAL CLASS AND SECRETS

Since social class is so seldom mentioned openly in families, the idea of considering its impact on secrets may be unfamiliar territory. Some of the questions I raise with clients about the hidden impact of social class can lift this taboo.

- Have there been social-class shifts up or down in your family and extended family that have led to silence and secrets?
- Have there been relationship breaks among grown siblings or between parents and adult children in your family because of unacknowledged social-class differences?
- How has class bias contributed to taboo issues?
- How have beliefs about money or education shaped secrets?
- Are financial assets and liabilities in your family and extended family known or hidden?
- Do you or others in your extended family disguise their social-class background? What would happen if you opened this concealed area in family relationships?

GENDER

A few years ago a journalist called me to discuss a piece she was doing on women's secrets. When I asked her what she meant by "women's secrets," she replied, "Like when a housewife has a fender bender but tells her husband that someone hit the car while it was parked." I asked her if she thought a husband would make a secret and tell a lie like that, and she said, "Of course not." Then we were into a most interesting discussion of secrets that are kept out of fear when relationships are shaped by differences in gender and power. If you want to understand the gender dimension of a secret in your life, ask yourself if a person of the opposite sex would keep this matter a secret. If not, then ask yourself what there is about this particular secret that is affected by gender and male-female relationships.

I Can't Believe She Did This to Me: Bill and Ellen's Story

Bill Korman stormed angrily into my office, while his wife, Ellen, followed meekly behind him. This was our second couples' therapy session for what each described as "too much distance between us." I quickly found out that after our first meeting Ellen had decided to tell Bill a secret she had been keeping for the twelve years of their marriage. "I wanted to get things out into the open. If we're going to have a marriage, I can't pretend in bed anymore," Ellen quietly stated. Ellen had been faking orgasms for their entire marriage. Bill was furious. "How could she deceive me this way?" I began to draw his attention to why Ellen felt she needed to pretend, and Ellen replied, "I felt ashamed of myself as a woman, and I felt I needed to protect your feelings as a man." For a dozen years Ellen had kept this secret out of the contradictory beliefs that she was somehow defective and that her husband would not be able to tolerate feeling like "less of a man" because his wife didn't have orgasms when they made love. Her personal shame, coupled with fear for her husband's vulnerability, created a toxic secret that permeated their entire relationship.[11]

Ellen's secret, standing at the heart of this couple's intimate life, is a painful illustration of the impact of gender on secrets. Until very recently, all manner of physical and sexual abuse of women was kept secret. While such abuse is now known within the culture, many individual women still remain mute when they are being beaten by their partners or when their daughters are being sexually abused. Until very recently, women who were raped were most often blamed for the rape. Humiliation by medical, police, and judicial authorities guaranteed that women would keep silent about a rape.

In many parts of the world, the degradation of women following a rape still occurs, driving women into secrecy. Historically, rape has been used as a weapon in wars. In captured countries, women are forced to have sex with the occupying soldiers and are forbidden from speaking out. Long after the end of a war, many women shamefully hide that they have been violated, fearing that telling will put them at risk of being ostracized among their own people. These dangerous secrets are examples of the more powerful coercing the less powerful into silence. While such secrets are made within intimate family relationships, their continuity is supported by the deeply rooted and only recently challenged historical assumption that women and children are the property of men. The ongoing tension between maintaining such secrets or opening them is directly related to women's shame, self-blame, and centuries of training to protect their men, coupled with uncertainty regarding the responses of police, courts, social agencies, and extended family.

To maintain jobs, women often keep the secret of sexual harassment by male superiors in the workplace. When Anita Hill came forward to declare that she had been sexually harassed by Clarence Thomas, a spotlight suddenly was turned on this national secret. The life of this spotlight was painfully brief. Not only did we discover that a highly educated attorney had been frightened that she would endanger her career if she didn't keep the secret of being harassed by her male supervisor, we sadly found out that she was correct in her assumption. As Senator Barbara Mikulski said, "To anybody out there who wants to be a whistleblower, the message is: Don't blow that whistle because you'll be left out there by yourself. To any victim of sexual harassment or sexual abuse or sexual violence either in the street or even in her own home, the message is nobody's going to take you seriously, not even in the United States Senate."[12] Sexual harassment has shifted from a secret that particular working women kept to a secret that we all know but pretend not to know.

Some secrets are kept by men from women because they feel entitled to do so. I am often amazed, over a quarter of a century after the start of the women's movement in the United States, by the number of men today who maintain secrets from their wives about money. Often these secrets are conveniently redefined as "private matters." While women collude in such secrets when they accept not knowing about the couple's finances, I've seen many men who feel entitled to keep financial information secret from their wives.

An audacious model of how secrets can be used to protect men at the expense of women is apparent in the first recorded case of donor insemination. In 1884 a husband and wife consulted their doctor, complaining of infertility. While anesthetized, the woman was inseminated with the sperm of a medical student without her knowledge. Clearly believing that men were entitled to keep such a secret, the doctor told only her husband about the insemination. She gave birth and raised a child she believed to be her husband's. This secret hid yet another secret—the husband had had syphilis and didn't want his wife to know about this as the likely cause of the infertility.[13] While a secret with these particulars would not occur today, the belief in male power and privilege that underpinned such a secret over a century ago still persists and enables other secrets that men feel authorized to keep from women.

Men also keep secrets to enhance an otherwise unsupportable image or to cover vulnerabilities and weaknesses that are considered "unmanly." Many men keep secrets regarding work insecurities, lack of competence, or outright failure. When Tom and Sonia Gorham came to see me, their marriage was in an extreme crisis. Tom's business had been failing for many months, but he had kept this a secret from Sonia. Unknown to her, he had been using money put aside for their children's college education to keep his business afloat. Most recently he had taken a loan at a very high interest rate, thereby jeopardizing the financial safety of their home. Only when Sonia opened a piece of mail from the bank did she begin to discover what Tom had been doing with their money.

When we first began to talk about what was happening in

their lives, Tom appeared arrogant and angry with Sonia for what he called "snooping." Only later in the session did he break down crying and say, "I'm the man. I'm supposed to take care of my family. I didn't want her to know. I didn't want anyone to know." Tom's father was a successful businessman, and he grew up with the message that "men take care, women are taken care of." Shame regarding his business failure drove him to keep secrets that nearly wrecked his marriage.

Social constructions of manhood influence men to keep secrets even from themselves. Sometimes such secret-keeping can be personally dangerous. Forty-three-year-old Charlie Gooden came to see me two years after his divorce. Lonely and quite sad, Charlie talked about his inability to find the "right" women to date. As we moved along in therapy, I found out that Charlie had met one woman he seemed to care for, but the relationship had "mysteriously" ended several months earlier. When I pressed Charlie for his views on what happened, he changed the subject. Then in our eleventh session Charlie told me that a friend wanted to arrange a date for him, but he had declined. What was going on for this man who so much wanted a new relationship?

I asked Charlie what he imagined would happen if he agreed to meet this woman. Suddenly he broke down and began to cry. He wanted to bolt from the session, but I implored him to stay. With much stammering, Charlie told me that toward the end of his last relationship, he suddenly couldn't sustain an erection. With anger and recriminations, the woman he was seeing had ended the relationship. Charlie went into hiding. He threw himself into work and came to see me only at the urging of his best friend. He told me he "forced himself to forget" about what had happened with his woman friend. I asked Charlie if he had gone to see a doctor. He scoffed and said a doctor would just tell him that he had a problem with women. Explaining that erectile difficulties could be related to many different physical conditions, I urged him to get a checkup. Two weeks later Charlie discovered that the reason he couldn't maintain an erection was that he had previously undiagnosed diabetes.

Our beliefs about what it means to be a man or to be a

woman underpin one of the most painful and closely held secrets of men, the secret of sexual abuse. While some women have begun to open the secret of being sexually abused as children, very few men have done likewise. Like female victims, young boys are intimidated into silence at the time of the abuse. By the time a boy has grown independent of his abuser, he has also learned the loud social message that being a victim of abuse has made him "less of a man." The deeply held gender belief that being a man is clearly superior to being a woman functions to promote secrecy about the abuse. If the perpetrator was a man, homophobia surrounds the secret. "If others know this happened to me," a man tells himself, "they will think I'm homosexual." Rather than opening the awful secret, many men respond by becoming hypermasculine, eschewing any responses in life that might appear vulnerable or "feminine." Alcohol, drug abuse, and compulsive sexual behavior may numb the pain and drive the secret deeper.[14]

Over the years, I've worked with several couples in which the couple's initial complaints about a husband's substance abuse, sexual problems, or unmovable silence were ultimately discovered to be connected to the man's abiding shame regarding a never-opened secret of being sexually abused as a child. In every instance, the man's gender beliefs, learned from the culture and his family of origin, were the glue that sealed the secret shut.

In a 1995 series of episodes on *NYPD Blue*, the effects of two gendered secrets on a couple are portrayed with thought and care. The relationship of the newly married police detective Andy Sipowicz and assistant district attorney Sylvia Costas begins to erode under the weight of secrets each is keeping from the other. Recently mugged on the street, Sylvia begins to reexperience the trauma of having been raped many years earlier. She has kept this rape a secret from her husband, driven both by her own shame and by fear that Andy would be turned off by her if he knew. The dilemma experienced by many rape victims regarding whether to tell anyone, and if so, who to tell, is touchingly shown. As viewers, we are invited into her considerable turmoil as she considers the consequences of telling or not telling.

Simultaneously, we are shown the development of a new secret in Andy's life. Fearing that he may have cancer of the prostate, he keeps the secret of this medical problem from his new wife. We viewers witness the formation of a secret, fueled by the motive of protecting a loved one. As a man, Andy thinks he needs to hide any vulnerabilities from his wife.

In this context, not knowing her husband's secret, Sylvia finds the courage to risk telling Andy the secret about her being raped. While he is supportive of her, he withdraws from her sexually due to his own medical problem. Not knowing his secret, Sylvia assumes that her worst fears have been confirmed. Much later, when Andy is assured that he does not have cancer, he reveals his secret.

This carefully crafted subplot takes but several minutes to portray, and yet we are shown the deleterious impact of secrets on a new marriage, the distance that important secrets can create in intimate relationships, the doubts and fears that people experience when they consider opening a secret, the shame attached to particular secrets, and how learning the content of one secret may affect another. The particular secrets shown and Sylvia and Andy's motivations for keeping them are richly imbued with gender dimensions. Sylvia's secret is a secret of rape and, like women throughout time, she fears that her husband will think less of her or blame her because she was raped. The content of Andy's secret is associated with male sexuality—will he be less of a man if he has prostate disease? He responds the way men have been socialized to respond for centuries, with denial of his own fears and "protection" of his wife through silence and withdrawal.

GENDER AND SECRETS

As you think about secrets regarding physical abuse, sexual harassment, sexual abuse, war, infertility, new birth technologies, parentage, and abortion, think about the ways that gender patterns and beliefs in the wider culture impact such secrets.

- What has your experience been as a woman or a man with secrets that spring from gender?
- If you are part of a couple, whether heterosexual or homosexual, how have positions of men and women in the wider culture influenced secrecy and openness in your intimate life?

BRAIDED SECRETS

While race, ethnicity, religion, social class, and gender can each stand alone to shape the context of any secret, often two or more of these dimensions intertwine. For instance, both religious and gender issues underpin the secret of sexual abuse of an altar boy by a priest. Or ethnicity and religion and gender might all be pertinent to a secret regarding homosexuality.

"When Is Your Mother Coming?": Margaret's Story

In Margaret Castle's life, race and racism, child-rearing beliefs derived from ethnic "rules," religious hypocrisy, social-class elitism, and choices constrained by gender combined to make a secret that has haunted her forty-six years of life.

"One Sunday when I was sixteen," she told me, "my mother sent me across the street to Mrs. Ellis with some flowers from our garden. Mrs. Ellis thanked me and said offhandedly, 'I haven't seen your mother for a long time. When is your mother coming?' 'My mother? My mother's across the street—you see her every day.' She looked frightened. After a long moment she asked, 'They've never told you that Lucy is your mother?'"

With this conversation, brief and shattering as an earthquake, Margaret Castle's life was at once confused and clarified. Raised in Barbados by a middle-class black family, Margaret was the younger of two children. "As a small child, I always sensed that something wasn't right. I was always told I asked too many questions, that I was too outspoken. Lucy was a very light-skinned woman who visited our home often when I was little. She was bossy to me, but not to my older sister. I never understood why my mother let her order me around. She used to change my hairdo, take down my braids, put a big bow in my hair, and announce, 'This is more high-class.' I hated it, but I had to let it be."

When Margaret discovered the secret of her adoption, she confronted her adoptive parents, who denied it and angrily refused any further discussion. "In Barbados, children were raised the British way—to be seen and not heard. Children were like cats—you picked them up, you put them down where you wanted them. You owed them no explanation about anything and they had no right to ask or feel," Margaret told me. "To this day, the worst part is that no one ever apologized to me."

What stood behind this secret would take Margaret many years to unearth, understand, and ultimately forgive. "For many years I never spoke to anyone about it. I was consumed by anger. My focus in life was to grow up and leave as soon as I could." Discovering the secret in her mid-teens, in a context where no one would talk to her about it, seemed to disrupt Margaret's young-adult life. She left Barbados at eighteen for New York and didn't return for two decades. While she is a successful businesswoman today, she spent several years floundering. "I lived angry. I had no faith that I could go to college. I wasted many years in a relationship with an older, unavailable man," Margaret said.

When I met Margaret, I was struck that all of her remarks about the people in her life were prefaced by descriptions of their skin color, religion, and social class. It turned out that these were the dimensions driving the secrets that had affected her life so profoundly.

Lucy's father, Michael Rose, was a white Barbadian whose grandfather was a slaveholder. Lucy's mother, Ruth, was black and descended from slaves. Michael Rose, a respected landowner and deacon in his church, fathered many out-of-wedlock children with several different women. Margaret said, "The secrets continue today, you know. Just last year I found out that a seventy-two-year old woman I thought was a maid in the Rose family was one of Michael Rose's children. In other words, she's my aunt!"

Lucy was Michael Rose's favorite child. "She was raised to think she was white. When she got pregnant with me in her early twenties and Michael Rose found out that my father was a working-class black man, he pressured her to give me up," Margaret said. "I was born premature, and I found out that when Michael Rose heard about my birth, his first question was, 'Will it live?' I think he hoped that I would die and the whole thing would be put right."

Fearing her father's wrath and longing for his approval, Lucy gave Margaret to her distant cousins, the Castles. She told Margaret many years later that she assumed the arrangement to be an informal one. "The Castles got me a new birth certificate—they legally adopted me," said Margaret. "To this day, I don't know who or what to believe. I've never been able to get straight information about who my father was. It took me many years to find the courage to ask about him. Lucy tells me he's dead. Perhaps, perhaps not. Just last year she asked me, 'Do you know you have a half-brother who's a doctor?' Of course I didn't know that. The important thing to Lucy was that he's a doctor, not that he's my brother. I feel like my life's been spent finding out one secret after another."

When Margaret and I looked at the many ways secrets moved her life and the lives of her family members, we began to connect these secrets to the complex social context in which she grew up. Barbados, a British colony at the time of her birth, was a society steeped in painful incongruities related to race and class. These disparities resounded in the life of Michael Rose. A highly placed white man, Michael Rose married a black woman, Ruth, and felt no compunction about his many extramarital affairs, including one with Ruth's sister. These kinds of liaisons were not unique to Michael Rose and comprised a kind of open secret in the culture. However, while a highly placed white man's behavior in this regard was tolerated, his daughter's similar behavior was not. A double standard regarding women's sexuality, combined with the race and social class of Lucy's lover, led to the secret of Margaret's origins.

A strange combination of arrogance and shame adhered to this secret. In any society, community, or family where beliefs in the superiority of some people over others abound, little if any thought is given to keeping secrets that directly affect a person who is considered "less worthy." Making and keeping the secret maintains the social order and amplifies the power of the secret-keeper. Shame is surgically removed from the secret-bearer and reattached to the person whose life story is hidden from her. In all of her interactions with Lucy when she was a young child, Margaret was made to feel that there was something wrong with her—her skin was too dark, her hair was too curly, her manners were unruly.

The motivations of the Castles in keeping the secret were complicated. They badly wanted a second child. In order to get Margaret, they promised to keep her origins a secret. They also wanted to protect her from feeling stigmatized. And in the Barbados of the 1940s, as in most other places at that time, children were not considered to have any rights either to ask questions or to receive information. As an adult, Margaret asked her older sister what she had been told. Her sister responded, "They just came home with you one day. I was thirteen. No one told me anything, and I never asked."

Both the impact of discovering the secret in the way that she did and the lack of candor when she tried to pursue the truth devastated Margaret for many years. Nonetheless, she pulled her life together with amazing courage and integrity. "I made a decision that I was going to be an open, up-front person, no matter what," Margaret told me. "That's brought a lot of good people into my life. If I even sense hypocrisy, I run the other way."

More than twenty years after leaving Barbados, Margaret decided she needed to reconnect with both her birth mother and her adoptive family. She does a lot of giving to the older generation now. When I commented on her generosity, she said, "Truthfully, it gives me peace of mind. It fits my spiritual beliefs." Then she smiled and said wryly, "Maybe it also gives me a certain pleasure to know that I'm in control."

OLD SECRETS IN NEW TIMES

In a recent conversation with my mother, we were discussing a cousin of hers who had died at age twenty of complications related to undiagnosed anorexia. We have talked about this cousin many times throughout my life. This time, my mother said, "You know, I think it was quite related to her parents' divorce." "Divorce?" I said. "What divorce? You never told me about any divorce." "Well," my mother quietly replied, "people used not to talk about such things, and I guess I just forgot about it."

Certain secrets that were made and kept one or two generations ago, such as cancer, mental illness, alcoholism, adoption, out-of-wedlock births, or divorce, are much less likely to be kept secret today. When I was a young child, my uncle Nathan had epilepsy, which the community at the time considered a mental illness. He lived most of his life inside his parent's home. While he was loved, protected, and well cared for, his bedroom was in the back of the house, a metaphor for a life kept secret. When you think about the secrets in your childhood and compare these to the secrets that are made currently, you will immediately notice profound changes in what the broader culture deems shameful and stigmatizing. These changes have occurred both in the content of secrets and in our beliefs about secrecy and openness.

The experience of Watergate called into question an entire generation's ideas about secret-keeping. The Freedom of Information Act, passed in direct response to Watergate, presented the nation with the concept of the right to know and raised serious questions about the ways secrecy may enhance illegitimate power. Simultaneously, social movements of the last twenty-five years, particularly the women's movement, the civil rights movement, the patients' rights movement, the gay rights movement, and the recovery movement, have brought many previously hidden aspects of American life into the open.

Our culture's newfound facility to challenge taboos does not, however, mean that toxic and dangerous secrets have disappeared. For many families, secrets that were made in the past now involve increasingly complex dilemmas in a context that seems to demand openness at any price. I speak often with people who experience confusion and enormous loyalty conflicts about what to do with these old secrets. Members of younger generations may have little or no appreciation for the constraints on candor that existed until quite recently, leading sometimes to angry confrontations when secrets made long ago finally emerge.

Some secrets were created under earlier "rules," and now those rules have changed. Generations of adult adoptees, for instance, were adopted under a system that maintained secrecy concerning biological parents. Mothers who gave their babies up were promised anonymity at a time when both out-of-wedlock births and the infertility of adoptive parents were highly stigmatized. Now we live in a culture that largely values open adoption, including the possibility of later contact between birth parents and child. What about all of the people born, giving birth, or adopting on the cusp of the change? What road map tells them what to conceal and what to reveal?

Even when previously taboo topics are widely acknowledged within society, individuals may remain trapped in secrecy. Many gay and lesbian people still feel compelled to conceal their sexual identity from their families. When "don't ask, don't tell" became the national policy about gays in the military, another partially opened door was slammed shut. Dramas about domestic abuse appear on prime-time TV even as women beaten by their partners continue to be driven by humiliation and lack of social support to hide the abuse. Right-wing politicians, cynically heralding "family values," call for the resurrection of shame and secrecy as the antidote for impoverished teen moms.

And even as we congratulate ourselves on our seeming openness, new secrets are being created, unimaginable a generation ago. Consider the painful conundrums of HIV/AIDS and the panoply of questions surrounding the new reproductive technologies. We still struggle with whom to tell, who has a right to know, and at what price such secrets are kept or opened.

4

"We Know What's Best for You to Know": *Secrets and Institutional Arrogance*

The people who came in were not told what was being done. We told them we wanted to test them. They were not told . . . what they were being treated for or what they were not being treated for. . . . We didn't tell them we were looking for syphilis. I don't think they would have known what that was. (Emphasis added)
—*Dr. J. W. Williams, referring to the Tuskegee Study of Untreated Syphilis in the Negro Male*

FROM 1932 TO 1972, nearly four hundred poor, mostly illiterate African-American men were placed in a research project that kept its very purpose a secret from the subjects. Unknown to them, each had been diagnosed with syphilis. Now they would be studied throughout their inevitable decline. The U.S. Public Health Service seduced the men with free physicals, rides to and from the clinic, hot meals, and the macabre promise of a burial stipend. One subject in the experiment recollected the original deception in 1932: "They told me I had bad blood. And that's what they've been telling me ever since. Charlie, you've got bad blood. . . . They never mentioned syphilis to me. Not even once."[1] Another man said, "I don't know what they used us for. I ain't never understood the study."[2]

Disregarding the men's health and well-being, the study also withheld all known treatment from them. The men were warned not to take any treatments elsewhere or they would be dropped from the study and lose their promised benefits. Cynical and useless curiosity to discover the effects of untreated syphilis on a group of poor black men continued unabated even when penicillin—a definitive cure for syphilis—was discovered in the 1940s. Many of the men died. Those who lived often went blind or insane.

Secrecy, denial, lying, and deception extended to levels beyond the manipulative actions toward the men. When the study was talked or written about among the white public health officials, it was described as a study of the effects of untreated syphilis on the Negro male. When, however, the study was referred to by these same officials communicating with the black leaders of the Tuskegee Institute, where the study was located, it was called a study of the effects of syphilis on the "human economy." Thus in biracial conversations about the experiment, race disappeared. Since it was clear that the leadership at Tuskegee knew that all of the subjects were African-American, this linguistic sleight of hand facilitated not just deceit but self-deceit and complicity. Social class differences between the Tuskegee officials and the impoverished research subjects mattered more than racial sameness in preserving this dreadful secret.

In the mid-1960s some members of the medical profession outside of the study tried to challenge the legitimacy and ethics of the experiment. As is true with many initial attempts to open institutional secrets, these queries to the U.S. Public Health Service were met with silence, stonewalling, and unanswered letters. Preserving the secret, no matter the consequences, took on a life of its own.

When the press ultimately broke open the secret of the Tuskegee study in 1972, those connected to it in the U.S. Public Health Service went into high gear to justify what had been done. Apologies, admissions of wrongdoing, or anything resembling ethical reflections never materialized at the time.[3] Finally, in 1997, a quarter of a century after the public learned of this terrible secret, President Clinton issued a formal apology to those few men from the study who were still alive, and to the descendants of those who had died.

The Tuskegee experiment is a useful template for understanding all institutional secrets. Underpinned by the arrogant belief *"We know what's best for you to know,"* such secrets permeate governments, corporations, police, the military, health and mental health systems, child welfare and adoption agencies, and organized religion. Examples are legion: the Watergate break-in and all of its subsequent lying and secret-keeping, ironically recorded on audiotape in the Oval Office of Nixon's White House; the Central Intelligence Agency's search for a truth serum, beginning with secret experiments with marijuana, cocaine, heroin, and amphetamines and culminating with tests of LSD on unwitting subjects across the country;[4] the contamination of workers in the asbestos industry, an industry that was able to cynically deny asbestos's carcinogenic effects since the cancer it caused appeared decades after exposure; the Pentagon denial that soldiers were exposed to poison gas during the Gulf War; child sexual abuse by clergy; and patient abuse in state hospitals for the mentally ill and the mentally handicapped. Facilitated by power differences that enable secret-keeping, these secrets lead quickly to outright abuse of power. As we saw with the Tuskegee experiment, the makers and keepers of institutional secrets adopt a position of superiority toward anyone they deem lower on the social ladder—the poor, the ill, the elderly, minorities, children. Such hierarchy is used to justify the deliberate withholding of information from others, even when such information is vital to make informed choices in life or to provide safety.

Some institutions not only are cloaked in secret practices, but also urge secrecy upon their clients. The authority vested in "experts" often influences the decisions about secrecy that families make. Adoption and the new reproductive technologies are two instances where the beliefs and attitudes of professionals have shaped decisions about secrecy and openness for millions of families. As we'll see in both cases, secrecy that began as protection for children had the capacity also to cover over ugly and corrupt practices.

ADOPTION: FROM BENIGN
SECRETS TO MALIGNANT SECRETS

When I first became a family therapist, it was gospel that secrets were necessary in any adoption. True, adopting parents were usually counseled to tell a child he or she was adopted, often with an emphasis on the child's specialness in being "chosen." But an even louder message accompanied this advice: adoption professionals urged parents to assume that their adopted child was *no different* from a biological child.[5] Agencies went to great efforts to match physical characteristics between adopting parents and adopted child. Sameness in hair color, eye color, and skin tone were thought to minimize and deny the otherwise enormous fact of adoption. Birth parents and adopting parents never met or even corresponded. All parties were told by adoption agencies and courts that records were sealed. Adoption of an infant began with secrecy and was expected to remain secret. Laws were passed to prevent adoption agencies from giving out any but the most cursory information to adopting families, such as the birth mother's height or grade level in school. Birth mothers, in turn, received even less information about the people who would raise their children. They were simply expected to take their secret and disappear. With no research to support their position, adoption experts insisted that women would not give up their babies for adoption unless secrecy prevailed.[6] Although the secrecy aspect of adoption law is in a state of transition today, the majority of states and Canada still maintain sealed adoption records.

Such secrecy probably began with benign intentions: It seemed to insulate children from the stigma of "illegitimacy," offer confidentiality to birth mothers, protect adoptive parents from the shame of infertility, and ensure no future intrusion on either biological or adoptive parents. But it resulted in many unintended consequences. Beginning with the creation of a new birth certificate, where the names of their adopting parents replace that of their birth parents, adopted children and their families are forced into a conspiracy of silence and denial of difference. Thus anything about an adopted child that makes him or her different from the adoptive family must be denied, including personality differences, physical traits, and temperament.

Paradoxically, the very denial of difference that is intended to make parents and children feel close and connected often shapes a child who feels unacceptable or a youngster who shows more and more of the very traits the parents don't want to see. What gets talked about in adoption circles as "problems with identity," or an adopted adolescent's confused or chaotic self-image, springs directly from lack of information about the child's self and the child's history, and from disconfirmation of his or her links to biological origins. I've worked with families formed by adoption where anything expressed by the child that didn't fit with being a member of the family the child was adopted into was either minimized, not noticed, or, more dramatically, eradicated through punishment. When these strategies didn't work, especially in adolescence, these families sometimes went to the opposite extreme, maximizing difference and blaming all behavior on the fact of adoption. Both positions hide the complexities attached to adoption.

The conspiracy of silence also extends to the deep emotions involved in every adoption—especially the natural process of grieving. Adoption involves gains and losses. When only a fiction about a "chosen child" can be expressed, then the loss for the birth mother of her biological child, the loss for the child of his or her birth parents, and the loss for the adopting parents of the ability to give birth all go underground.

The North American adoption scene is very different today than it was a decade or two ago. Several forces have combined to challenge many of our earlier notions about the need to make and keep adoption secrets: the burgeoning field of genetics, leading to the right to know our medical heritage; the diminishing of the twin stigmas of out-of-wedlock births and infertility; the lack of available white babies for adoption, resulting in an increase in international and transracial adoption, in which difference cannot be denied; and an increasingly sophisticated knowledge of adoptive family dynamics.[7]

Social movements of adult adoptees and of birth mothers

searching to reconnect; open adoption in which birth and adopting parents might meet, correspond, and never seal any records; changing state laws to facilitate reunions—all speak of a new openness. Nonetheless, there are still many thousands of adoptees who were adopted under earlier rules and assumptions. Secrecy continues to stalk their lives, presenting enormous dilemmas.

PEELING BACK THE LAYERS OF AN ADOPTION SECRET

I first met Shari Dardan when she was twenty-four years old. While very bright, she had dropped out of three colleges and could not seem to hold a job. Just before coming to see me, Shari had moved back home because she was unable to pay the rent on her studio apartment. "I can't seem to get on track," Shari said. "My parents say I'm a late bloomer, but no one else in my family bloomed late." When I asked Shari what she believed about her situation, she said, "We all know it's because I'm adopted, but no one would ever say so."

When I asked Shari what she knew about the circumstances of her adoption, she responded like many adoptees. She knew she was born in New Jersey and adopted by her parents in Pennsylvania. She had very sketchy information about her birth mother, and no knowledge about why her parents adopted her five years after giving birth to her older and now very successful brother, Howard. "I grew up hearing that my adoption made no difference, that Howie and I were just alike," Shari said. "Anytime I tried to find out more, my parents looked hurt and changed the subject." In short, Shari had no story about her origins, and no context to deal with her enormous sense of loss and difference. Her presently unsuccessful life seemed to be a painful way to tell her family that she was not fully a Dardan.

My work with Shari involved many layers, beginning with sessions involving her parents and older brother and extending to the adoption agency, the courts, and a group designed for adult adoptees who want to search for their birth parents. At first Mr.

and Mrs. Dardan resisted my invitation for them to join the therapy, insisting that they didn't want to intrude on Shari's privacy. When Shari made it clear to them how important it was that they come, they agreed.

In our first family meeting, Shari's mom said, "I knew you and Shari had to be talking about her adoption. Twenty-four years ago, when we brought Shari home, our adoption agency told us just to tell her that we especially chose her and to reassure her that she was one of us. I never knew what to say beyond that." Behind this fiction of the "chosen child" lay the secrets of three miscarriages, an emergency hysterectomy, and the extended family's disapproval of the Dardans' decision to adopt a baby. Neither Shari nor Howie had ever heard about any of their parents' turmoil. "We were just so happy when we got Shari that we wanted to put it all behind us," said Mr. Dardan. "And anyway, our social worker told us that telling Shari our struggles would probably make her feel bad, like she was our second choice." The Dardans' resolve to close off stories of their adoption decision left Shari to grow up in an atmosphere where the very reason for her being in this family was a mystery.

During our early work Shari got to hear, for the first time in her life, how she entered the family. As her parents revisited those years before her birth and adoption, she witnessed both their pain and their courage. We talked a lot about the advice they had received from the experts to minimize any reference to difference. "I knew I was different in certain ways," Shari said in our fourth family meeting. "The more you ignored it or pretended it wasn't so, the worse I felt, and the more determined I became to show just how different I was."

Opening the Dardans' half of Shari's adoption story was the easy part. As Shari began to feel accepted for who she was, and similarities and differences with her adoptive family could be openly acknowledged, she returned to college. She came back to see me two years after her graduation, now ready to work on the harder part: searching for her birth mother.

Initially I coached Shari to reveal to her parents her desire to search. Her mother and father were reluctant to support this effort at first. They invoked what they had been told by their agency years ago: that birth mothers don't want their lives disrupted. We met and talked over some of the newly emerging information showing that many birth mothers do, in fact, want to meet their offspring. I also drew distinctions for them between secrecy and privacy, explaining that what was couched by the agency as Shari's birth mother's "privacy" had actually created a profound secret in Shari's life. I took the position that Shari had a right to know *who* her birth parents were, but that knowledge of her origins did not necessarily extend to a right to a relationship. Shari and the members of her birth family would have to work that out together. For her part, Shari assured her adoptive parents that searching in no way diminished her love for them.

Shari's search proved difficult and frustrating at many turns. Like many adult adoptees, Shari was stonewalled by the adoption agency. They insisted they could give her no information, even though the laws in her state had changed, allowing agencies to release some identifying information. Shari was also told by two social workers that her wish to search was an indication that she needed therapy. Angry at what felt like condescension from these workers, Shari remarked to me, "I've liked being in therapy with you, but what I need is to find my birth mother." When Shari persevered, the agency finally capitulated, but then they insisted that one of their workers would have to serve as a go-between. At that point Shari quit trying to work with the agency. "I need to do this. The people at the agency act as if I'm still an infant in need of their care. I'm an adult, fully capable of handling whatever information I discover, fully able to act responsibly," Shari said to me. Full of confidence and resolve, Shari was now a very different woman from the tentative, frightened person I had met two and a half years earlier. Shari joined an ongoing group of adult adoptees who are searching for their birth parents. At this juncture we determined together to stop therapy. Like many adult adoptees, Shari found strength and support in a social movement that affirmed her right to know her origins. A different kind of institution with far fewer bureaucratic axes to grind would now be her ally in a quest for openness.

Shari's story is typical in the world of healthy-infant adoption. In fact, it represents a relatively benign outcome under the old system. The Dardans were a loving family, filled with goodwill, who followed the prevailing wisdom given to them by the adoption professionals. And they finally were able to support their daughter in her search. But the secrecy embedded in the adoption system can lead to darker scenarios—to exploitation and even tragedy.

The last decade has seen more and more adoptions termed "special-needs," a euphemism for children who are "hard to place." Currently one fourth of domestic adoptions of an unrelated child involve older children, often with significant physical and emotional problems. Many of these children were born to drug-addicted parents and have spent the better part of their young lives in multiple foster homes and residential treatment. Far too often parents willing to adopt these children are not told their true history.[8] The existence and effects of parental drug addiction, neglect, repeated rejection, fractured foster home placements, chronic illness, and years of severe physical and sexual abuse may be kept secret or minimized. Adoptive parents are left to discover the impact when they try to love a child whose primary response is rage or withdrawal or both. Such misguided and manipulative secret-keeping leads to lawsuits and interrupted adoptions. The consequences are devastating, both for the well-intentioned adoptive parents, who are racked with self-blame, and for the children, once again consigned to the scrap heap of foster care and group homes.

SECRET BABY-STEALING: A TACTIC IN WAR

Secret-keeping in traditional adoption originated at least in part with an intent to protect children. As with many institutional practices, the solution became the problem. No such claim of protection can be made in the distorted and self-serving secrets attached to the surreptitious adoption of children deliberately stolen from their parents as a tactic of political terror.

In the 1970s, during Argentina's "dirty war," hundreds of children were abducted by the military. Some were put in orphanages, some were abandoned, and some were secretly adopted by the very people who murdered these children's parents. The Argentine police ran a baby-trafficking network, giving infants born to women in prison to childless military officials.[9]

Similarly, during the 1979–1992 civil war in El Salvador, children were kidnapped by the Salvadoran military and placed with families in El Salvador, France, Italy, and the United States. Stolen babies became war booty. Unlike the Argentinian adoptions, in which the families knew full well that they were adopting stolen children, American families were not aware that the Salvadoran children they were adopting had been kidnapped. However, it has since been revealed that the United States embassy in El Salvador *knowingly* accepted false birth certificates and kept this a secret from adopting families.[10]

Opening these terrible secrets has been slow and difficult. Postwar governments in Argentina and El Salvador have resisted efforts to track down these children. For many years, the political and social movement in Argentina, called the Mothers of the Plaza de Mayo, comprising mothers whose adult children were killed or disappeared and whose grandchildren were kidnapped by the military, labored in vain to open the secret. Finally, in 1988, technology emerged to support their claims for these stolen grandchildren when a blood test capable of identifying the children's genetic heritage was developed.

In Argentina, only fifty-four children have been traced as of 1996. For most of these children, discovering the deceit corroding their entire existence is extremely traumatic. These children, now adolescents, must deal with the certainty that the people they love and regard as parents may well have participated in killing the people who gave them life. Some respond by rejecting their biological kin, no doubt the only available metaphor for rejecting horrifying and unacceptable knowledge. Such an intense loyalty split and fragmented identity is likely beyond our human capacity to repair. The majority of the stolen children have remained with the families who were complicit in their kidnapping.

Some children, however, had sensed deep secrets in their lives prior to discovering the truth. One young Salvadoran woman adopted by Americans insisted that she had another family. Sent to a therapist to deal with this belief, she was told this was a "fantasy" that she needed to overcome. Her family was dead—or so her adoptive parents had been told by Salvadoran officials. In 1996 she was reunited with her biological parents and siblings, all very much alive. No doubt because her adoptive parents were not complicit in her abduction or in secret-keeping about her biological parents, and because they supported her reconnection with her biological family, she was able to stay connected to both families.[11]

Secrecy in adoption is, first and foremost, secrecy about a human being's very existence. While child kidnappings, murders of biological parents, and false families are the extreme expression of political terror, they exist on a continuum with other official secrets. Underlying every case from best to worst is the presumptuous notion that one person has the right to withhold another person's birthright.[12]

NEW REPRODUCTIVE TECHNOLOGIES: SECRETS BEFORE BIRTH

During the last forty years, well over a million children have come into the world through the assistance of reproductive technology. Donor insemination was introduced after World War II, and the last fifteen years have seen a proliferation of new methods, such as in-vitro fertilization (IVF) and gamete intrafallopian transfer (GIFT). It's now possible that a given child may have a total of *five* "parents": three mothers—genetic, gestational, and child-rearing; and two fathers—genetic and child-rearing. Add in the fertility treatment centers where all this takes place, and the arena for secrecy is enormous.

Today in the 1990s, the nearly five million American couples with fertility problems would seem to have many options open to them. Their encounters with almost all fertility treatment centers, however, begin and end with secrets. Couples desperate to have a baby, and often willing to spend tens of thousands of dollars to do so in a multimillion-dollar unregulated industry, are seldom told the general success rate of a given program.[13] Compared to the hyperbolic hope such programs hold out to infertile couples, their success rate is dismally low. And some programs keep the secret from couples that their particular chance of bringing home a baby is nil, allowing them instead to spend their money and undergo treatment after treatment.

In the case of donor insemination, nearly all programs across the United States keep sealed records of sperm donors, in which are listed only anonymous numbers and no names; this eliminates any possibility of tracking down biological origins or even vital medical history. In addition, couples are usually advised to keep donor insemination a secret from their extended family, the child's pediatrician and teachers, and especially their child. When one adult man tried to track down his biological father's medical records, he was told by the clinic that this was "private information" and, furthermore, that his mother had violated her contract with them by informing her son of his origins.[14] Some donor insemination programs carry denial and secrecy one step further. Mixing a husband's sperm with donor sperm, these programs make the high-handed assumption that lack of clarity will foster forgetfulness.

Prior to today's work of DNA identification and genetic testing, such sperm mixing might support a lifelong pretense of biological paternity. The impact of such ambiguity on family relations over time is given short shrift. Adults created through donor insemination have told of sensing secrets all of their lives, of wondering if they were perhaps the result of an extramarital affair, or of experiencing confusing distance from an otherwise loving father, but their stories never seem to reach programs that insist their doors remain shut tight.[15]

To unpack the secrets surrounding reproductive technology is to touch some of the deepest feelings in human nature. Shame has been attached to infertility throughout time. Today infertility may be spoken about on talk shows but still remain taboo in the heart of a given family. In some cultures and religions, not producing offspring has long been blamed on the woman and considered grounds for divorce. Supposedly "modern" psychological theories of infertility also disparaged women. Now women suffered doubly: Not only were they not producing children, but they were told by the "experts" that their hostility toward their husbands and ambivalence toward motherhood was the reason. While recent scientific discoveries about the biological origins of infertility have mostly debunked these theories, their influence remains a potent aspect of the self-doubt stalking infertile couples. And the biological explanations are by no means free of stigma. Men who discover their own biological functioning to be a contributing factor to infertility often feel deeply ashamed, believing this reflects on their manhood.

Infertility often creates extreme distress for a couple who must deal with the pain of not being able to do what other couples simply take for granted. Just at a time when greater communication is vital, far too many couples respond with distance, conflict, or mutual protection through silence. Couples who do bring home a baby but follow the advice of the experts to keep the baby's origins a secret must live with that secret at the heart of their marriage and family life.

Some religions proscribe assisted reproduction, preventing couples from turning to their clergy or church community for support. One couple I worked with insisted that they had to keep their daughter's origins a secret, lest their parish priest deny them the sacraments.

Finally, certain members of the medical community have an opportunity to make huge amounts of money. In an industry where physicians can make a million dollars annually, maintaining certain secrets, such as success rates, is embedded in self-interest.

While all of these factors contribute to secret-keeping, the secrecy is once again initiated by the "experts," the doctors who warn couples not to tell *anyone* about their child's origins. In instances where children are born from donated sperm or eggs, couples are advised to "pretend" the baby is fully biologically theirs. Parents are told their child is the result of "collaborative reproduction." Exactly who is collaborating is never made clear. Operating with extreme arrogance, fertility specialists tell parents, "You'll forget." Such advice plays on a couple's already existing sense of shame and enlarges it. The spoken message, "Don't tell anyone," surely links to the unspoken and therefore unchallenged belief, "There is something wrong about what you did."

Because conception is couched as a medical event and there-fore *private*, much of the fertility industry's advice to couples also ignores the fact that infertility and its remedies have a profound and long-lasting impact on relationships. I've worked with couples a decade or more after fertility treatment only to find that their feelings about the experience are as raw as if it occurred last week. As with adoption, couples who keep their struggles with infertility a secret can't mourn the loss of their own biological child. Even when they bring home their long-wished-for baby, the ordeal of infertility needs to be openly acknowledged if it is ever to be inte-grated. The glib prediction "You'll forget" makes such reconcilia-tion less likely.

If a couple tells some relatives and close friends but follows so-called expert advice not to tell their child, the likelihood that this youngster will discover the truth from others is very high. As we saw in Leanne Bowers's story in chapter 2, families engulfed in secrecy about something so profound as a child's origins drag this baggage from one stage of family life to the next, shutting down opportunities for authentic connection.

Like many institutional secrets, those in the reproductive technology industry are simply presented as "necessary." But a few programs have taken a courageous step toward openness. The Sperm Bank of California, located in Oakland, currently keeps identifiable records of donors who agree that they may be con-tacted when a child reaches age eighteen. A program called Yes-

Donor challenges all of the conventional wisdom about the need for secrecy in donor insemination. The accepted belief that such openness would drive people away has turned out to be a myth, as nearly 80 percent of this program's clients request a yes-donor. Similarly, the Center for Surrogate Parenting and Egg Donation, in California, now identifies egg donors to their recipients and urges them to meet.[16] The position of these programs underscores a dual belief: that individual participants are their own best judge of how to handle information, and that children have a right to know their biological origins. While it will be many years before the impact of such openness can be assessed, the position represents a critical shift away from the cavalier stance of "doctor knows best."

Wrapped tightly in a blanket of secrecy, the lethal formula consisting of desperate infertile couples, enormous financial gain for doctors and infertility treatment programs, and the godlike aura surrounding highly successful fertility specialists can lead to perverted results. In 1992 Dr. Cecil Jacobson, a physician specializing in fertility treatment, was convicted of fifty-two counts of fraud.[17] For years Jacobson had lied to his patients, telling them he had used anonymous sperm for donor insemination when in fact he had used his own sperm. For many of the families who had kept the donor insemination a secret from their children, a double secret now exploded in their lives. All of the families were given a choice whether or not to seek DNA testing or participate in the court case against Jacobson. However, even if they chose not to do so, the weight of what Jacobson had done could not disappear from their lives in a puff of denial.

In a more horrifying example of creating life without consent of the living, charges are pending against Drs. Ricardo Asch, Jose Balmaceda, and Sergio Stone, formerly at the University of California at Irvine, for prescribing unapproved fertility drugs, performing research on infertile women without their consent, altering consent forms, hiding nearly a million dollars in income, and, most egregious, stealing women's eggs and embryos and giving them to other unknowing women. Eggs and embryos of thirty-five unconsenting couples were given to others, and at least seven children are known to have been born as a result.[18]

One patient of Asch's who brought home a baby after twelve years of infertility proclaimed, "I believe he works for God."[19] In fact, the extremes of secrecy enabled him to play God. As of 1997 Asch and Balmaceda had fled the United States. But, in a confounding invocation of patients' privacy, they continued to refuse to turn over their records. Sergio Stone is under house arrest in Orange County, California.[20] Not unlike the Tuskegee experiment, medical "privacy" is a convenient cover for malignant secrets. And, as we saw in the military kidnappings and adoptions, secrecy at the heart of institutional practice can become a weapon in autocratic hands.

LEGACIES OF MISTRUST: WHEN INSTITUTIONAL SECRETS BREAK OPEN

On a cold and snowy February night in St. Louis in 1993, I entered a room filled with thirty people who were strangers to one another. We were theologians, ethicists, lawyers, canon lawyers, social scientists, therapists—and priests who had sexually abused children, along with those now grown who had suffered such abuse. We came together at the invitation of the Bishops' Committee on Priestly Life and Ministry from the National Conference of Catholic Bishops. I was invited by the convenor, Father Canice Conners, for my knowledge of families, institutions, and secrets. We were a think tank with a heavy task: Over the next three days, we were to hammer out recommendations to address the enormous crisis of child sexual abuse in the Catholic Church.

Seven years before our meeting, a secret in the American Catholic Church had begun to break open. In 1986 Father Gilbert Gauthe was convicted in a Louisiana Court of sexually molesting thirty-seven boys and was sentenced to twenty years of hard labor. Soon after, two more Louisiana priests were similarly charged.[21]

Quickly a pattern emerged across the country, a pattern soaked in secrecy.

Stories abounded of children, now adults, who had never come forward about their abuse. They spoke of keeping the secret for multiple and complex reasons: their priest was caring toward them; their priest threatened them with God's punishment if they told; their priest told them it was their own fault for being "seductive"; their priest was respected, even revered; and certainly no one would believe them if they told.

But some abused children *had* told. It was the response of the institutional Church to the voices of these children that had brought us to St. Louis in 1993. For decades, priests who were accused of child sexual abuse were quietly removed from one parish and placed in another, with neither community being told the reason. Instances of abuse were never reported to child-welfare authorities or to the police. Children who tried to tell other priests or nuns in their own parish were ignored or punished.[22] Accusing families were intimidated into silence. Jeanne Miller, the mother of an abused boy, said, "We were sent to every mucky-muck in the Archdiocese that you can imagine—anyone who had a title. And one by one, they lined up to tell us everything from we're over-reacting to we could be excommunicated."[23] When Miller sued in civil court, a detective hired by the Church went through her garbage, interviewed her son's teachers, and approached her neighbors in an attempt to discredit her.

These strategies for silencing appeared again and again across the country. Church payment for a victim's therapy, for instance, stopped if the person decided to bring a civil suit. When cases did come to civil court, they were far too often settled with secrecy agreements in which the Church admitted no liability. The case records were sealed, and the plaintiff promised there would be no publicity and no disclosure of the amount of money received. This was hush money in its truest sense.

In 1992 the three-decade-old secret of Father James Porter broke open in the media. James Porter had been released from his priestly vows in 1973, but not before he had sexually abused dozens and dozens of boys and girls. Many church officials had known of Porter's abuse and continued to recycle him from parish to parish, maintaining the secret. After Porter spent time in a treatment center for abusive priests, his bishop, who knew of his abuse in four parishes, recommended him for reassignment to yet another parish. Letters attesting to his "recovery" proliferated in his file. In each new setting, Porter's history of child sexual abuse remained a secret from parish families. Through a media exposé, victims who had long thought they might be the only one began to discover one another. Only a few months before the St. Louis think tank convened, ninety-seven people in locations all around the country had filed charges of sexual abuse against James Porter. In this context we began our work.

In our meeting, the voices of those who had been abused were strong. They spoke poignantly of the long-term effects of secret sexual abuse, of lives derailed by depression, alcoholism, broken relationships, shattered beliefs. As I listened to individuals describe how the Church hierarchy had first denied the abuse and then demanded secrecy, I heard expressions of outrage, betrayal, loss of faith and community, and feelings of renewed violation.

Throughout the meeting, I was deeply aware of tensions between those of us who framed the issue primarily as one of secrecy at all levels of the institution and those who wanted to locate the problem essentially inside the offending priest. The Church of the 1990s had adopted the label of "sexual addiction," with its concomitant requirement of psychotherapy. This had replaced the earlier view of sexual abuse as a "moral lapse," to be treated solely by penance and prayer. Neither definition of the problem, however, addressed the institutional response of secrecy and cover-up. While all of us agreed that the policy of moving an offending priest from one parish to another must stop, and that no priest who abused children should ever be reassigned to parish work, there was strong disagreement about how much openness was required. Several of us insisted that multiple layers of secrecy would need to be addressed in order to make lasting change. Others, particularly the lawyers involved with civil suits against the Church, responded with warnings that too much openness might lead to more lawsuits. As we grappled with the issues I realized that addressing the secrecy meant going much deeper than the scandal of sexual abuse, since secrecy was embedded in and supported by the hierarchical structure of the Church.

Many of our final recommendations dealt with ending secrecy in all arenas, including telling parishes why a priest had been removed and informing the community of the aftermath of any allegations; actively searching for other victims when sexual abuse had been substantiated; conducting open hearings on child sexual abuse regionally and nationally; holding National Conference of Catholic Bishops meetings on this subject in public, rather than in executive session, as had been the practice; ending secrecy agreements in civil suits; and opening the history of a priest who had sexually abused children to Church authorities in any location to which he was reassigned.

I left this meeting feeling enormously satisfied. We had worked hard. Our recommendations were clear and strongly worded. A Bishops' Committee on Sexual Abuse was set up to deal with our recommendations. In a short while, however, my satisfaction vanished. Our recommendations were edited, watered down, and sent on to the National Conference of Catholic Bishops *before* those of us involved saw the final text. What happened to openness? I wondered. What happened to accountability?

In 1996 I went searching for some answers to my questions about the impact of the St. Louis meeting on Church policies and practices. I was especially interested in what had changed about secrecy. I spoke to Father Canice Connors, the original convenor of the think tank and president of St. Luke's Institute, a treatment center for clergy, and to Tom Economus, president of Link-Up, a national support group for victims of sexual abuse by priests. The answers I received were confounding and contradictory.

"There is zero tolerance for secrecy now," Father Connors told me. "Victims are interviewed immediately. Counseling is arranged for victims and paid for by the Church. If the abuse is recent, it is reported to child welfare authorities. Priests are sent to treatment and not reassigned to parish work." Tom Economus presented a far less sanguine picture. "We're worse off now than before the think tank," he told me. "It all *looks* better, but truly it isn't.

In 1997 I spoke with Sue Griffith, the mother of Scott Griffith, who charged Father Ted Llanos with sexually abusing him when he was a child.[24] She and her husband come from generations of religious Irish Catholics and devoted many years to volunteering in Marriage Encounter. She told me the Church claims it is not responsible for Father Llanos's abuse of twenty-six victims, because the California Supreme Court has held that an employer is not responsible for the behavior of an employee. The Church says there are no records of prior accusations against Father Llanos, but Sue Griffith believes this is a lie. Whether it is or not, the historical context of lies and secrets has simply not been expiated. "We can't be Catholics anymore," she told me sadly. "Spirit can't work when there are secrets."

More recently, a Texas jury ruled that the Dallas Roman Catholic Diocese was responsible for ignoring all warnings and covering up the evidence about the sexual abuse of eleven altar boys by a former priest, Father Rudolph Kos. While the abuse ended in 1992, shortly before the convening of the think tank, the 1997 jury decision held that the diocese concealed information, and was therefore guilty of gross negligence, malice, conspiracy, and fraud. Ordered to pay nearly $120 million and told by the jury, "Please admit your guilt and allow these young men to get on with their lives," the diocese has responded that it plans to appeal the decision.[25]

While Father Connors maintained that the bishops now understand that they and their priests are also *public officials* who are required to address this issue openly, Tom Economus insisted that they have simply learned to be expert public-relations players. Both agreed that the false accusations of sexual abuse against Chicago's Cardinal Bernardin in late 1993 had halted much of the media focus on this issue, but while Father Connors believes that the issue is better addressed without a lot of publicity, Tom Economus thinks that media attention is critical to stopping the secrecy.

I asked Father Connors if "zero tolerance for secrecy" extended to what parishes are told when a priest is removed. He responded that there was still no guarantee of openness and that practices differ from parish to parish. Since each diocese sets its own rules, a sexually abusing priest might still disappear under cover of night while the reason for his disappearance remains a mystery to his parish. And he admitted that the think tank's recommendation against secrecy agreements in civil court settlements had been largely ignored.

I also attempted to get a perspective from the Bishops' Committee on Sexual Abuse. My calls and faxes were met with delays, stonewalling, and lack of response. Finally I was told I would be contacted by their general counsel. I never heard from him. And try as I might, information about an invitation-only international meeting of bishops held in 1996 to address sexual abuse by clergy worldwide was impossible to uncover.

In my conversations with Father Canice Connors and Tom Economus, I was struck by each man's sincerity—and by how much each man's view was shaped by his own position and experience. Father Connors works with priests who have abused children; Tom Economus works with victims and their families. In the end, each one's "facts" seemed less important to me than the enormous legacy of mistrust rising from decades of high-handed secrets. This legacy will continue, and the pain of these secrets will not be healed, until genuine responsibility is claimed by the Church.

SECRETS IN THE MAKING: MANAGED CARE

Secrets kept by doctors from patients or the general public have a long history. Until the death-and-dying movement of the late 1960s, which brought with it a new openness, diagnoses of cancer and other terminal illnesses were routinely kept secret. Medical mistakes resulting in injury or death, mistakes that could lead to lawsuits, may also be kept secret from families.[26] Until very recently, any doctor who assisted a patient's suicide certainly kept this a secret, and, due to the illegal nature of such actions, most still do. Not so long ago, patients were not even allowed access to their own medical records. And arguments are rife today in the medical community over whether or not patients should be told the results of genetic testing, especially if an illness can't be treated.

None of these secrets, however, has the potential to contaminate the doctor-patient relationship on a wholesale level the way secrets attached to the managed-care enterprise do. In late 1995 the previously secret existence of "gag clauses" in contracts between large managed-care corporations and physicians was opened in the press. Such clauses require doctors to keep their financial arrangements with these companies secret from their patients, including monetary benefits that accrue to doctors for sharply limiting care. For instance, under the secret incentive system of many managed-care companies, a doctor receives monthly bonuses based on how few specialist referrals, hospital stays, and emergency-room visits his or her patients use.[27] Under a system where money disappears from doctors' pay when more treatment is given, quality of care is surely sacrificed. Doctors are also enjoined in their contracts from telling patients about possible treatments that are not covered by the managed-care contract, even when these treatments may be in the patient's best interest. Sharing misgivings or criticisms of a managed-care company's policies with a patient or the public can result in a doctor's dismissal as "managed-care-unfriendly." When Dr. David Himmelstein first opened managed-care secrets to the media in 1995, he was immediately dismissed by U.S. Healthcare.[28] In the long tradition of institutional secret-keeping, the managed-care industry claims the right to maintain secrets from those considered lowest in the hierarchy and to punish anyone who opens such secrets.

Managed-care executives justify secret-keeping by blaming doctors, calling it a way to prevent doctors from sharing their frustrations with patients about a changing health care scene. Making the paternalistic assumption that patients have no legitimate interest in knowing what's in contracts between the doctors who care for them and managed-care companies, Dr. Daniel A. Gregorie, president of Choice Care, said, "Physicians are angry, frustrated and, to some extent, depressed because the world as they've known it is changing rapidly and radically. But physicians should not take out that frustration in a nonconstructive way by sharing it with patients. This does not help the patients; it just makes them more anxious about the care they are receiving.[29] In other words, patients don't know what's good for them to know.

As the secrets demanded by managed care have been revealed to the public, the doctor-patient relationship has been profoundly affected. Doctors experience a lack of trust from patients they have known and treated well for years. As one physician told me, "Now patients are angry before we even start. They believe I'm withholding something from them. The other day I was all set to order a test for a patient. Before I could tell him, he was yelling at me to get this test. I've been this man's physician for eleven years and we always got along well. His faith in me is shot, not because I'm any less qualified, but because he knows I answer to someone else about his care and he can't know the details."

The managed-care industry wields a double-edged sword where secrets are concerned. On one side, doctors are required to keep secrets from patients. On the other side, they are required to *open* patients' secrets to the system, particularly in mental health and substance abuse care. The essential secrets that shape and support a therapeutic relationship are now grist for the managed-care computer mill.

Traditionally psychotherapy has been a confidential relationship. Therapy should be a sanctuary, a place where it's safe to confront our demons, expose our deepest shame, experiment with new alternatives, and struggle to heal our most penetrating wounds. There are legal limits to confidentiality in the case of child abuse or potential harm to others, but most people assume that what they told their therapist remained between them. If, however, they are using their insurance benefits to pay for all or part of their therapy, this assumption no longer pertains. Managed-care companies demand the right to see a therapist's files, including access to whole records when far more limited details would suffice. Such intrusion is rationalized as an antifraud measure, but in fact it gives the managed-care industry the license to shape the entire relationship among therapists, patients, and third-party payers. The power to require that secrets open against someone else's wishes—and without their knowledge—is a profound power indeed.

Managed-care companies frequently ask for electronic transfer of therapy records. A clerk at the other end of a fax machine may read a client's most intimate revelations. Such previously confidential material is then stored in computers and made available to many people, including employers. Therapy records are now released for purposes of payment, treatment evaluation by nonprofessionals, plan administration, and research—in other words, for any purpose whatsoever. Such records have been used to deny other insurance, including health, life, and automobile coverage, both to the individual in therapy and to other family members who are mentioned in their records.[30] Sensing a pending backlash against this corporate attack on privacy and misuse of personal information, the managed-care industry is now moving swiftly to influence legislation that would guarantee them an eavesdropping role in the therapy room. What is already true in practice with many managed-care plans would be codified in law. Employers would be guaranteed the right to obtain treatment information when an employee enrolls in a plan. No further authorization would be necessary. The employee's right to keep information revealed in therapy confidential, to create essential secrets, and especially to decide whether to allow anyone else to see their records would be totally eroded under this law.

A RECIPE FOR TOXIC INSTITUTIONAL SECRETS

All of the examples in this chapter add up to a recipe for institutional secrets that destroy the integrity of the secret-keepers, perpetuate harm in the unknowing, and corrupt relationships. The ingredients for this recipe include:

- A rigid hierarchy of relationships, both within the institution and between the institution and those it serves
- All power located at the top of the institution
- Tight boundaries that manage information entering or exiting the institution
- A sense of arrogance adhering to those in power
- Silencing strategies as a way of maintaining power
- Avoidance of scandal, regardless of the cost to individual lives
- Required deference and obedience to those who have power by those who do not
- Unquestioned loyalty to the institution
- Lack of accountability by the institution to those it purports to serve

A RECIPE FOR CHANGE

Toxic institutional secrets are best rectified in two ways. First, responsible journalistic investigations and insider whistle-blowing have historically opened such secrets. When knowledge is released to a previously unknowing public, the possibility for change begins. Just as when a secret opens in a family, new information has the potential to lead to new relationships. But opening the secret is not enough. The power differential between institutions and individuals or families is enormous. Such power, including the power to define the issues, is seldom ceded willingly. Rectifying the excesses and exploitations born of institutional secrets most often requires a social and political movement whose own power can begin to rebalance the relationship between an institution and its constituents. It took a patients' rights movement to gain access to medical information formerly kept secret. It took a movement of adult adoptees to begin to eliminate decades of adoption secrecy. The movement of adults who have been sexually abused by priests, as exemplified by Link-Up, keeps the pressure on the Catholic hierarchy to deal with this painful reality. Mental health professionals and consumers are just beginning to organize to address the excesses of managed care.[31]

The secrets made and kept in some institutions are a template for certain kinds of family secrets, those maintained by power imbalances. The claim to keep harmful secrets while silencing marginalized voices turns an already closed institution or family ever more inward, closing off possibilities for growth and complexity. Mutuality disappears, and our vision of each other becomes more and more stereotyped.

As we'll see in chapter 5, one vast institution, the broadcast media, has profoundly affected the ways we think about and act toward the secrets in our lives.

Chapter

5

Talk Show Telling Versus
Authentic Telling:
The Effects of the Popular Media
on Secrecy and Openness

Well, my guests today say that they can't bear to keep their secrets locked inside of them any longer. And they've invited their spouse or lover to come on national television to let them hear the secrets for the first time.

—*Montel Williams*

THE YOUNG WOMAN entered my therapy room slowly, with the usual hesitation of a new client. I settled her in a chair, expecting to begin the low-key question-and-answer conversation that usually takes the entire first session. Almost before she could pronounce my name, she began telling me a deeply personal and shameful secret. In an effort to slow her down and start to build a relationship that might be strong enough to hold her enormous pain, I gently asked her what made her think it was all right to tell me things so quickly. "I see people doing it on *Oprah* all the time," she replied.

Throughout history human beings have been fascinated by other people's secrets. In great literature, theater, and films we view how people create and inhabit secrets and cope with the consequences of planned or unplanned revelation. Life-changing secrets are central to such ancient dramas such as *Oedipus* or Shakespeare's *Macbeth*, as well as to twentieth-century classics such as Ibsen's *A*

Doll's House, Eugene O'Neill's *Long Day's Journey into Night*, Arthur Miller's *Death of a Salesman* and *All My Sons*, or Lorraine Hansberry's *A Raisin in the Sun*. Like me, you may remember the poignancy of the sweet secrets in the O. Henry tale "Gifts of the Magi," where a wife secretly cuts and sells her hair to buy her husband a watch chain for Christmas, while he, unbeknownst to her, sells his watch in order to buy silver combs for her hair. Contemporary popular films, such as *Ordinary People*, *The Prince of Tides*, or *The Wedding Banquet*, also illustrate the complexity of secrets and their impact on every member of a family. Literary and dramatic portrayals of perplexing secrets and their often complicated and messy resolutions help us to remember that keeping and opening secrets is not simple. Perhaps most important, they help us appreciate our own deep human connection to the dilemmas of others.

Since the advent of television, however, we have begun to learn about other people's secrets and, by implication, how to think about our own secrets in a very different way. Exploiting our hunger for missing community, both afternoon talk shows and evening magazine shows have challenged all of our previously held notions about secrecy, privacy, and openness. While such shows have been around for nearly thirty years, in the 1980s something new began to appear: Celebrities began to open the secrets in their lives on national television.[1] As we heard about Jane Fonda's bulimia, Elizabeth Taylor's drug addiction, or Dick Van Dyke's alcoholism—formerly shameful secrets spoken about with aplomb—centuries of stigma seemed to be lifting. Other revelations enabled us to see the pervasiveness of wife battering and incest. The unquestioned shame and secrecy formerly attached to cancer, adoption, homosexuality, mental illness, or out-of-wedlock birth began to fall away.

This atmosphere of greater openness brought with it many benefits. In my therapy practice I experienced an important shift as the people I worked with displayed a greater ease in raising what might never have been spoken about a decade earlier. Frightening secrets lost some of their power to perpetuate intimidation. Those who had been silenced began to find their voices and stake their claim as authorities on their own lives.

But as the arena of the unmentionable became smaller and smaller, a more dangerous cultural shift was also taking place: the growth of the simplistic belief that telling a secret, regardless of context, is automatically beneficial. This belief, promulgated by television talk shows and media exposés, has ripped secrecy and openness away from their necessary moorings in connected and empathic relationships. Painful personal revelations have become public entertainment, used to sell dish soap and to manufacture celebrity.

If cultural norms once made shameful secrets out of too many happenings in human life, we are now struggling with the reverse assumption: that opening secrets—no matter how, when, or to whom—is morally superior and automatically healing. The daily spectacle of strangers opening secrets in our living rooms teaches us that no distinctions need be drawn, no care need be taken, no thought given to consequences.

TALK SHOW TELLING

From a *Sally Jessy Raphael* show in 1994, we hear and see the following conversation:

> *Sally:* Let's meet David and Kelly. They're newly-weds. They got married in December. . . . As newly-weds, what would happen if he cheated on you? What would you do?
>
> *Kelly:* I don't know.
>
> *[Before David begins to speak, the print at the bottom of the screen reads, "Telling Kelly for the first time that he's cheating on her," thus informing the audience of the content of the secret before Kelly is told.]*
>
> *David:* I called Sally and told the producer of the show that I was living a double life. . . . I had a few affairs on her.
>
> *Sally (to Kelly):* Did you know about that?
>
> *[Camera zooms in on Kelly's shocked and pained expression; she*

is speechless and in tears, and she shakes her head while members of the audience chuckle.]

Sally: Kelly, how do you feel? On the one hand, listen to how awful and bad this is. On the other hand, he could have just not ever told you. He loves you so much that he wanted to come and get this out. . . .

In the late 1960s the *Phil Donahue Show* began a new media format for sharing interesting information and airing issues. This shifted in the late 1970s and 1980s to celebrity confessions and the destruction of taboos. In the 1990s talk TV brings us the deliberate opening of secrets that one person in a couple or a family has never heard before. In a cynical grab for ratings and profits, the format of such shows has changed rapidly from one where guests were told ahead of time that they were going to hear a secret "for the first time on national television" to one where guests are invited to the show under some other ruse. These programs are referred to as "ambush" shows.

According to former talk show host Jane Whitney, "Practically anyone willing to 'confront' someone—her husband's mistress, his wife's lover, their promiscuous best friend—in a televised emotional ambush could snare a free ticket to national notoriety. *Those who promised to reveal some intimate secret to an unsuspecting loved one got star treatment*" (italics added).[2] Presently there are over thirty talk shows on every weekday. Forty million Americans watch these shows, and they are syndicated in many other countries.[3] Even if you have never watched a talk show, you live in an environment where assumptions about secrets have been affected by talk show telling.

Opening painful secrets on talk TV shows promotes a distorted sense of values and beliefs about secrecy and openness. While viewers are drawn into the sensational content of whatever secret is being revealed, the impact on relationships after the talk show is over is ignored. Indeed, when there has been severe relationship fallout, or even tragedy following the opening of a secret, talk show hosts and producers claim they have no responsibility, intensifying the belief that secrets can be recklessly opened without any obligation to be concerned about the aftermath. Consider the following:

- In one notorious incident in 1995, a young man named Jonathon Schmitz murdered an acquaintance, Scott Amedure, following an unwelcome revelation on the *Jenny Jones* show.[4] Schmitz had been told that he was coming on the show to meet a "secret admirer." He was *not* told that the show was about "men who have secret crushes on men."[5] When his shock and humiliation resulted in Amedure's murder, the host and producers insisted they had no responsibility.

- On the *Montel Williams* show, a woman heard for the first time that her sister had been sleeping with her boyfriend for several years. She came on the show after being told it was a show about "old boyfriends."

- Former talk show host Jane Whitney describes a show she did called "Revealing Your Double Life." A mother was invited on who had no idea why her son had cut himself off from her for two years. Whitney, of course, knew that the son was about to reveal his pending sexual reassignment surgery. When she met the mother just before the show, the woman implored her, "Do you know what's wrong? We were always so close. I don't know what's happened. Is he sick? Does he have AIDS?" Assuring the mother that "everything would be all right," Whitney lied and kept the secret in order to maximize its revelation on the show.[6]

- Ricki Lake invited on a man who had been keeping his homosexuality a secret from his family. His roommate announced that he had taken it upon himself to tell the man's family this secret.[7]

When such actions occur over and over again on talk TV, we lose our capacity to ask a critical question—namely, under what circumstances do we have the right to open another person's secret?

On talk television, husbands hear for the first time that their wives want a divorce; mothers are told the secret of their daughters' sexual abuse; wives discover that their husbands tell friends about their sexual relationship. And all of this occurs in a context in which the host disingenuously denies any responsibility for what is set in motion in the complex ecology of family relationships.

Talk show telling ignores the importance of committed relationships. Telling can be anonymous and disguised. A studio audience and a viewing audience consisting of strangers hear the previously hidden details of our lives. Commercial breaks cavalierly interrupt the opening and hearing of a painful secret. Eavesdropping stands in for sincere listening. Voyeurism substitutes for witnessing. The host's pseudo-intimate hugs and caresses replace genuine healing.

When secrets are opened on television, several peculiar triangles are created. The relationship between the person telling the secret and the person hearing the secret is immediately invaded by the audience, the host, and the "expert," each with a calculated and repetitious role. These roles are imbued with arrogance: the belief that one knows what is best for other people to do about the secrets in their lives. Talk show telling involves opening secrets to a huge group of uninvolved, faultfinding listeners who have no responsibility for the relationship after the talk show ends.

When a secret is about to be revealed, captions are placed below the image of the person who has not yet heard it. The audience sees such words as "About to hear that his wife just had an abortion" or "Jim is not Ellen's biological father." Thus the audience knows the content of the secret before the person whose life the secret affects. A context of humiliation is constructed. Often the audience laughs or gasps while the camera catches a close-up of the perplexed face of the listener. The recipient of the secret is, in fact, the last to know. This structure reduces empathy and enables the audience to feel separate from and superior to the ambushed guest.

The audience encourages further revelations through applause.[8] As viewers, we get the message over and over that opening a secret, regardless of consequences, gains attention and approval. Loudly applauded, cheered, jeered, and fought over, secrets are in fact trivialized. On talk shows, a secret of sexual abuse equals a secret about family finances equals a secret about being a Nazi equals a secret of paternity.

Once a secret is revealed, both the teller and the recipient are immediately vulnerable to the judgmental advice and criticism of strangers. Blaming and taking sides abound. Not a moment elapses for reflection on the magnitude and gravity of what has occurred. Every secret is instantly reduced to a one-dimensional problem that will yield to simplistic solutions.

Soon after a secret is opened, the host goes into high gear with some variation of the message that opening the secret can have only good results. Sally Jessy Raphael tells the young wife who has just discovered the secret of her husband's affairs in front of millions of unasked-for snoopers, "He loves you so much that he wanted to come and get this out." The message to all is that telling a secret, in and of itself, is curative. There is no place for ambivalence or confusion. Indeed, guests are often scolded for expressing doubt or hesitation about the wisdom of national disclosure of the intimate aspects of their lives.

The host's position as a celebrity can frame the content of a given secret and the process of telling as either normal or abnormal, good or bad. When Oprah Winfrey joins guests who are exposing secrets of sexual abuse or cocaine addiction with revelations of her own, the telling becomes hallowed. No distinctions are drawn between what a famous person with a lot of money and power might be able to speak about without consequences and what an ordinary person who is returning to their family, job, and community after the talk show might be able to express. Conversely, some hosts display initial shock, dismay, and negativity toward a particular secret, its teller, or its recipient. When a guest on the *Jerry Springer Show* who has just discovered that a woman he had a relationship with is a transsexual hides in embarrassment and asks the host what he would do, Springer responds, "Well, I certainly wouldn't be talking about it on national TV!" A context of disgrace is created, only to be transformed at the next commercial break into a context of understanding and forgiveness.

Toward the end of any talk show on which secrets have been revealed, a mental health therapist enters. A pseudo-therapeutic context is created. The real and difficult work that is required after a secret opens disappears in the smoke and mirrors of a fleeting and unaccountable relationship with an "expert" who adopts a position of superiority and assumed knowledge about the lives of people he or she has just met.[9] While we are asked to believe that there are no loose ends when the talk show is over, the duplicitousness of this claim is evident in the fact that many shows now offer "aftercare," or real therapy, to deal with the impact of disclosing a secret on television.[10]

The time needed even to begin to deal adequately with any secret is powerfully misrepresented on talk television. In just under forty minutes on a single *Montel Williams* show, a man told his wife he was in a homosexual relationship; a woman told her husband she was having an affair with his boss; another woman told her boyfriend that she was a transsexual; a wife revealed to her husband that they were $20,000 in debt; and a woman told her boyfriend that she had just aborted their pregnancy. An ethos of "just blurt it out" underpins these shows.

Talk show telling also erases age-appropriate boundaries between parents and children. Children are often in the audience hearing their parents' secrets for the first time. On one show an eight-year-old boy heard his aunt reveal that he had been abandoned by his mother because she "didn't want" him. Children may also be onstage revealing a secret to one parent about the other parent, without a thought given to the guilt children experience when they are disloyal to a parent.[11] The impact on these children, their sense of shame and embarrassment, and what they might encounter when they return to school the next day is never considered.

Ultimately, talk show telling transforms our most private and intimate truths into a commodity. Shows conclude with announcements: "Do you have a secret that you've never told anyone? Call and tell us"; "Have you videotaped someone doing something they shouldn't do? Send us the tape." A juicy secret may get you a free airplane trip, a limousine ride, an overnight stay in a fancy hotel. While no one forces anyone to go on a talk show, the fact that most guests are working-class people who lack the means for such travel makes talk show telling a deal with the devil.

TALK SHOW MYTHS ABOUT SECRETS

Talk shows have created a powerful model for secret-telling in our culture, but this model contains many *toxic myths*.

- Painful secrets can be opened without regard to committed relationships.

- Telling a secret per se is automatically healing.

- Any issues contained in secrets are resolved instantaneously.

- There is no legitimate sphere of privacy.

- Pseudo-intimacy and pseudo-community can replace genuine connection.

- Strangers have a right to judge and criticize you without knowing your full story.

- Telling your secret on TV will make you an instant celebrity.

- Five minutes in an unaccountable relationship with an "expert," who presumes to know what is best for another person's life, can resolve all the problems a secret has created.

- Relationship obligations, loyalty, and personal and social responsibility are of no importance.

- The historical context of a secret and the potential future consequences of opening it can be disregarded.

- Age-appropriate boundaries for secret-telling can be ignored.

Has talk show telling permeated the ways you think about secrets and how secrets are managed in your own interpersonal world?

FAMILY SECRETS ON MAGAZINE TELEVISION

In addition to afternoon talk shows, the 1990s have seen a proliferation of evening "magazine"-style programs. Such shows usually include three or four segments ranging from an angle on the week's news to an exposé about business or government to the portrayal of a family's story. The revelation of a family secret often makes for a compelling mini-drama. Sound-bite interviews with family members and apparently informal—though highly staged—shots of the family in their kitchen, living room, or strolling down a road are tied together by a narrative voice-over filled with hyperbole. The *content* of the particular secret, be it new reproductive technologies, paternity, or sexual abuse, usually takes center stage over the relationship complexities in which it is embedded. The drama emphasizes the pain and distress of those who have been kept in the dark. Through careful editing and narration, the viewer is shown whom to blame and whom to sympathize with. The picture may be in color, but the story is reduced to black and white, "good guys" and "bad guys." Distinctly missing is any framing that might help the viewer think critically about keeping and telling secrets. Lacking any reference to social context or wider cultural meanings, these programs draw our attention only to the inflammatory content of the secrets portrayed.

Let's look at one example of a family secret that made its way onto two magazine programs in 1995. First *American Journal* and then *20/20* portrayed the story of the Lang family. Following a bitter divorce and custody battle in the 1980s, Marcia Lang gained custody of the family's two children, Chelsea and Robert junior, and her ex-husband, Bob Lang, remarried. Several years later, in 1991, during an angry telephone conversation, Marcia told Bob that the children were not his biological children but were actually the children of his former boss, Jim Pickens, with whom she had had a seven-year extramarital affair.

American Journal begins the story by telling us that we are about to hear a "shocking" secret that has led to "an unprecedented lawsuit that will affect American families for years to come." In what follows, we are told about the sudden opening of the paternity secret during a conference call among father, mother, and the two children on Christmas Eve, while Bob Lang, his new wife, and the children baked gingerbread cookies. We see the children crying; hear about a blood test initiated by the young son to establish paternity; listen to Jim Pickens, the biological father, talk about the ruin of his medical practice and loss of his own family when the secret was revealed; hear that father and children have grown closer after learning the secret; see the stepmother tell the interviewer that Marcia Lang revealed this secret because "she's really an abusive woman"; hear Chelsea call her mother chronically "cold" and "neglectful"; watch the interviewer chase a fleeing Marcia Lang into her car, demanding to know how she could "do this to her children"; and hear finally that this "scandal" has left father and children with "pain and emotional scars."

The ratings for this *American Journal* segment must have been excellent, because a few months later the Langs' story was repeated on *20/20*. In the introduction, we are told that we are about to hear "a family saga you'll never forget" about a "secret love affair" and a "devastating secret." The basics of the story are the same, but father and children offer quite different details than they had told on *American Journal*. Instead of a conference call, we now hear that the father took the call with the children listening to his end of the conversation and getting increasingly upset. Rather than the son asking for the blood test to establish paternity, we are told it was the father who "needed to know the truth." Father and daughter, we are told, are not close, but alienated; the interviewer tells us that the "revelation of this secret has torn father and daughter apart." While Marcia Lang is not chased down the street, we again see shots of her refusing to be interviewed, and again see Chelsea invited by the interviewer to excoriate her mother on national television. In contrast, Bob Lang and son, Robert, are shown as warm and loving with each other. The court case, in which Bob Lang sought damages for fraud and back child support and which *American Journal* assured us would be "precedent-setting," has by the time of the *20/20* piece been thrown out of court.

During the segment, the interviewer asks rhetorically, "Why would someone keep a secret that nearly devastated the lives of three people?" Why indeed? At no time in either piece are we helped to consider this question. Rather, our vision is constrained to see victims and victimizer, absolutes of right and wrong. Following the piece, the *20/20* anchor, Hugh Downs, comments, "Such drastic and different reactions of son and daughter—we have to wonder why." This thoughtful question is immediately followed by a commercial break.

In both of these segments, the complex motives for keeping a secret are nowhere to be found. Is the secret kept because of shame, stigma, fear, intimidation, protection of self or others, purposeful deception, arrogance and the misuse of power, powerlessness—or plain confusion? The equally intricate reasons for opening a secret—including anger, revenge, a desire to split loyalties, alleviation of guilt, wish to shift a burden from self to others, an honest hope to repair and heal relationships, or a need to regain one's sense of balance, identity, and integrity—are likewise missing.

No distinctions are drawn between the reckless opening of a secret and the opening of a secret that is done with thought and care. Questions such as "Who has a right to information contained in a secret? Whose life does a secret affect? Who cannot properly make decisions or use resources if a secret is kept?" have no place in magazine TV.

Television stories of family secrets frequently contain a person who refuses to be interviewed. Never is such a refusal framed as an appropriate desire for privacy. When Marcia Lang rejects both interviewers' entreaties, we are given further license to heap blame and guilt upon her.

As I watched these shows my mind raced with unanswered questions. What, for instance, could have been going on between the Langs during their ten-year marriage that enabled a seven-year extramarital affair to be kept secret? Were there other secrets? Did the Langs come from families in which important secrets were kept in marriages? While a ten- or twelve-minute television segment cannot possibly include all of this background, the consistent absence of such information in pieces like this suggests that it never even crosses the producers' minds.

I was particularly struck that the gender dimension of the Lang family secret was never mentioned. Men have fathered children secretly since time began. They may have abandoned them, supported them without the knowledge of their wives, or claimed them publicly on their deathbed, but they have seldom reaped the scorn and humiliation placed on a woman who has done a similar thing. If Bob Lang had done what Marcia Lang did and kept it a secret, would the media hang a scarlet letter on him, as they did with her? Not likely. While in both segments we see Jim Pickens suffering the loss of his family and medical practice, he is also framed as a victim who "didn't know" he had fathered two children. Only Marcia Lang is portrayed as the true villain of the story.

This focus on innocence and blame gives us no way to think about the future resolution of relationships after a secret has been revealed. When Chelsea Lang is encouraged by the interviewers in both pieces to trash her mother, no thought is given to the impact of this on any possible reconciliation with her mother. Secrets are portrayed without past or future, and without social and cultural frames of reference.

Above all, magazine TV wants us to keep it simple. How are we to think about a "psychological" father who clearly loves his children and yet is suing in court for back child support? The contradiction is never considered. And what about a mother who both hurt her children by opening the secret and yet seems to have provided a loving father for them? Marcia Lang is simply demonized, and we are never asked to consider the incongruities.

AUTHENTIC TELLING ON TELEVISION AND IN OUR OWN LIVES

When secrets are portrayed on television with eloquence and concern, as viewers we witness complicated emotions: anxiety, anger, guilt, shame, sadness, and relief. We see relationships marked by protectiveness, betrayal, mistrust, and reconciliation. The benefits and consequences of keeping and opening secrets on each individual and on relationships are carefully drawn, enabling us to reflect on such results in our own lives. As in real life, ambiguities remain after a secret is revealed.

The 1995 made-for-television documentary movie *Before Your Eyes: Angelie's Secret* is an exemplar of authentic telling of a secret in the media. Ten-year-old Angelie Dias, a fifth grader from Jupiter, Florida, has AIDS. Born to a drug-addicted mother in Puerto Rico, Angelie and her baby brother were adopted. Her brother died of AIDS as a toddler. Angelie and her adoptive parents have kept her diagnosis a secret from both adult and child friends, teachers, and their community. Her parents enable us to understand how a decision to keep the diagnosis private, made in order to protect Angelie when she was a small child, has become a toxic secret in their lives.

Angelie poignantly tells us, "I've been keeping this secret because I didn't want to lose friends."

But in fact the family has been compelled to live with a high wall between themselves and others. That wall is constantly penetrated by the anxiety of unplanned disclosure. As Angelie's mom says, "The fear is that you tell somebody and they don't keep that secret for you." If the family decides to open this secret, they recognize that they must open it to their entire community.

In a film that spans over a year in Angelie's life, we witness her struggle regarding whether or not to open her secret. The film is not a re-creation of events. The real time that it takes to make a decision to open a secret of great magnitude is powerfully depicted. Her parents' fears about opening the secret are integrated with their weariness in keeping it. Angelie's mother speaks exquisitely of the pain of lying to friends and the school. But we are also vividly reminded of what has happened to other families who have opened this aching secret, only to see their dog murdered or have their house burned down or be driven out of town by neighbors. Angelie and her best friend, Jamie, "tell each other everything," as ten-year-old best friends do, but "everything" excludes Angelie's illness. Her frequent absences from school in order to go for treatments make Angelie's favorite teacher suspect that something is seriously wrong, but, like many people who sense powerful secrets, she'd rather not know and she never asks.

Gradually Angelie makes her decision over a summer between fourth and fifth grade. We see her during a week at Camp Heartland, a camp for children with HIV/AIDS where everyone is open—in striking contrast to the constraints of her life at school. As viewers, we are helped to imagine a world where AIDS is a disease to be fought, not a secret to be kept.

While Angelie gathers her courage at camp, she hears from children who have had very positive outcomes from telling their secret. She also talks to children who experienced terrible consequences when they told others, including her biggest fear, losing friends.

In scenes that resonate with agonizing over secrets in our own lives, we see Angelie and her mom and dad try to predict how people will respond as they get ready for the first telling, to their closest friends. The actual initial responses confirm their worst fears. Friends are angry. They distance themselves from the family. A telephone is slammed down on Angelie's mom as she tries to explain why they kept the secret. Angelie's parents are accused of putting other children at risk. Parents forbid their children to play with Angelie. One mom tries to justify herself: "Our child won't be allowed to play with other children if she continues to play with Angelie." Angelie's best friend's mother takes her daughter to be tested for HIV. Medical facts regarding the transmission of HIV are ignored by many. We see Angelie's pain and anger as her best friend begins to ignore her. The prejudice and ignorance that fuel the AIDS secret are stunningly shown.

Yet something else begins to occur. The family's minister

blesses them from the pulpit and calls for caring responses from their congregation. The school principal supports the family and paves the way for Angelie to tell her secret to the entire school over closed-circuit television in each classroom. The teachers are carefully prepared ahead of time. As viewers, we are able to consider the critical impact of the context in which a secret is opened. The school system's advocacy of Angelie and her family and the principal's determination to meet bigotry with education make a huge difference in how the secret is received.

With dignity and courage far beyond her ten years, and with the principal at her side for support, Angelie finally tells her secret. Her classmates respond to her mettle and spunk with affirmation. "Angelie, I think you are so brave," says one little girl. Others marvel at how difficult it must have been to keep this secret.

It would have been easy to end with the children's honest and empathic responses, but the film goes on to explore the multiple and complex effects of opening a secret. At a parent-teacher meeting in which Angelie and other children are also present, a potent mixture of anger, defensiveness, fear, friendship, loyalty, and caring spills forth. One father angrily demands to know why Angelie's family had a right to keep this secret and continue to send her to school. Angelie's pediatrician responds that all people with AIDS have a right to privacy regarding their diagnosis and attempts to place this in the scientific context of what is known about HIV transmission, but clearly the father is not convinced. Facile answers are decidedly missing, as they often are in our own lives when we struggle to locate the borders between privacy and secrecy.

As with the opening of most important secrets, Angelie's and her parents' lives are more complicated after the telling. Some children come to her birthday party, but some children stay away. She loses her best friend but says she has "more friends than ever" since she told the secret. The family's openness leaves them vulnerable to a charming promoter who wants Angelie to be his "poster child" to raise funds for his "cure" for AIDS. Another little girl with AIDS in a nearby town hears of Angelie on television and decides to open her secret, even though she and her father had been hounded from their previous home in the Northeast when they had been open. Neighbors respond with unimagined support. Angelie joins a cavalcade from Camp Heartland traveling all over the East Coast, from New York to Florida, to speak openly about AIDS with children and young adults at schools and churches. The possibilities of a social movement defying a politically and culturally created context of shame-driven secrecy are apparent. Angelie and others on the cavalcade gather strength from one another to tell their stories, to open their secrets.

The film ends with a powerfully thought-provoking comment: "Since Angelie revealed her secret, her immune cell count has stopped declining. She feels well." While there is certainly no linear relationship between opening this secret and Angelie's well-being, we are left knowing that she and her family have achieved a deeper kind of healing—which we have been privileged to witness.

OPENING A SECRET AUTHENTICALLY

In sharp contrast to talk show telling of secrets, in authentic telling secrets are handled differently.

- Painful secrets are opened in a context of committed relationships.
- Accountability, loyalty, and mutual obligations in relationships are the necessary requirements to open secrets well.
- The past, present, and potential future of relationships are carefully considered before deciding to open a secret.
- Reliable support is sought prior to opening a secret.
- An empathic and receptive atmosphere is created in which to tell a secret.
- Concern for the impact on others stands alongside one's own need to speak.

- Healthy privacy is respected.
- The issues contained in any secret are not resolved simply by telling; healing occurs over time through dealing with these issues.
- Age-appropriate boundaries are respected.
- Courage is honored, both in telling and in listening.

The successful resolution of secrets requires that we challenge the television model of reckless telling and arrogant, voyeuristic listening and build instead a model marked by thoughtful telling and humble listening, a model that assumes we are mutual witnesses of one another's struggles with the truth of our lives.

Chapter

6

Concealing and Revealing:
Choices and Changes

> *As lightning to the children eased*
> *With explanation kind—*
> *The truth must dazzle gradually*
> *Or every man be blind—*
> *—Emily Dickinson*

WHO OWNS MY SECRET? :
DAMON'S STORY

"I was a psychology intern, just learning to practice psychotherapy. My patient worked in the hospital where I was receiving medical care. I had already found her difficult—confrontational, argumentative, demeaning. But when she walked into a session several months into her therapy with me, I was totally unprepared for what she said," Damon told me. "Even now, three years later, I can still feel my shock and anguish."

Damon's patient had gone into his medical records. Without permission from anyone, she simply looked him up on the hospital computer. When she began her next psychotherapy session, she looked at him slyly and said, "So, how are your T cells?" Damon's patient had ripped open the secret he had chosen to keep during his internship training: that he is HIV positive. With utter disregard for his privacy or for the boundaries of their relationship, she claimed ownership of a secret that did not belong to her.

While anything even resembling further therapy was, in fact, impossible, the woman threatened to expose Damon's secret if he terminated his work with her. "It was like being blackmailed by a very disturbed person," Damon said. "I felt I couldn't even tell my supervisor, because I had entered the program keeping this secret. I was stuck working with this woman for almost a year, feeling like she was my jailer."

As Damon and I began a conversation about secrets one summer morning, he started with this painful story. Slowly he then recounted other terrifying and courageous decisions in his life regarding concealing and revealing.

Damon grew up as the youngest of three children in a country where being different from the majority could put a person in extreme danger. Laws against homosexuality combined with family, religious, and cultural taboos made the decision to come out in any way enormously complex. Like most homosexual people, Damon spent his childhood and adolescence maintaining the secret of "feeling different."

Before telling anyone else, he needed to tell the secret to himself. "First I wrote it in my journal—in code, if you can imagine. I was terrified of anyone else finding out. Then I made a couple of tries at telling therapists. The first therapist responded with utter silence and then changed the subject. I felt I had said something I shouldn't have said. I tentatively told a second therapist that I thought I might have had some homosexual fantasies once in a while. When I felt his disapproval, I went back the following week and told him it wasn't true. He looked at me and said, 'Good.'"

For a long time Damon felt completely alone. Like many people struggling with secrets that go to the heart of who they are, Damon needed to meet many other gay people in order to begin to feel comfortable in the world. With this support, in his early twenties he began to tell family and friends. "I decided to tell people one at a time over a couple of days. I told everyone except my parents," Damon said. During the process of telling, Damon's sister said, "Don't tell Mom and Dad. You never know—you might change. Why upset them?" That was all Damon needed to hear. "The minute she supported the fear in me, I decided not to tell them," Damon told me.

Several months went by before Damon's mother came to him to confront his secret. She gently told him about another gay young man she knew and asked him if he ever felt that way. As they talked, however, she advised him not to tell too many people and told him definitely not to tell his father.

For Damon, the process of opening the secret of his homosexuality to the most important people in his life took nearly a year. As is true with many secrets, other people's discomfort with his disclosure led to their attempts to control the information. Damon heard many variations of "Don't tell so-and-so," which amplified his own ambivalence about telling. An older sibling saying, "Don't tell Mom and Dad," or a mother saying, "Don't tell your father," easily confounds the question of whose right it is to open a particular secret. It took Damon several more months and lots of courage to finally tell his father. "I had to remind myself that he was both my father and the husband of my mother and that each of these relationships was vital and deserved respect," Damon told me. When Damon finally told him, his father struggled to be accepting. And he was quite annoyed at being the last to know.

A few years went by before Damon had to deal with decisions surrounding a second secret, that of his HIV-positive diagnosis. In 1985 during a medical workup for enlarged lymph nodes, a physician tested Damon for HIV without asking or informing him that this was being done.[1] Several health care providers and religious leaders in Damon's life were told *before* he himself was told. Foreshadowing the stolen discovery of his illness by his patient many years later and thousands of miles away, Damon's doctor then warned him that he'd better tell his mother, because she worked in the same medical institution and was likely to find out.

Damon's mother responded with care and concern. However, once again she implored, "Don't tell your father. It'll kill him to know. You might outlive him. He might never need to know."

This time the secret stayed solely between Damon and his mother for many years.

"It became a secret from myself," Damon told me. "I just blocked it out." In so doing, he paid an enormous price. Previously a warm and caring man who was deeply connected to others and fully engaged with life, Damon became silent, distant, cold, and shut-down. He alienated all of his friends and became disinterested in life. Finally a new relationship required that he confront the secret in himself and begin to open it to others. Dear friends who thought he had become hateful toward them immediately understood his years of silence. But when he told his siblings, they responded, "Don't tell Dad and please don't tell our kids. They love you so much—let them enjoy their childhood."

"My decision to finally tell my father came when I realized that if I was going to have a real relationship with him, he had to know," Damon told me. This time his father was upset and angry with all of the people who had insisted that he not be told. He responded to Damon, "I lived through the Second World War. I surely can cope with anything you have to tell me."

I wondered with Damon why everyone in his family had wanted to keep his father out of both secrets. It was not, as one might suspect, that his father was especially vulnerable or intolerant, but rather because his father was the most emotionally expressive and direct member of the family. For his father to know meant that the adults in Damon's family would have to deal straightforwardly with the information.

Damon's family, however, lived very far away. For a long time Damon lived well with his decision to tell his HIV diagnosis to people who loved and cared for him, while keeping his illness private in his work setting. After his patient violated his confidential medical records, however, Damon needed to struggle with the slippery boundary between secrecy and privacy. "While my diagnosis was indeed no one's business at work, I realized that keeping it secret made me vulnerable to blackmail," Damon told me. "If I could be open about it, then no one would ever again have the power to use my illness to hold me hostage."

Damon thoughtfully prepared himself for various responses

to his revelation. Nonetheless, there were some surprises. Some people disappeared from his life. Some quickly changed the subject, acting as if they never heard what Damon had said. A few demanded that he take care of them emotionally, rather than vice versa. Some acted better toward him than they ever had, leaving Damon to wonder what that meant. Most were quite wonderful, supportive, and caring, taking their lead from what Damon needed.

As he developed more and more courage through telling and dealing with all of the different responses, Damon made a decision to give a paper at a national professional meeting detailing his own journey from secrecy to openness regarding HIV/AIDS. As with many secrets, this complex journey is not completed. "It's never just one liberation and then it's over," Damon declared. "There's such social pressure to make it a secret again in some new context."

Currently Damon is struggling with the dilemma regarding telling his niece, who is now eighteen. Her parents have asked him not to tell her. When she visits, he hides his medication from her. She knows he's gay, but neither of them mentions HIV. His niece witnesses her father, Damon's brother, sobbing every time they part at the end of a visit. Damon said, "It's clear to me that I can't have an authentic adult relationship with my niece unless she knows. It's less clear to me whose right it is to decide whether I can tell her."

DECIDING TO CONCEAL OR REVEAL A SECRET

Damon's story brings us to the heart of the complex decision-making process attached to concealing or revealing any secret. Reflecting on several key questions can help you in this process.

WHO "OWNS" A SECRET?

When you are keeping a secret that *primarily* and *essentially* regards your life, then you are the owner of the secret, and decisions to keep it or open it rightfully belong to you.

It's always important to think about the effects of concealing or revealing on other people. However, when a secret truly belongs to you, you don't need anyone else's permission to open it. If you feel you need permission to open a secret, this should be a signal either that the secret doesn't belong to you or that you're caught in a web of relationships that need to be reexamined. If your best friend tells you she is going bankrupt, that secret does not belong to you. If, on the other hand, you are going bankrupt, you don't need your sister's permission to tell your father.

Deciding to open a secret is often very anxiety-provoking. Visions of who will approve and who will disapprove may plague your decision. Such images are a good indication that you need to work on lowering your own anxiety in your relationship network *before* opening a secret.

While adults really don't need anyone else's approval in order to live their own lives with integrity, most of us want and need acceptance from the people we love. The palpable risk of losing acceptance through revealing a secret often does battle with the feelings of loneliness that arise when we keep a secret.

You also shouldn't feel compelled to keep a secret because other people urge you not to tell. Frequently people claim owner-ship of a secret that really doesn't belong to them, opening it when they have no ethical right to do so or insisting that you keep silent about your own secret.

You may need to think through whether you have sole pro-prietorship of a secret, as Damon did with his homosexuality, or whether it is co-owned with others, as would be the case in the birth of a child by artificial insemination.

WHO HAS A RIGHT TO KNOW?

The content of certain secrets goes to the core of other people's lives. Secrets about birth origins (including paternity, adoption, and the new birth technologies), secrets about medical diagnoses that may require informed decisions about treatment options or preventive care, and secrets regarding terminal illness all involve another person's *right to information*. While secrets like these have powerful relationship implications, they pertain first to another person's autonomy. When such secrets are kept from the person whose life they directly affect, the secret-keeper is operating from a position of arrogance, saying, in effect, "I know what's best for you to know—even in your own life." If you're keeping such a secret, you'll need to be prepared when you open it for an *initial* response of profound anger. You'll need to listen and respect these feelings in order to begin the complex process of integrating the secret into your relationship.

WHOSE WELL-BEING IS AFFECTED?

While you may indeed be the sole owner of a secret, keeping or opening the secret may affect the well-being of many other people. Maintaining certain secrets can put other people in jeopardy. While a person may own the secret of their HIV-positive status, the health of a sexual partner is at stake when such a secret is kept.

Some secrets disable the people in your life. If others are unable to use resources that they need, or cannot make decisions adequately because you're withholding information from them, it's time to consider how to open the secret. If the people you care about are living their lives based on a set of assumptions that you know to be false, then keeping the secret breaks a fundamental trust.

WHAT RELATIONSHIPS ARE HANDICAPPED BY THE SECRET?

You may be the owner of a secret that may not directly affect anyone else's physical or mental health or their capacity to make good decisions. Nonetheless, you may find that relationships are negatively affected. Damon's HIV secret belongs to him. His niece's individual well-being is not particularly affected by this secret. Damon's ability to have an authentic relationship with her, however, is handicapped by the secret.

To consider the impact on a relationship of a secret you are keeping, ask yourself two questions: What are the effects of my keeping this secret on our relationship? In what ways would our relationship change if I were to open this secret?

As you examine ownership, the effects on others, and the effects on relationships in regard to any given secret, you'll begin to see that there can be no simple formula for making your decision, and no guarantee that it will be risk free. Secrets reside in a complex geometry. Opening a secret whose maintenance is having a poor effect on someone you love may indeed throw the relationship between the two of you into turmoil for a period of time.

DOES THE SECRET VIOLATE SHARED ASSUMPTIONS IN A RELATIONSHIP?

Intimate relationships, whether between spouses, lovers, or dear friends, are based on shared assumptions about what will and will not occur in the relationship. Sometimes these premises are clearly spelled out, but often they are implicit. In North America spouses most often expect monogamy, whether or not they discuss it. Best friends often assume each other's secrets will be safeguarded and that neither will hide significant matters.

When a secret violates such shared assumptions, the person outside of the secret is left living his or her life with expectations that no longer apply. If you believe that you and your spouse openly and honestly share money matters, but your partner is keeping an important financial secret, your actions are based on a faulty premise. This kind of secret-keeping, often based in arrogance, disables another person from "playing life with a full deck."

Such secrets are often maintained because the secret-keeper accurately perceives that disclosure will be met with anger. If you're keeping a secret that robs someone else of key information they need to make good decisions, you're probably violating shared assumptions in your relationship.

HOW IS YOUR BEHAVIOR AFFECTED BY KEEPING THE SECRET?

Does keeping the secret use lots of energy that could be going to other things? Has the secret taken over your life, requiring so much caution and hypervigilance that your spontaneity is sacrificed? Do you avoid topics that might remotely touch upon the content of the secret? Has the secret led you to deny what is really going on in your life? Are you distancing yourself from people with whom you wish to be close? Does the secret cause you to lie and erode trust in important relationships? Is your life marked more by duplicity than authenticity? Answers to these questions can help you to see the impact of a given secret on your life. When secret-keeping begins to distort *who you genuinely want to be*, then it is time to consider careful ways to change.

COMPLEX MOTIVES: MAKING AND KEEPING SECRETS

When I first met the Katziki family, I was bewildered by the intensity of Faye Katziki's responses to her daughter Elena's seemingly ordinary behavior. What appeared to me as fairly benign and garden-variety adolescent mischief, including being caught smoking in the girl's bathroom, putting on forbidden eye makeup, and, most recently, returning an hour late from a school dance, had become the basis for a war between Faye and her fourteen-year-old daughter. In our initial session Faye's husband, George, expressed confusion over what was happening in his family. "Elena's our only child," he told me. "Faye and Elena have always been so close, but this last year it seems everything Elena does upsets my wife." As George spoke, Faye hung her head, looking more ashamed than angry.

I asked the Katzikis about their extended families, just as I would do in any initial meeting with a family. George readily told me about his parents, who lived nearby. The elder Katzikis were Greek immigrants who had done very well and were extremely loving and generous to all of their grandchildren. "I have to say,

Elena is their favorite," George told me. "And they love Faye so much. They're very upset by all the fighting. My mother tries to calm Faye down, but it doesn't seem to help."

When I turned to Faye to find out about her family, I could feel the tension rise in the room. George moved closer to Faye and put his arm gently around her shoulder when I began my inquiry. "I don't see my parents," Faye remarked quietly. When I tried to find out why this was so, Faye said, "I don't want to talk about it, if you don't mind." As Faye spoke, Elena began to fidget in her chair. A moment later Elena said, "I have a headache—could we just stop for today?" While this mother and daughter were often battling, Elena knew when it was time to protect her mother. In the next two sessions, I witnessed the repeat of this same pattern—Faye would begin the session, complaining about some behavior of Elena's; mother and daughter would argue; George would look pained and express confusion; and every time I raised a question that even remotely addressed Faye's life, Elena would come to the rescue with a host of distractions. What was going on here? It would take many failed attempts to lower the temperature between Faye and Elena before I would know.

At the end of our fourth meeting, Faye asked me if she might see me alone. "I've asked my husband and Elena if they would mind, and they said it would be okay," Faye said. I agreed.

Faye came to our meeting looking drawn and very sad. "If I don't talk about this to someone, I don't know what I'm going to do," she began. I listened quietly as Faye told me the secret that was driving her intense reactions to Elena. Tears rolled down her face as Faye spoke. "My husband doesn't know, my in-laws don't know, Elena certainly doesn't know—I got pregnant when I was fifteen. My parents sent me away to a home for unwed mothers and made me give the baby up for adoption. I had a son—they never even let me see him. He would be twenty-five now. I think about him every day. And I feel driven—I have to stop this from ever happening to Elena."

I gently began to ask Faye more about what happened to her as an adolescent. Her parents were very traditional, very strict. And, in a typical pattern, the more they restricted Faye, the more she found ways to break their rules. There were no conversations about sex in her family. Her three older brothers all had girlfriends, but she was not allowed to date. Nonetheless, when a handsome senior took an interest in her, she found ways to see him, telling her parents she was at her best friend's house. When Faye became pregnant, she was terrified and told no one for five months. When her parents found out, they were furious. Her father called her a whore. Their priest arranged for her to go away for the rest of her pregnancy. When Faye returned, the entire incident was never spoken of again. Faye left home after high school and never went back.

"After I met George and fell in love with him, I just knew I could never tell him," Faye said as she wept. "Now I'm just so confused. I keep thinking my son might show up at my door. I want him to, but what would happen to my life?"

I slowly began to connect Faye's responses to Elena's behavior to what had happened in her own life. As Elena approached the age that Faye was when she became pregnant, Faye started to be hypervigilant. And while she allowed Elena to go on dates, which her own parents had forbidden, she did so with an unspoken message of lurking danger. Faye's daily life now was a swirl of fear and anxiety: Might her secret son show up unannounced one day? Would George leave her if he found out? Would Elena get pregnant? As our meeting ended that day Faye said, "I can't keep living this way." I told her we would work on ways to change her circumstances.

I met alone with Faye for several sessions. As we talked about her life and she experienced compassion rather than harsh judgment, her responses to Elena became far more measured. As her own shame lifted, she became ready to explore opening her secret. "I feel ready to tell George," Faye said, "but I feel very confused about telling Elena, and I don't want my in-laws to know." I told Faye that, in my experience, secrets were best opened one step at a time.

Telling her husband did not mean she had to tell anyone else. However, while this secret belonged to her, a piece of it also belonged to Elena—she had a half-brother somewhere. I felt confident that we would get to that issue once Faye opened the secret to her husband. I had experienced George as a loving and concerned husband, and I had little doubt that he would find a way to accept Faye's secret.

I coached Faye to tell George all of the stories she had told me. His first response was relief. "I knew all along that there was something Faye was keeping from me, something about her family," George said to me when we met following Faye's revelation. "I never really understood why we never saw her parents. They didn't even come to our wedding. I thought maybe she was sexually abused or beaten. I didn't know what to think. I wanted to respect her privacy, but I was always wishing she would trust me enough to tell me. She thought I would stop loving her—that'll never happen."

During the time I worked with the Katzikis, George convinced Faye to open her secret to Elena. Not wanting to put Elena in a position to have to keep a secret from her grandparents, they also told George's parents, who responded well. I tried to interest Faye in reconnecting with her parents, but she declined.

Secrets are kept or opened for many complex and intricately braided motives, from self-serving abuses of power to altruistic protection of others. Exploring your motives for making and keeping a secret can help you decide whether and how to open it.

WHO AM I PROTECTING?

Any secret may be made to protect yourself, another person, and/or a relationship. You may be telling yourself that a secret exists only to protect another person. As you begin to ask yourself what would change if you were to open the secret, you may discover that you are also protecting yourself.

When you say to yourself, "I could never tell Dad," are you protecting Dad from knowing something you believe he could not handle? Where does the idea come from that this information is beyond his capacity? Look carefully for exceptions to the myth that Dad would "collapse" if he knew. You may discover that in fact you are protecting yourself from Dad's responses or from Mom's responses to your decision to tell Dad.

You may fear that a relationship will explode if you open a secret. Faye, for instance, was certain she would lose George if he knew her secret. But what is happening to the relationship as a result of *keeping* the secret? Is it enhanced by the secret? Is it becoming encrusted with lies? Or is it dissolving because the secret is requiring more and more distance?

When emotional protection of self, others, or relationships is invoked as a motive for secret-keeping among adults, it's a good sign that relationship issues need to be addressed before a secret is opened.

AM I INTIMIDATED INTO SILENCE?

Some secrets are kept because of fear and threats. If you would like to open a secret but hesitate because you are overwhelmed with fear of the consequences, you need to establish support that you can rely on before moving forward.

When one person is intimidated into keeping a secret, then another person is misusing or abusing power in a relationship to enforce secrecy. Such power may involve physical threat, potential financial ruin, or profound emotional coercion. Since people seldom give up power easily, secrets that are held captive by power imbalances most often open when the person being intimidated decides it's time to take the risk.

In the case of dangerous secrets—those involving physical harm—the secret-keeper is often paralyzed by fear, since telling can bring further injury. Opening such secrets requires a plan for safety first, including, at times, police protection and an alternative place to live.

AM I CONFUSED ABOUT WHEN TO TELL?

Many secrets are made "temporarily" and then kept indefinitely because of uncertainty about the right time to tell. If, for example, a parent keeps a secret from a young child, when is the child finally "old enough" to hear it? Or a secret is made during a time of family crisis and no one opens it after the storm has blown over, fearing that to do so may resurrect the earlier turmoil. Such doubt and confusion usually support the status quo of maintaining the silence.

AM I KEEPING A SECRET BECAUSE I FEEL TOO ASHAMED TO OPEN IT?

Sharing a secret often requires facing shame.[2] We live in a time when conservative voices speak about "the need to bring back shame" in order to control people's behavior, particularly in the arenas of sex and substance abuse. In my own experience witnessing people struggle with secrets, shame is all too alive and well, oftentimes driving the very behavior popularly connected to lack of shame.

Since the experience of shame can be so painful and debilitating, many people seek to deny it through secret-keeping. Paradoxically, the more we try to escape shame through secrets, the more ashamed we often feel. Shame and certain secrets exist in an escalating dance with one another: the more shame, the more secrecy; the more secrecy, the more shame.

COMPLEX MOTIVES: OPENING SECRETS

Just as there are varied and complicated reasons for making and keeping a secret, so the motives for opening a secret can range from revenge, on the one hand, to a genuine desire to heal relationships, on the other, with many other reasons intertwined.

AM I OPENING THE SECRET OUT OF ANGER?

Placing previously hidden information into a relationship is a powerful act. Some secrets are opened in anger or with a desire for revenge. If you are opening a secret that rightfully belongs to someone else, you may be acting with anger even while telling yourself that you are doing this "for someone else's good."

In the play *Mrs. Klein*, the daughter of famed psychoanalyst Melanie Klein opens the secret of her brother's suicide with the deliberate intention of causing great pain to her mother, with whom she's enraged because of a lifetime of perceived hurts. Opening the secret becomes her weapon to get even.

When a secret becomes a pawn in a game of escalating anger, opening the secret is more likely to damage than to heal the relationship.

AM I OPENING THE SECRET IN ORDER TO DIVIDE LOYALTIES?

It is all too easy to use opening a secret with one member of your family in order to turn them against another member. When a divorced father, Alan, opened his ex-wife's secret love affair to his teenage son, Bruce, he did so deliberately to erode Bruce's loyalty to his mother, even while rationalizing that he simply wanted an "open" relationship with his son.

AM I OPENING THE SECRET IN ORDER TO GET THE BURDEN OFF MY BACK AND ONTO SOMEONE ELSE'S?

In my therapy practice with couples, I have frequently seen one spouse tell his or her partner about an affair not out of a genuine desire to heal the relationship, but "because I couldn't stand the guilt of her/his not knowing any longer." When an affair secret is opened in this way, the person having the affair usually wants the initial telling to be the final conversation about the matter.

When you imagine opening an important secret and the scenario you fantasize is your own great relief followed by the other person's complete and utter acceptance with no further work to be done, recognize this as a warning flag. Ask yourself how much you are being motivated by a desire to alleviate your own guilt at another person's expense. The outcome is almost sure to be more complex than you anticipate.

AM I OPENING THE SECRET OUT OF A SENSE OF SELF-RIGHTEOUSNESS?

Some people believe that they have a corner on the truth and that secrets need to be told regardless of the consequences to others. In Ibsen's play *The Wild Duck*, Gregers takes it upon himself to "free" his old friend Hjalmar from his "self-delusion." Without regard to the outcome, Gregers brutally reveals to Hjalmar that the daughter he so loves is not his own and that he was tricked into marrying his wife when she was already pregnant. The biological father is, in fact, Gregers's father. Gregers's motive for telling is his own vindictiveness, which he cloaks in the banner of "telling the truth." In *The Wild Duck* this self-righteous telling leads to tragedy. With no explanation to his daughter, Hjalmar rejects her. Devastated by the unexplained loss of her father's love, she commits suicide.

While this example may seem extreme, it certainly illustrates that opening a secret because you think you know best what others should know is as problematic as keeping a secret for this reason.

DO I WANT TO OPEN THE SECRET IN ORDER TO REGAIN MY OWN INTEGRITY AND SENSE OF BALANCE?

Living with certain secrets can make you feel you are living a lie. A kind of psychological laryngitis can capture your voice, and only opening the secret will enable you to reclaim it. Since many secrets can exact a great price in how we experience ourselves, you may need to open a secret in order to restore your own sense of yourself as honest, sincere, and genuine.

Both opening secrets to alleviate guilt and opening secrets to regain integrity may initially be motivated by a desire for relief. When we open secrets simply to erase guilt, we expect that relief to be immediate and final. Opening secrets to regain our integrity involves a recognition that opening the secret is just the beginning, and a commitment to deal honestly with all of the issues that arise once a secret opens.

DO I WANT TO OPEN THE SECRET BECAUSE I TRULY BELIEVE THE INFORMATION BELONGS TO ANOTHER PERSON OR WILL ENHANCE ANOTHER PERSON'S LIFE?

The content of a secret may involve another person's core identity. You may decide that a secret belongs to someone else and that he or she has a right to the information. You may also decide that opening a secret that lies deep in your family's history will allow family members to live fuller and more informed lives.

When Alyse Butler came to see me she was struggling with whether to open a secret to her brother, Kyle, that she had known for many years. Their father died in 1968. Alyse was seventeen at the time, and Kyle was ten. The children were told that he had a heart attack. Alyse suspected that their father, who had suffered from depression for several years, had committed suicide. She doggedly pursued the truth. Her mother kept insisting that he died naturally. When Alyse was twenty, her suspicions were confirmed by her paternal aunt, who then swore her to secrecy. "My aunt said, 'You must never tell Kyle—he idolized your father.' To this day I've obeyed her injunction," Alyse said. "But now I see Kyle so consumed with his own health, so afraid that he'll die of a heart attack. It's driving his wife crazy—he refuses to have children because he's convinced that he'll die and leave them. For the last couple of years, he's been constantly checking his pulse, his blood pressure, running to the doctor for every little thing."

As I listened, it became clear to me that as Kyle grew closer and closer to the age at which his father died of a supposed heart attack, the more frightened he became that he too would die an untimely death. He needed the missing information about his father's life and death in order to live his own life well.

I confirmed Alyse's intuition and told her that the promise she made her aunt when Kyle was just thirteen was intended to protect him. Keeping that same promise now was, in fact, causing him harm. I told her I didn't think she needed her aunt's permission to open the secret, but that out of respect she should let her aunt know her new decision. Alyse said she wanted to bring her brother to therapy to open the secret.

In a session with Kyle, Alyse told him what she knew about their father's death by suicide. He was stunned and initially quite angry that this had been kept from him. Alyse explained the promise she'd made to their aunt and her subsequent confusion about who had the right to know. Their mother's refusal to talk about what really happened added to Alyse's dilemma. We met together several times to piece together the story of their father's life and death. I coached them to talk to their mother, but she remained adamant in her refusal to acknowledge her husband's suicide. Nonetheless, Kyle became less and less obsessed with his own health and more and more interested in who his father was. Kyle and Alyse went to the cemetery together for the first time to visit their father's grave. "I feel terrible that my father killed himself," Kyle told me, "but I also feel free now to live a full life." Two years after I finished seeing Kyle and Alyse, I received a birth announcement from Kyle and his wife.

DO I WANT TO OPEN THE SECRET IN ORDER TO REOPEN A RELATIONSHIP?

Distance, narrow and repetitive conversations, lack of passion, and loneliness all travel alongside certain secrets. Sometimes the only way to resuscitate a dying relationship is to find the courage to open a secret. When a secret is opened out of a genuine desire to reopen a relationship, you have to be willing to slog through the possible pain, confusion, blame, anger, disappointment, and sadness in order to reach trustworthy healing and reconciliation.

Our motives for making, keeping, breaking, or opening a secret can sometimes be elusive. You may see your motives one way, while your partner may experience them quite differently. What you view as protection, your adult daughter may see as disloyalty. Carefully listening to another person's point of view, without defending yourself or attacking the other person, enables you to appreciate the exquisitely braided motives attached to any secret. Such an appreciation, while certainly not simplifying your decision, will enhance the likelihood that you are approaching secrets with the care and responsibility that are their due.

A TIME TO SPEAK, A TIME TO WAIT, A TIME TO MAINTAIN SILENCE

While there is no such thing as the absolutely perfect moment to open a secret, there are certainly better and worse times.

Since deciding to open a secret often raises anxiety, many people seek to reduce such feelings by rushing headlong to reveal without taking the time needed to plan, to build support, to anticipate possible reactions, and to think through their own responses.

In my many years as a family therapist, I've been astounded by the number of people who choose to open a secret to their entire family on a major holiday, such as Thanksgiving or Christmas. Everyone is together in one place. It feels like a good opportunity to get it all over with at once. However, since these rituals are already fraught with the tensions of intense family gatherings, including decades of good and bad memories and all of the family's unfinished business, this is usually the worst time to open a secret. Doing so will catch you up in the relational crossfire of all of the preexisting family relationships. You may find yourself remembered forever as the son or daughter "who ruined Thanksgiving" by your revelation of a pending divorce, homosexuality, financial failure, sexual abuse, or other issue. Your desire for connection, support, or reconciliation will be harder to achieve.

Similarly, major life cycle rituals, such as weddings and graduations, are not a good time to open secrets. When Steve Bunting chose his younger sister's college graduation to tell his family he'd been secretly married to a woman of a different religion for nearly a year, his sister was furious with him. They had always been close, and Steve assumed she would be supportive. Instead she felt angry that his news spoiled what should have been her day, as everyone's attention turned away from her graduation to their upset at her brother's intermarriage.

Life cycle rituals are intended to make and mark transitions for individuals and your family. Since family relationships are shifting, such rituals may seem to offer a perfect invitation to open a secret. Yielding to this temptation will confound your purpose in opening a secret, as the process of telling will get all tangled up in the ritual event. Either the importance of the secret will get lost or it will overwhelm the ritual. In short, use regular time, not ritual time, to open a secret.

If you or a member of your family has already opened a secret during a major family ritual and you now find yourselves dealing with cutoff relationships and heaps of blame, you may want to initiate a conversation or write a letter to family members in which you distinguish between the ritual and the content of the secret. Steve Bunting was able to regain his sister's support after he apologized for opening his secret on her graduation day. "I told her I hadn't thought carefully about the way my news would affect her graduation. I was scared and anxious and tired of keeping my marriage a secret," Steve said. "Everyone was together, and so it seemed easier. Instead it just made things worse. I sent my sister a carefully written letter and said I had been wrong to choose her graduation day to tell everyone the secret of my marriage." After Steve wrote to his sister, she came and met his wife. The rest of Steve's family had been using the timing of Steve's telling in order to avoid dealing with the substance of his revelation. Once his sister let everyone know that "spoiling" her graduation was no longer an issue and that she supported her brother's marriage, the rest of the family had to begin to deal more with the content and less with the timing.

When a person is terminally ill, he or she may decide to open a secret in order to have one last chance to resolve relationships or complete unfinished business. Great literature and history are replete with such deathbed confessions. Conversely, family members may decide that a terminally ill family member needs to hear a secret for the first time. Think very carefully if you are faced with such a situation. Does a dying husband really need to hear that his wife had an affair seventeen years ago, or is the wife simply making a last attempt to alleviate her guilt? While long-standing relationship issues that have remained secret can be resolved when a person is dying, you want to ask yourself just whose needs are being met.

Funerals are often a time when family secrets emerge. All that could not be spoken when a person was alive may come tumbling out upon their death. Family members may have promised to keep a secret and no longer feel bound by the promise.[3] Secrets may emerge through the discovery of letters or papers belonging to the person who died. When family secrets open just before, during, or immediately after a funeral, the process of grieving becomes more complicated.

When Angie Alonzo's powerful father, Anthony, died suddenly at age seventy-four, she flew home for his funeral knowing that she would finally speak to her brother, Tony, about a secret she had harbored for over thirty years. When Angie was thirteen, her father's brother, Uncle Bernard, began to sexually abuse her. The abuse continued for two years. Angie tried once to tell her mother, but her mother seemed to disbelieve her and told her never to mention it to her father. Shortly afterward the abuse stopped, leaving Angie to wonder if her mother had in fact intervened. Angie's mother died a year later. While Angie never forgot the abuse, it was never mentioned again until one hour before Anthony's funeral, when Angie finally told her brother.

"For me, it was like all of the mysteries in our family began to clear up," Tony said. "There were generations of women in my father's family who were always coming unglued. You always felt like there was an unhingedness in the family, like things could fly apart at any moment. And then there was my father's authority and all the things you could never say because one raised eyebrow from him would wipe out you and your words. My sister knew she couldn't speak while he was alive. This was his brother. Men counted more. Women were viewed as hysterical. My father would never have believed her. She couldn't risk his discounting her reality, but the moment he died, she had to speak out."

In the aftermath of Anthony's death, Tony and Angie unearthed generations of sexual abuse of women in their father's family of origin. While not abusing anyone himself, Anthony, the patriarch, played a powerful role in maintaining the silence and intimidation.

I asked Tony how his sister's revelation had affected his grief over his father's death. "My grieving went at a different pace," Tony said. "First there was lots of anger—anger that my father's tyrannical place in our family kept my sister and cousins from being protected. Parents are supposed to take care of children. It didn't work that way in our family. It's so complicated—losing my father meant my sister could finally speak. My sadness over his death is all knotted up with loyalty to my sister. Still, I have no regrets that she spoke up when she did—I'm only sorry she couldn't have told me earlier."

When secrets are discovered upon the death of a family member, it may mean that the person who died played a powerful role as the enforcer of silence. It's astonishing to see how quickly another family member tries to step into this role. Secrets that open following a death can offer an opportunity for increased closeness, greater openness, and more flexibility, or they may send family members scurrying to their positions in preexisting and rigid alliances. This is often a good time for some short-term family therapy in order to deal with grief, changing family relationships, and assimilating the new knowledge that has emerged.

MANY SECRETS, MANY WAYS TO TELL

Secrets can be opened anonymously or in the context of committed relationships. They may be revealed to strangers we will never see again or to the person who shares our bed for life. Throughout history, human beings have established special means to tell secrets outside of their committed relationships. Such telling may be motivated to relieve guilt, to seek guidance, to gain absolution, to rehearse, or to assuage loneliness. The various methods of telling bring both opportunities and perils.

CONFESSIONAL TELLING

Secrets told in certain circumstances are protected by law, ethics, and customs. Many of the world's religions have established methods to reveal shameful secrets to a member of the clergy, within a religious ceremony, or on a special holiday. For centuries observant Catholics have used the confessional as a place to tell secrets with the absolute promise that the priest will never reveal what he hears. Such telling spans a continuum from the routine to the sacred. While not intended as such, religious confession can provide a "rehearsal" for opening a secret to family members.

In contemporary times, we may reveal our secrets to psychotherapists, physicians, or our comrades in a twelve-step program. This secular "confessional" has been predicated on the protection of confidentiality. As we saw in the discussion of managed care, such confidentiality is no longer guaranteed.

Similar to revealing a secret in a religious context, doing so in a mental-health context can be the first and final telling, or it can enable a safe beginning to opening the secret back home in family relationships. If you choose to open a secret in therapy, it is important to ask your therapist for help in clarifying what you want to do next. Far too many therapists err either on the side of neglecting further disclosure or on that of encouraging disclosure without a careful plan. If you are struggling with a secret, look for a therapist with expertise in family relationships and the ability to offer careful coaching.

ANONYMOUS TELLING

Many of us have had the experience of hearing a secret from a stranger on a plane or train. You may have done such telling yourself. People who will never see each other again share secrets with no ongoing responsibility for relationships. Such telling may be a way to experience another person's response to something that you have never spoken, an attempt to hear yourself speak just to see what it feels like, or a trying out before opening a secret in your family.

Manicurists, hairdressers, and bartenders find that they become the recipients of many secrets. Beauty salons and bars offer a contradictory combination of intimacy and anonymity. "When I do a woman's nails, I'm touching her, holding her hand, really. Then I begin to hear stories, things she might not tell anyone," Sara Callahan, a manicurist, told me. "Then the next week, it's like she never said it. Believe me, I know a lot of people's secrets."

You may see such people again and again after telling a secret, yet they remain outside the meaningful network of relationships in your life. Telling and hearing secrets can be done with no responsibility for an ongoing relationship, no sense of threat, and no promise of confidentiality. Anonymous telling may serve as a rehearsal, or it may be the only time a secret is told.

COMPUTER TELLING

A father posts a message on a computer bulletin board: "My daughter has cancer. . . . We are preparing ourselves for the worst, which her doctor hinted we should expect. . . . I do not know how to tell her grandparents, or even our friends."[4] Before telling this painful reality to family and dear friends, this father has reached out to tell hundreds of faceless strangers. Adoptees searching for their biological parents, husbands planning to leave their wives, women with depression, people with HIV—all are traveling the information superhighway, telling their secrets to persons they do not know and will never see.

Many gay adolescents who have never told anyone about their homosexuality are telling for the first time on the Internet. Ryan Matsuno, seventeen, turned on his computer one night and reached out with the message "Does anyone else feel like you're the only gay guy on the planet?" His question brought this gay teen, who had never told anyone else his secret, more than a hundred supportive responses. Feeling a sense of community for the first time in his life, Ryan developed enough courage to open his secret to his mother. His friends in cyberspace shared their own coming-out processes, and Ryan derived courage from their stories.[5]

Computers have entered our lives with a power to communicate to hundreds and thousands of faceless others. As a child, you may have written a secret on paper, placed the note in a bottle, and cast it out into the ocean, never knowing who would find and read it. And no matter who did, you would never get an answer. In today's culture, you can still cast a secret out to unidentified recipients, but they are a multitude and they will probably write you back.

Similar to talk television, computer telling has furthered the breakdown of taboos. If you choose to tell a secret on the Internet, no one else can be the guardian of your life story. No one edits it, no one limits who you may tell. Like television, the revelation of secrets on computers occurs without commitment for an ongoing relationship. Unlike with television, however, personal computer telling is not packaged into a commercial production. People using their modems to send out *their own* secrets are not someone else's commodity.

While computer telling may give us access to a world where it seems safe to explore even previously unmentionable topics, telling our secrets to an unaccountable crowd has important limitations. Computer telling offers the seeming control of anonymity. But at the same time, once you have put a secret out via your computer, you lose ownership of the content of your secret.

Computer telling can be a wrenching and heartfelt attempt to open shameful and painful secrets. It can also be an invitation to make up sensational stories. We need to think about how such revelations impact our ability to draw distinctions among secrets. If secrets come to us through the same medium that brings us our bank accounts, recipes, stock quotes, travel tips, and a kaleidoscope of material from the profound to the banal, what must we do to maintain respect for the magnitude of other people's pain?

Certain computer bulletin boards are defined as being for a particular population. For instance, an adoptees mailing list is described as being exclusively for adult adoptees, their spouses, significant others, and children/grandchildren; birth siblings; and persons who are separated from their birth parents but who are not technically adopted. Birth parents, adoptive parents, and anyone else who is not in the above categories are asked not to use this particular mailing list. An artificial boundary is created. Part of the directions for this service read, "Messages posted are intended only for distribution to subscribers on this list. Unless you have explicit permission from the author, please DO NOT redistribute messages posted to this list elsewhere. *Many subscribers are sharing feelings with others that they've never discussed with others before, and often their shared experiences are highly personal*" (italics added).[6] These instructions are predicated on the false assumption that all people are ethical, that no one will lie or misrepresent themselves. Trust, an element in human relationships that is usually associated with long-term, face-to-face relationships, is invoked in a context where mutual obligation is in fact a fiction. Is the subscriber truly an adult adoptee, or perhaps a novelist, a researcher, or a voyeur? Who knows?

When real names are used, bulletin board readers may find themselves in the peculiar position of knowing another person's secret without that person knowing that they know. For example, a woman, Karen Alexi, was diagnosed with metastatic cancer. She told her best friend but had not yet decided to tell anyone else. Her friend wrote the sad news on an organizational bulletin board, mistakenly thinking she was writing to just one other person. An acquaintance of Karen's remarked to me, "I'd like to call Karen and give her my support, but she doesn't know I know about her illness. I don't know what to do."

Computer telling can also rip open secrets without your permission. Your own medical records are likely for sale to the highest bidder, without your knowledge.[7] Sold to researchers, pharmaceutical companies, health maintenance organizations, or market analysts, your confidential medical information is no longer between you and your doctor. In Maryland, every contact between a patient and doctor is entered into a state computer. The 1996 health insurance bill passed in the United States Congress provides for the establishment of a vast computerized medical records database to be used for billing, research, and other unspecified purposes without the knowledge or consent of patients.[8] In many parts of the country, your mental health records are put into a computer that any hospital employee can examine without your knowledge and without your consent. Such records will remain a secret from you, however, if professionals deem it not in your "best interest" to see them. The very same computers that democratize secret-telling by putting us all on the same level are capable of creating an authoritarian hierarchy that excludes us from our own secrets.

Computer technology clearly has moved faster than our capacity to imagine adequate ethics or to create enforceable laws. At the same time, computers are playing an increasingly intimate role in our lives. Before using your computer to tell a secret, spend a bit of time asking yourself what you intend to have happen. Are you clear about what you can and cannot control once you open a secret this way? Is a computer community a substitute for family and friendship connections, or a step along the way?

COERCED TELLING

Just as people are sometimes intimidated into keeping a secret, so they may be coerced into opening one. One recent form of coerced telling is "outing," when a homosexual person's secret is told without their permission and against their wishes. Once a person is "outed," he or she has lost control of the secret and has little choice but to tell others.[9] This kind of telling is often done in the context of a "cause," but it ignores the individual human dimensions involved in every secret. Opening secrets is exquisitely connected to core aspects of one's self and relationships. Coerced telling rips this connection.

Coerced telling occurs when someone else tells your secret before you are ready to do so. You may also feel compelled to tell a secret because you feel threatened or blackmailed. It is important to distinguish between coercion and influence. If your best friend threatens to tell your husband a secret that you have told her, that is coercion. If she debates with you, pointing out all the good reasons to open the secret, she is using her influence with you. Coercion is also not the issue when safety is in question. It is not coerced telling if you open someone else's secret when not to do so would put another person at grave emotional or physical risk.

PLANFUL TELLING

Once you have determined that you want to open a secret, you need to reflect on ways to do so with care.

In order to avoid *reckless telling* and to prepare yourself for *planful telling*, you may want to try the following exercise.

1. Think about the advantages and disadvantages of opening your secret for every *individual* in your significant circle of family and dear friends.

2. Think about the advantages and disadvantages of opening your secret for each *relationship* in your significant circle of family and dear friends (for example, you and your mother; you and your father; your mother and your father; you and your brother; your brother and your mother; your brother and your father; you and your husband; you and your daughter; your husband and your daughter; you and your best friend, and so on).

3. Think about the advantages and disadvantages of opening your secret for your entire *family*.

This exercise places you in an imagined future in your network of relationships. It enables you to consider not only the catastrophes that we often imagine will follow upon opening a secret, but all of the good possibilities as well. You will see where relationship work may need to be done *before* opening a secret. You will gain a sense of how you can use the order of telling to build support. If your secret will have major impact on your mother, for example, would it be a good idea to tell your sister first? And as you imagine opening the secret and the changes that will ensue, you'll have a renewed sense of the possibilities for authentic relationships in your family.

Very few secrets are told once and resolved. Many secrets require telling and retelling. Secrets about your own identity, such as homosexuality, parentage, and illness, may require a new decision about openness each time you develop an important relationship. Secrets told to children at a young age often require more sophisticated retelling as children grow. Remember, too, that telling a secret involves drawing a new boundary, one that demarcates privacy. Opening a secret within your family seldom involves telling your entire neighborhood. What was secret is transformed to that which is private.

Opening secrets planfully does not mean that their impact will diminish or that issues and relationships will automatically and magically change for the better. We live in a time when everything is speeded up, leading us to expect that human predicaments should be resolved instantly. Deciding what to do about a secret is only the first step in a process. As we will see in part 2 of this book, when this process goes well, it leads to deeper, more complex, and more connected relationships.

Part II

Secret Passages

Self-Secrets

I'd decided there would be no genetic test in my life, that I didn't need to know. I would drive all night to get back home—to get back, in a sense, to my own unknown. I had a right to that.

> —C. Siebert, on deciding whether to be tested for
> the gene causing an incurable heart condition

This is my nightmare—I'm a person created by donor insemination, someone who will never know half of her identity. I feel anger and confusion, and I'm filled with questions. Whose eyes do I have? Why the big secret? Who gave my family the idea that my biological roots are not important?

> —M. R. Brown

There is a more intimate and personal issue involved in AIDS, and that is the right to keep knowledge from oneself—in other words, to keep a secret from yourself.

> —Alida Brill

"THERE WERE MANY SECRETS in my family when I was growing up," Kathleen Ellington told me. "To this day, I don't know what all of them were. We lived in a small town, where my father was a respected businessman and community leader. He was away a lot. I suspect he was having affairs. I realize now that my mother was an alcoholic. Her drinking was *never* discussed. Their marriage was displayed to our town as *Ozzie and Harriet.*

"As children, we knew we weren't allowed to ask any questions or make any comments about our family. As a young teen, I began making secrets of my own." As we talked one autumn evening, Kathleen, now thirty-eight, told me a secret that she had kept to herself for twenty-five years.

"When I was thirteen, I became fascinated with speech and drama. A good friend of mine was taking voice lessons, and I wanted to join her. When I asked my parents, who could well afford the lessons, they refused. My father said it was a waste of money, that nobody needed to be taught how to speak. My mother sided with him, and said voice lessons would make me sound phony," Kathleen said. "There was so much covered up in my family that my mother's fear about phoniness seems quite bizarre to me now."

Determined to have the lessons, Kathleen began to baby-sit in order to make the money herself. She quickly realized that baby-sitting would not yield the money she needed. At that point she began to steal from the families for whom she was baby-sitting. "I was very careful," Kathleen told me. "I stole small amounts at a time so that it wouldn't be noticed. I sat for lots of families, so the money added up. I never told anyone and I was never caught." When she had enough money, Kathleen surreptitiously began voice lessons.

"My parents never knew. I became quite adept at lying about where I was. My voice teacher thought I was very good. I felt proud of myself, but I couldn't let anyone else know. I lived like this until I went away to college," Kathleen said. In college, with no more baby-sitting available and no more voice lessons, Kathleen began a different combination of paradoxical activities, secretly shoplifting from stores while participating in social action on campus. Today Kathleen is a voice teacher who works with adolescent girls. With some bewilderment she told me, "Once or twice a year, I shoplift some small, unnecessary item. Until tonight, it's been my ongoing secret with myself."

How do we make sense of Kathleen's story? As she and I talked we began to make connections that she had never made.

Kathleen came from a family where visible pride and invisible shame lived side by side. Without Kathleen realizing it, this contradictory alloy was mirrored in her actions. A knot, consisting of irreconcilable strands, was pulled tighter and tighter. Kathleen stole in order to develop her voice. Discovering her talent in speaking required that she remain silent about her lessons and how she obtained them. When I commented to Kathleen that her compelling desire for voice lessons as a teen and her career path as a voice teacher made a lot of sense for someone coming from a family infused with silence and denial, she was astounded. "I can't believe I never thought about that," she said. When I told her I'd known many children and teens who respond to family secrets with petty theft, stealing from their families and shoplifting, she silently nodded.

Like many people who live with self-secrets that arise within a wider context of family or social secrecy, Kathleen's abilities to see certain connections were occluded. Stealing, which she kept as a secret with herself, intertwined both with family secrets, whose presence she sensed, and with knowledge about herself that remained just out of reach.

Kathleen's story held two kinds of self-secrets: those she kept *with* herself and those she kept *from* herself.

SECRETS WE KEEP WITH OURSELVES

Each of us has many stories that we easily tell other people. These are the stories that we relate over and over in many different contexts. They shape and define our public selves. Other stories are available only to particular people, including certain family members or special friends. Sharing these stories marks a turning point in a marriage, a relationship, a friendship. We feel more known, more vulnerable, and more available than before for responses from those who hear us and affect our most intimate sense of ourselves. And still other stories remain deeply hidden in the recesses of our hearts; these are the stories that we have never told another living soul.

When Paddy McGarrity, thirty-one, first came to see me, I quickly realized he would rather be anywhere but in a therapist's office. His supervisor at work had strongly urged him to make the appointment. Paddy felt he had no choice. Shortly before I met him, Paddy had started a fistfight with a coworker at a construction site. He was determined to work on "anger," but he remained enormously guarded, telling me just the bare minimum about his life. I knew he had been born in Ireland and was now living in the Bronx. Everything in between was off-limits for conversation. He refused to talk about his family, friends, past, or present life. "I came here to talk about controlling my temper. It's getting me into trouble," Paddy said. "Let's get on with it."

What could be happening in this man's life, I wondered, to make him so wary? Week after week he came to see me, diligently "working on his anger," while refusing me access to anything but the most superficial aspects of his life. For three months I respected the limits he drew, and taught him some techniques for anger management. When Paddy described two incidents within one week where he avoided fights and felt he handled his anger well, I assumed our work together was over. To my surprise, Paddy asked for another appointment.

"Is it true," he began, "that what I tell you, you can't tell anyone else?" After I explained the limits of confidentiality, Paddy looked at me and said, "I'm illegal." For the next two hours he poured out the story of his migration from Ireland three years earlier and his subsequent hidden life in New York.

Paddy handled being undocumented by pretending to himself and others that he didn't have a secret. "I know lots of guys who come here and change their names. They end up more confused about who knows what about them. I decided to keep my name. I just act like I'm legal. No one here knows the truth." All of Paddy's energy went into protecting his secret. He lived an isolated life, terrified of making any friends, because he had seen men at work turned in to the Immigration and Naturalization Service by friends who had some gripe against them. His mother had relatives in Brooklyn, but he had never let them know he was in New York, fearing that any little argument might lead them to call the authorities. For three years he hadn't gone out on a date with a woman. He had a college degree and dreamed of being a teacher, but he worked in construction because it was easier work to get without a green card. In Ireland he had played a banjo and performed in clubs. Here he went home to his studio apartment every night after work and closed the door. Advanced schooling was out of the question. "I came here because I wanted more opportunities than I had in Ireland," Paddy told me. "Instead I feel like I'm in a cage."

Just before coming to see me the first time, Paddy had learned that his mother had been quite sick in Ireland. He couldn't go home to check on her. "I overstayed my visa long ago," Paddy said. "I still think I want to be here, though I feel like I've been running this around in my own head for so long I can't be sure what I think anymore. I just knew I couldn't go home if I ever wanted to come back again."

What, I wondered aloud, prompted Paddy to finally open his secret with me? "You didn't push me," he said. "You accepted what I told you I wanted. I needed to control my temper. I trust you as much as I can trust anybody." When I asked Paddy how I might be able to help him now, he said he really wasn't sure. He explained that he just needed to tell me his story, needed to have another human being know about his life. I think he needed the validation of his experience that comes only when another person hears our story, when talking to ourselves is no longer sufficient.

When I got ready to make another appointment, Paddy hesitated and said he'd call me. Several weeks went by. He didn't have a phone, and I knew I couldn't risk calling him at work. I never heard from him again.

Paddy's story, though specific to him, is but one variation of the lives of men and women from Mexico, South America, Asia, Ireland, and other places around the globe who make their way to the United States without documentation and then must live secret lives. Just like documented immigrants, some come in desperation, some come to escape terror, and some, like Paddy, come seeking opportunities for a better life. Their secrets make them vulnerable to exploitation and blackmail, limit their work and educational possibilities, and create lives steeped in anxiety and mistrust.[1]

KEEPING SECRETS TO OURSELVES TO PROTECT OTHERS

Not all secrets we keep to ourselves are made for sheer self-protection. Sometimes they are kept to protect another person. Such loyalty may extend beyond a lifetime. Keeping such secrets constrains us; rather than knowing, tolerating, and embracing one another, with all our complexities and contradictions, we cling to simplistic stereotypes.

Jeremiah Simms was forty-five years old when he came to see me for therapy. He was African-American, born and raised in a small town on the Mississippi Delta. Now he had a Ph.D. in mathematics and was teaching at a university in upstate New York. "I haven't been back to Mississippi since I left for college twenty-seven years ago," he told me in our first meeting. He described himself to me as a man who liked clear and precise answers in life.

Jeremiah grew up as an only child with his father and paternal grandmother. His mother and father had never married. He started out life with his mother but went to live with his father and grandmother when he was four, following his mother's marriage to another man. "My grandmother raised my father alone. His father had another family nearby. My grandmother never had another man in her life. She devoted herself to my father, and he lived with her his whole life," Jeremiah said.

Our therapy began shortly after the death of Jeremiah's grandmother at age ninety-three. He was feeling sad and anxious. His wife suggested that he consult a therapist. When I asked him why he thought she wanted him to see me, Jeremiah said she was worried about him and that she had been upset that he hadn't gone back to Mississippi for his grandmother's funeral.

As I got to know Jeremiah, he told me many stories about his grandmother, focusing particularly on how she had helped him and encouraged his education. He felt passionately that he would not be where he was in life were it not for her. "My father only went as far as third grade. School meant nothing to him," Jeremiah said. "He wanted me to drop out after eighth grade. Grannie fought with him and insisted that I go to high school." He told me that high school cost money because the students had to wear uniforms and buy their own books. His family was quite poor and his father refused to give him any money for school. "I don't know how she did it," Jeremiah said, "but Grannie got that money. I had one uniform instead of two like most of the kids, but Grannie saw to it that it was always clean. And she gave me money for books. It was the only time I ever saw her argue with my father about anything."

Jeremiah told me this story calmly, with little emotion. Why, I wondered, had this man not been back to his hometown in twenty-seven years? Why had he seen his grandmother only twice in that time—once when she came north for his college graduation and once when she came for his wedding? And why had he not returned for the funeral of this woman who had so powerfully contributed to his academic and professional success? It would be many months before we figured this out together.

After we began our work, Jeremiah's sadness deepened. While I thought that his grandmother's death had affected him profoundly, he didn't want to speak about her after our first few meetings. He wanted to continue therapy, but he seemed more and more remote. I asked if it would be okay for his wife to join us for a session or two and he agreed. When I am confronted with mysteries in therapy, I generally find that inviting more people provides an opening.

At our next session, Sandra Baker-Simms told me she was growing increasingly alarmed about her husband. "Something is troubling him. I don't know what it is," Sandra said. "I don't know if he knows what it is. He's sad. He's silent. I've never seen him like this. It's all come about since his Grannie died, but whatever it is, he won't talk about it." Jeremiah looked bewildered while his wife spoke. I began to think that the death of Jeremiah's grandmother had left him with something profoundly unfinished: something to which he had yet to give words.

At my next session with Jeremiah, I told him that many times when someone dies we're left with things we wish we'd said, questions we wish we'd asked. I told him I thought it might be helpful if he wrote a letter to his grandmother. I said, "The letter is just for you. You won't have to share it with anyone unless you decide you want to." Looking quite pained, Jeremiah said he would think about it and call me.

A month went by before Jeremiah wanted another session. He hadn't written the letter, but he'd thought about writing it. He told me he was still feeling very sad, but he spoke with no visible emotion. He felt Sandra was being very understanding, but he worried that she would lose patience with him. I told him to take his time.

Three weeks later Jeremiah came for our next meeting. With his hands shaking, he took a tightly folded letter out of his breast pocket. He handed it to me, but I suggested that if he was willing, it might be better if he read it to me aloud. He agreed and began:

> *Dear Grannie,*
>
> *I want to thank you for seeing to it that I went to school. I never would have gone to high school, college, graduate school if not for you. I know you worked hard for me. I hope I made you proud. Other people did tell me you were proud of me, though you never said so yourself.*

After that much, Jeremiah stopped reading and looked over at me. "I've never told this to anyone. It's not in my letter, but since I began the letter I can't stop thinking about it. I've thought about this through the years. Whenever I see paisley material, I remember."

I sat quietly while Jeremiah spoke. "I must have been five or six. On nights when my father was out drinking with his buddies, my grandmother came out of the shower wearing a paisley robe. She got into my bed next to me, opened her robe, and told me to suck on her breasts. After fifteen or twenty minutes she would leave." As Jeremiah spoke, tears ran down his face and his hands were tightly balled.

As we sat together that afternoon Jeremiah told me that he had never told anyone this story, because he wanted to protect his grandmother. He knew people would think badly of her if they knew. His loyalty and gratitude to her were profound. As we talked, a far more complicated picture of his grandmother emerged. She was a lonely and isolated woman. She was determined to see to Jeremiah's education, to give him opportunities for a better life than she or her son had, but she had little understanding about what else a child might need. "I'm sure she had no deliberate intention to abuse me," Jeremiah said. "I really don't think she had any sense of what a child thinks or feels."

Jeremiah's grandmother had never told him he must keep a secret. He simply knew. When he turned seven, his grandmother no longer came to his bed. These memories occupied only a very small corner of his consciousness until she died. "I've had so many talks with her in my head since she died," Jeremiah remarked, "and they're all about this."

After he became an adult, Jeremiah maintained his silence in part because of what he had heard and read about sexual abuse of children. "What all of those books were saying simply did not fit my life or my experience," he said. "I have a wonderful marriage, an accomplished work life, a sense of humor. I'm a good father. I don't drink or use drugs or overeat or do any of the things those books predict. I don't have flashbacks. I'm simply not dysfunctional," he said with a laugh, his mood beginning to lighten. "I kept hearing, 'You're only as sick as your secrets.' I definitely felt pain over this, but I never thought I was sick." Reading the popular literature about how he was *supposed* to feel had driven Jeremiah's secret further underground. He feared that if he opened his secret, others might impose a construction of his life that simply didn't match his experience. "My own story was just more complicated than 'perpetrators' and 'victims.' Probably that's true for a lot of people," Jeremiah concluded.

Jeremiah's self-secret caused him little difficulty in life until his grandmother died. Unable to open the contradictions about her life and her relationship with him, and with no more chances to resolve any of it directly with her, Jeremiah grew despondent. Opening the secret, first with me and subsequently with his wife, Sandra, led to other changes. He made his first trip back to Mississippi in twenty-seven years. He visited his grandmother's grave, where he read his letter aloud and then, carefully choosing his words, told his grandmother he forgave her *misuse* of him.

I met with Jeremiah and Sandra several months later in a follow-up session. His depression had totally lifted. He and Sandra were planning to take their children to a family reunion of Jeremiah's extended family—an annual reunion that Jeremiah had always avoided.

KEEPING SECRETS TO OURSELVES
TO MANIPULATE OTHERS

When I first met Rebecca and Sam Underwood for therapy, they told me that they couldn't wait to sell their successful upholstery business and retire to California. "I would leave tomorrow," Sam said, "but Rebecca is worried about our son, Ira, and to tell you the truth, the way he needs money from us makes retirement seem far away."

The Underwoods' thirty-one-year-old son, Ira, had "a good job," they told me, but over the past three years they had heard from their son at least monthly with one financial crisis after another. In each instance, checks flew from Philadelphia, where Rebecca and Sam lived, to Pittsburgh, where Ira resided. A year earlier the Underwoods had promised each other that they would not continue to bail him out financially. But a month before they came to see me, during yet another "emergency" of Ira's, each had discovered that the other was clandestinely sending him money. This discovery precipitated their call to me.

During our first meeting, I also learned that Ira had been born after three miscarriages and one stillbirth. "I knew when I had Ira, I would give him the world if I could," Rebecca said. Clearly, Ira had grown up with a sense that he was very special and very entitled.

I was curious about what could be going on in Ira's life. The Underwoods told me that he earned $54,000 a year and yet he never seemed to have enough money. "It's one crisis after another," Rebecca explained. "He's very busy. He forgets to do things like pay parking tickets, so last month his car was towed in by the police. He's very good-hearted. Once he let a girlfriend use his credit card, and she ran up several thousand dollars in bills. I didn't want him to have to pay all that interest, so I sent him the money. I'm sure someday he'll pay us back." As Rebecca spoke, Sam silently shook his head from side to side.

I asked Sam and Rebecca whether their son could be in some real trouble with drugs or gambling, but they insisted that this could not be so. "Ira is a college graduate," Sam declared. I laughed and said Ira wouldn't be the first college graduate who abused drugs or gambled, but they quickly closed off my inquiry. Then I asked if they would invite Ira to the next meeting. Sam and Rebecca agreed, but it would be a long time before their son appeared. His many stories about his money troubles were quickly embellished by excuses for not coming to a therapy session with his parents.

Over the next ten weeks of our work together, Sam and Rebecca decided that they truly wanted to stop sending Ira money. They were convinced that at thirty-one, Ira should be supporting himself. Furthermore, Sam had had a mild heart attack shortly before I met them, and they were determined to retire. Together, they wrote Ira a letter telling him of their decision. Within two days Ira called with yet another crisis. For the first time ever, the Underwoods turned down his request for money.

Nine days later the Underwoods called me in a panic. Ira's phone had been disconnected. He hadn't been to work for three days. They had called Ira's neighbor, who reported that his car was nowhere to be found. Rebecca told me that all along she had feared he would kill himself if she ever stopped sending him money. They called the police, drove to Pittsburgh, and began a search for him among his friends. After ten days of fear and anxiety, one of Ira's friends told Sam that Ira was staying with another friend. It appeared that he had deliberately gone into hiding to frighten his parents into sending him money again. At that point the Underwoods told their son that he had to meet them at my office, and he reluctantly agreed.

At the beginning of our meeting, Ira continued to insist that his "money matters," as he called them, were minor. "I don't know what the big deal is," Ira said, glaring first at me, then at his parents. "You've always sent me a little extra when I needed it. It all changed with this therapy business." As we had rehearsed, Sam and Rebecca calmly showed Ira an accounting of all the money they had sent him over the last three years. They had hidden this knowledge from themselves and were shocked to discover that they had sent their son nearly $36,000. Ira became more and more nervous, and laughingly referred to "receiving his inheritance early." I half expected Sam and Rebecca to join in the joke, but this time they remained silent.

After an hour and a quarter of temperate and steady confrontation from his parents, Ira began to tremble. He turned to me and said, "I owe a lot of money—a lot, a lot of money." Alternately defiant and pleading but obviously very frightened, Ira finally spoke to his parents about his gambling. He owed several thousand dollars to a loan shark. He was living paycheck to paycheck, using the money from his parents to pay interest on the loan—and to keep on gambling.

Rebecca and Sam were stunned. "All those stories," Rebecca said, "all those times you called us for money—it was all lies." Ira quickly began to make excuses, but his parents stopped him. Sam looked at me and said, "We all have a lot of work to do now."

I continued to meet periodically with Sam, Rebecca, and Ira for close to a year. Ira began to go to Gamblers Anonymous. He moved to a much cheaper apartment and severely curtailed his previously lavish style of living. With the help of a financial advisor, he was able to structure a legal loan. Our family therapy focused on reconstructing an adult son's relationship with his parents. While

Ira struggled to build a responsible life, Sam and Rebecca worked on holding him accountable. We needed to unpack years of lies and exploitation that, in fact, went all the way back to Ira's adolescence. It emerged that Ira had fallen in with a group of boys and girls in his upper-middle-class high school who convinced him that lying to his parents was the only way to avoid being "hassled." Sam and Rebecca's willing acceptance of anything their son told them, coupled with their compelling wish to make his life easy, merged with Ira's lies to create and sustain a web of manipulative self-secrets.

The last time I saw Sam and Rebecca, I gave them a framed picture of a voided blank check with a caption below it reading, "Protection Money—No Longer Available Here." I suggested that they hang it on the wall in their new home in California. "There may be times in the future," I said, "when you'll need a little reminder."

SECRETS WE KEEP FROM OURSELVES

A person with a terminal illness continues to talk about "getting better," perhaps dying without ever acknowledging what is happening. Another person, at risk for a genetic illness for which there is no cure, decides to forgo testing, preferring to live with the question rather than with the certainty.[2] An alcoholic father insists he's an upright citizen with no drinking problem because he gets to work every day. A woman who abuses tranquilizers tells herself the doctor wouldn't prescribe them if they caused trouble. A mother ignores sounds in the night and her husband's absence from her bed because confronting his incest means she must leave him. An adolescent girl wasting away with a severe eating disorder stubbornly says to herself and to her family that she is fashionably slim. A young man from a conservative religious family is unable to let himself know that he is attracted to other men.

We human beings have an amazing capacity to prevent ourselves from knowing what we know. We filter out what is right before our eyes. Distorting the most obvious information, we trick ourselves and sometimes pay a heavy price in our own well-being and relationships.

We keep secrets from ourselves by actively choosing not to know or by passively denying. Lack of readiness to know, paralyzing fear, self-justification, self-indulgence, the collusion of others, and overwhelming pressure to conform can all lead to secrets from ourselves.

Jonathan Whiteson was thirty-two when he first met my colleague, the family therapist and psychiatrist Gary Sanders.[3] When he was eighteen, Jonathan was diagnosed with grand mal epilepsy. His seizure disorder was severe, preventing him from working and requiring that he live at home with his parents. While medicine diminished the frequency of his episodes, the severity remained unaffected, including loss of consciousness and memory. Jonathan had serious attacks every month or so.

During a hospitalization for a complete workup, the nursing staff noticed that Jonathan had a seizure with absolutely no brain wave evidence that an attack had occurred. At this point Gary Sanders was asked to consult with Jonathan.

During their first meeting, Gary Sanders inquired about Jonathan's very first seizure, asking particularly what had been going on in his life during that time. Given that opening, Jonathan painfully and hesitantly told a story he had never told before. In high school, Jonathan had fallen in love with another boy, his best friend, who seemed to have similar feelings for him, even though they both were also dating girls. But when Jonathan tried to initiate a more intimate relationship, the friend attacked him. Jonathan was confused, devastated, and too ashamed to tell another living soul. Shortly after this incident, Jonathan had his first "epileptic" seizure, becoming so ill that he could not attend his own high-school graduation, an event at which he and his best friend had planned to double-date.

Jonathan spent the next fifteen years keeping the secret of his homosexuality both from others and from himself. His illness seemed to require that he stay close to home. He felt unable to function as an independent adult.

Following a seizure, he frequently would have amnesia for

anything that had occurred within a few days before the attack. A significant part of his life was missing from his conscious awareness. He continued to date women who were considered "proper" by his family and his church, but no relationship ever developed. He espoused antigay sentiments, insisting that gay and lesbian people were weak, sick, and inferior. He constructed a life in which a crucial dimension of himself was simply unavailable. His seizure disorder was not epilepsy, but rather a thunderstorm in his psyche.

In their work together, Gary Sanders gently challenged Jonathan's self-secret. Once he made the excruciating decision to tell the story he had never told, Jonathan could no longer keep the secret from himself. As he experienced true acceptance of who he was for the very first time, Jonathan began to let himself know and see more about his own life. As often happens, his toxic secret had come to control his entire existence. When he accepted his family's and his religion's mandate against homosexuality, he paid a terrible and dramatic price in his own health and ability to function as an adult. But with Gary Sanders's assistance, Jonathan began to see that he had choices. Once he refused to keep his homosexuality a secret, first from himself and then from those he loved, his seizure disorder gradually disappeared.

Like many secrets that a person keeps from him- or herself, Jonathan's secret was rooted in a social context that required conformity to a narrow notion of life and relationships. When being different from the majority in the culture puts us at risk for punishment, our variations go underground. Social demands for compliance coupled with the threat of penalties for rebellion can lead to an erasure of your most intimate reality. If you come from a family where conventionality and obedience are the reigning values, it is likely you will hide any departures from the family "program," first from others and finally from your own awareness.

COLLUSION IN SELF-SECRETS

While secrets we keep with ourselves appear to be located inside one person, their maintenance often requires the silent collusion of others. When I worked with the Underwoods after Ira's secret broke open, both Sam and Rebecca admitted that they had suspected that many of Ira's so-called crises over money were not true. Neither had raised this with the other, and both buried their suspicions, afraid to voice them out loud or to question their son.

Similarly, secrets we keep from ourselves are often obvious to others. If you choose to remain silent while someone you love keeps a dangerous secret from him- or herself, you may need to examine what's behind your own refusal to take a position.

When Penny James, twenty-five, and her fiancé, Victor Buckingham, thirty-two, came to see me three months before their wedding, they began our first session insisting that they had no problems. They had made the appointment, Victor said, because their minister thought it would be a good idea, and they both believed it was important to follow his recommendations. While they sat telling me every detail of their plans for an elaborate wedding suitable for the pages of *Bride's*, I was confronted by Penny's very visible but unmentioned secret. Sitting across from me was a five-foot-six-inch woman who weighed perhaps ninety-five pounds. Later in our meeting, when I asked her whether she had any problems with her weight, Penny quickly insisted that she planned to lose five more pounds before the wedding! Victor gazed out the window as Penny remarked that she was still a bit too "chubby" for her wedding dress.

As I got to know Penny and Victor, it was clear that her severe anorexia was both a secret that Penny kept from herself and an open secret in her entire social network of family and friends, none of whom ever commented on this young woman's virtual disappearance.

Penny and Victor had become engaged one year earlier. At the time of their engagement, Penny had weighed 130 pounds. Her mother and future mother-in-law criticized her for being overweight and expressed their hope that she would "slim down" for her wedding. Both Penny and Victor were from very wealthy families, and their engagement was regarded by family and friends as "perfect." Victor was an investment banker who was making a lot of money. Penny had graduated from an exclusive women's

college. Although very bright, she was not expected to work outside the home. Like her own mother and grandmother, Penny was
expected to maintain a beautiful home and do charity work. Paradoxically, as Penny became thinner and thinner, she both con-
formed to her family's quintessential model of womanhood and
silently demonstrated the grotesqueness of this ideal.

In our early work together Penny and Victor maintained an
impenetrable united front. "All of our friends say we're the best
couple they've ever known," said Penny. "We never fight. We
agree about everything. We're perfectly suited." After she spoke,
Victor patted her head as if she were a small child or a pet.

The power of Penny's self-secret and Victor's collusion in it
became obvious when I suggested that I wanted a separate meeting
with each of them. Our work went into a tailspin. Each of them
canceled individual appointments with me. They "forgot" agreed-
upon meeting times. They showed up together, stating it was
"easier" to do so. In asking to see each one alone once, I had powerfully threatened the myths that they had no conflicts and that
Penny's emaciated state was of no concern. Finally I asked to see
them with their minister, who had sent them to me. My choice to
widen our circle enabled Penny and Victor to hear a different version of their lives than the one they kept telling each other.

When Penny, Victor, the Reverend Allenby, and I met, I
asked the minister what had prompted his concern for this couple.
At first he hesitated, and then he began to speak about watching
helplessly as Penny had starved herself during the last year. His
attempts to bring his worry about Penny to the attention of her
parents or Victor had been met with dismissal. As he spoke of
knowing Penny from her birth and christening onward, of watching her grow into a bright and capable young woman, Penny began
to weep. "My life is over," she sobbed. "I want to go to graduate
school and study anthropology. I want to teach in a university. I'll
never do any of it."

Victor looked astounded. "I thought you wanted the same
things I want," he said angrily. "You lied to me." Victor rose to
walk out of the session, but I quietly asked him to wait and listen.

As we talked that afternoon, it became apparent that Penny

had lost all track of what she wanted. Her total attention had turned to her weight, to what was "wrong" with her body. As she became thinner and thinner and no one spoke out in protest, Penny became increasingly convinced of her worthlessness. Because she felt her own life was out of her control, food and eating became her last refuge of seeming control. When her family and Victor approved of her weight loss, Penny responded with increasingly bizarre rituals related to meals, including a growing list of foods that she felt "allergic" to, foods that could not be eaten together, foods that must not touch one another. She proclaimed there was a proper length of time that a meal must take. She refused to eat in restaurants. No one commented or challenged her.

With actions rather than words, Penny was expressing her pain. When no one listened or responded, she stopped knowing what she was feeling and what she was doing. Until our meeting when her denial finally cracked, Penny's dangerous anorexia was a secret from herself, a secret supported by her family, her fiancé, and his family, the values of her social world, and everyone's belief about what it meant to be a "good" woman.

My work with Penny and various members of her family went on for a long time. As in many families where eating disorders such as anorexia or bulimia emerge, real individuality and painfully unacknowledged desires had long been hidden under a veil of perfectionism, appearance, social status, and propriety. I had to remind Penny and her family many times that Penny nearly chose death rather than depart from her family and community's expectations of her.

Just as her anorexia was a self-secret, so all of Penny's wishes and desires for her life had become a secret from herself and everyone else in the family. Defeating anorexia required that Penny directly confront her mother and father's plans for her life. She broke her engagement to Victor, incurring the wrath of both families. The James family had spent several generations avoiding conflict at all costs. Penny's secret eating disorder had maintained the status quo at a time when radical change was needed. As Penny began to reclaim her self, her family painfully struggled to deal with other differences. Toward the end of our therapy, Penny moved out of her parents' home and began a doctoral program in anthropology. Mr. and Mrs. James contacted me ten months later—for the first time in their long and mostly silent marriage, Penny's mother was voicing opinions that differed from her husband's.[4]

Both Jonathan Whiteson and Penny James kept secrets from themselves that powerfully affected their own well-being. Each sacrificed health in order to conform to social standards that did not fit them. Trying harder and harder to adapt to lives that were impossible, each lost more and more knowledge of self, until the most essential aspects of their lives became secrets from them. And as for many who keep secrets from their essential selves, no one who knew them protested, challenged what was happening, or gave feedback, thus pulling the knot of secrecy ever tighter.

Some self-secrets run the risk of posing danger to others. When a self-secret involves alcohol, drugs, gambling, unsafe sex, or sexually transmitted diseases, personal blindness may directly harm both intimate and casual associates. Unlike self-secrets that spring from overwhelming pressure to accommodate, these secrets are self-indulgent. They involve moments of *choosing* not to know, regardless of the consequences to others. If you have ever kept such a dangerous secret from yourself, you know that when the fog lifts, a lot of relationship repair lies ahead.

MOTHERS, BABIES, AND HIV TESTING: A SELF-SECRET CONUNDRUM

Sandra Balik is a nurse-practitioner in a community health center who told me a story about talking one of her patients into having HIV testing at the start of her pregnancy. "She went to have the test, but she never returned for her results," Sandra said. "I kept after her, but it was one excuse after another. Finally I said to her, 'I thought you wanted to know your HIV status.' The woman looked at me sharply and said, 'No, *you* wanted to know.' "

The ethical dilemmas inherent in self-secrets find full expression in the question of whether and how to test newborn infants for the HIV virus. When an infant tests positive for HIV, it does not automatically mean that the baby is infected with the virus. Seventy-five percent, in fact, are *not* infected, but rather carry antibodies from their mothers. These babies will test negative several months down the road. But all mothers of babies who test positive *are* infected with HIV. In short, testing a baby is, in reality, testing the baby's mother, with or without her knowledge.

What appears at first to be a self-secret kept by a woman who chooses not to know her HIV status is in fact a marker of the unrelenting stigma and fear attached to this disease. If AIDS was considered to be a disease like any other, then secrets about it would be far less likely. Instead, new mothers who may be infected with HIV must struggle with receiving a diagnosis that can result not only in knowledge of a life-shortening illness, but also in censure from her entire community. The self-secret bound up in the issue of mandatory HIV testing of newborns is a powerful illustration of the need to question just where self-secrets are located. While such secrets may seem to be located inside one person, their meaning and consequences seldom reside only in our separate selves. Family, neighborhood, and institutions all crowd into this self-secret.

Shifting political and social policy in this arena painfully demonstrates that self-secrets rarely, if ever, simply affect the one person who is keeping the secret. Unwrap this particular self-secret and you will find conflicting beliefs about the relationship between mothers and children, pregnant women and their doctors, government and poor women. The enormous ethical and practical complexities attached to this issue quickly disappear in the sharply polarized debate between AIDS advocates and politicians. Do we trust or mistrust that mothers will do the best for their children? Do we extend this trust to some mothers and not to others? Do we protect a boundary of confidentiality around doctors and patients? Since 98 percent of pregnant women who receive prenatal care at public clinics agree to have an HIV test after hearing the risks and benefits, should law and social policy be governed by the 2 percent who refuse testing?[5] And what should the role of government be in determining what information may be given to, withheld from, or thrust upon a woman—whether she wants it or not? This particular self-secret is a template for the struggle between one person's readiness to know information about herself and another person's right to insist that, ready or not, the information must be known.

When HIV tests are anonymous, as they have been to date, statistics tracking HIV/AIDS can be gathered. From this we know, for instance, that 7,000 babies out of the 2.5 million who were tested in 1995 were initially positive for HIV. Of the 7,000, about 2,000 actually had the virus.[6] Such tracking gives no information to specific mothers about their own babies, leading some critics to compare anonymous testing to the Tuskegee experiments discussed in chapter 4.

The political debate centers on whether to pass state and federal laws that require both testing every newborn for HIV *and* informing the mother of the test results, whether she wants to know her own HIV status or not. Secrecy sits on both sides of this dilemma. Either the government possesses information that it withholds from mothers, or women who choose not to know are coerced into listening.

The frontline AIDS workers I've talked with tell me that the overwhelming majority of pregnant women they come in contact with want to know their HIV status in order to do the best for their babies. At the same time, a small minority of women simply do not want to know. A smaller subset of these women may be jeopardizing their infants.

Mandatory testing proposed by politicians, these workers told me, is based on creating a straw woman, either a monster mother who neglects her baby's well-being or an ignorant mother who needs the government to tell her what to do. AIDS activists insist that mandatory testing will scare some pregnant women away from necessary prenatal care and the opportunity for effective counseling. It will also make pregnant women the only civilian group designated for mandatory HIV testing.

Ironically, some of the politicians who want mandatory testing are the very same legislators who say they want the government out of people's lives. No doubt the self-secrets of some citizens are conveniently defined as "privacy rights" while the self-secrets of other citizens are defined as "the public's right to know."

DO YOU HAVE A RIGHT TO KEEP A SECRET FROM YOURSELF?

The enigma specific to testing newborn babies contains questions that touch on the special circumstances of keeping any secret from yourself that might harm another person.

- When does keeping a secret from yourself involve only you, and when does it affect others?
- When you are actively choosing to keep a secret from yourself, and doing so affects others, what is your responsibility?
- Who has a right to intervene in your choice to keep a secret from yourself? Family? Friends? Doctors? Government?

SECRETS ABOUT YOURSELF: LEARNING TO LIVE WITH MYSTERY

American culture promotes the belief that ultimately all things are knowable. Pop psychology in the second half of the twentieth century has championed knowledge of ourselves as a requirement for the good life. Self-help books and New Age philosophies entice us with the false promise that if we just work at it hard enough and long enough, we will achieve complete self-awareness. New genetic tests even hold out the double-edged promise of informing us about our future.

In all of this, the limits of self-knowledge are rarely appreciated. Acquiring some kinds of knowledge about yourself may prove impossible. Seeking to open particular secrets may lead to dead ends: The law or institutional policies may stand in the way, or relatives who might have given you some answers may have died. Or, as we have seen, you may decide that you would do better in life *not* knowing certain information, such as the likelihood of an illness. Many people are required to live with secrets—or choose to do so.

Cara Feldston was twenty-seven the first time she came to see me for therapy. She had dropped out of college when she was nineteen. As I listened I heard the story of a young woman who had been drifting through life for several years. Temporary jobs, short relationships, and brief friendships marked Cara's young adult life. When I asked her why she thought this was so, Cara responded, "I'm a donor insemination person—what do you expect?"

Cara went on to tell me that when she was fourteen she discovered that her biological father was a sperm donor. Her parents had decided never to tell her of her birth origins. She found out about the insemination from an aunt who was angry with her father. When Cara confronted her parents with this knowledge, they told her the truth. They related how their mutual deep wish for a baby had been frustrated by Cara's father's infertility.

Cara told me that she now understood why they had kept the secret, how they had hoped to protect her from a sense of being different and also wanted to protect her father from feeling bad about himself. But at fourteen she had been furious with them. Her adolescence turned stormy. Without asking further questions, Cara silently assumed that when she became eighteen she would be able to get information about the donor—she had an adopted cousin who had sought out her biological mother at that age.

Cara left for college at eighteen and immediately contacted the lab her parents had used. She quickly discovered that no identifiable records were kept; she would *never* be able to get information about her biological father. Over the next nine years, Cara became consumed with this issue. She thought about little else. At the time in a young adult's life that should be devoted to school, career choice, and beginning an intimate relationship, Cara's life seemed to have no room for anything but the question of her biological father. When I met her she was angry, depressed, and exhausted.

I began our work together by affirming the loss that Cara

had experienced. For the previous nine years, everyone in Cara's life had been telling her to "forget about it," to "get on with it," and that "you can't change what you can't change." All of this advice had left Cara feeling bad about feeling bad. She responded by withdrawing from well-meaning friends and family members, so that by the time I met her she was quite isolated. I asked Cara to bring me a symbol of her sense of loss. She brought me a small marble box that had no visible opening. "That's my life and I can't get into it no matter what I do," Cara said.

Gradually and gently I challenged Cara's idea that a box she couldn't open contained her entire life. I urged her to consider what was outside the box that also comprised her life. I asked her if she knew anyone who had complete and total knowledge of their history. I invited her to talk to friends about parts of their lives that were a mystery to them. She found that while her particular mystery was of greater magnitude than most, everyone had some aspects of their lives that were unknowable. To her surprise, a coworker told her about deliberately choosing not to know her genetic likelihood for developing breast cancer. She talked to an old friend who did an adoption search only to discover that her biological mother had died and that there was no way to get any information about her biological father. Cara finally acknowledged, "I knew in my head that I wasn't the only person facing this, but I always felt like I was."

For several years Cara had told herself that she was nothing like her family. I asked her to look more closely, to explore ways that she was like her family as well as ways that she was not. I suggested that she ask the same question about people she knew who were raised by both biological parents. The sharp distinctions with which she viewed herself began to soften.

An important part of our therapy involved letter writing. I suggested to Cara that she write letters to her donor father, expressing feelings and asking questions, and told her that since some of him was in her, she could also write what she thought his answers might be. This "correspondence" proved to be a critical dimension of our work. "My biological father will always be a phantom, and yet I can relate to him when I need to," Cara later told me. "I had idealized him and thought that the answers to all of my problems in life were in finding out who he was. Now I think he was probably a college student who needed some money—he gave me half of my genetic material, but I'm a hell of a lot more than a single sperm cell!"

I coached Cara to talk more deeply with her parents about their initial decision to have a baby with donor insemination. She had not spoken with them about any of this since she was fourteen, except to hurl anger at them. Her mother told her what it had been like, almost thirty years earlier, to find out about her husband's infertility. Her gynecologist had urged her to lie to her husband, to have the insemination and never tell him, but she refused. Her father told her how ashamed he had been, how he had been made to feel less of a man. As Cara listened to her parents' story, her focus on herself as a victim dissolved.

Slowly we began to make a different kind of meaning out of her dilemma. "I still wish it had been handled differently," Cara said, "but I realize now that my parents did their best with what they were given. I'm going to spend a bit of my time volunteering with foster children." By the time we finished therapy, Cara had returned to college, and she had reconnected with her best friend from high school.

She will never unearth the full knowledge about her biological father. She will never know half of her medical history, her ethnic origins, or whether she has any half-siblings. Nonetheless, the secret that drove her whole life when I first met her is now integrated as a significant *part* of her life. We're told that if we work hard at psychological issues in our lives, we'll reach something called "closure." But opening self-secrets is often less about closure than about expansion and reconnection, first with one's self and then with our intimates.

Making and Breaking
Commitments:
Couples, Intimacy, and Secrets

➤

It isn't that to have an honorable relationship with you, I have to
understand everything, or tell you everything at once, or that I can
know beforehand, everything I need to tell you. It means that most of
the time I am eager, longing for the possibility of telling you. . . .
That we both know that we are trying, all the time, to extend the
possibilities of truth between us. The possibility of life between us.
— *Adrienne Rich*

MARITAL AND FAMILY THERAPISTS have a special front-
row seat in the theater of social change. Even before a trend cap-
tures the public's attention, we see its intimate impact on the daily
lives of the couples we work with. New problems enter the therapy
room. Old problems disappear. And couples' expectations for
their relationships undergo radical shifts.

Twenty-five years ago I saw married couples almost exclusively. They entered therapy for one of two reasons: either they
were in the midst of a crisis, often relating to the discovery of an
affair, or they wanted help in deciding whether to remain married
or get divorced. It was the early 1970s, and so-called open marriage had swept parts of our culture, leaving many marriages in
shambles. The religious authority and family tradition that had
kept many poor marriages afloat were being challenged. Staying

together had once been a social and religious requirement; now it was increasingly seen as a personal choice. Going to couples' therapy or getting a divorce was no longer taboo.

From the late 1970s through the 1980s, I began to see more married couples who wanted to improve the quality of their relationship. These couples were entering therapy before a major crisis and well short of any thought of divorce. For middle-class and upper-middle-class couples, the full impact of changes wrought by the women's movement, including employment of women, postponed childbirth, and the need to realign male-female relationships at work and at home, posed unique challenges. Dilemmas attached to secrets about sexuality, abortion, miscarriage, infertility, and money found their way into my consulting room, joining earlier secrets involving extramarital affairs. During the same period secrets connected to premarital sex and births before marriage all but disappeared.

I also began seeing many more unmarried couples, both heterosexual and homosexual, who were living together. They often wanted to confront and resolve difficulties in their relationships before making a deeper commitment. Living together before or without marriage was no longer a secret from extended family for most heterosexual couples. Many gay and lesbian couples, on the other hand, were simultaneously dealing with relationship problems and with dilemmas attached to secrecy and coming out to their extended families.

Over the last ten years I have also begun to see increasing numbers of couples with religious, ethnic, and social-class differences. When these couples first come for therapy, they seldom locate their problems in these differences. They often keep secrets about diversity both from themselves and from each other. At the start of their relationship, while they may be initially attracted to each other *because* of difference, they find their dissimilarities too hot to handle openly. Like many new couples, they bask in all the ways they are alike. But by avoiding potential cultural and religious conflicts, they unknowingly set time bombs certain to explode in years to come.

Most recently I have started to get requests for therapy from dating couples—both young couples and people in their forties and fifties who have divorced and are reentering the dating scene after twenty or twenty-five years of marriage. In an earlier time, many of these men and women would have entered individual therapy. Why now are they sitting with me six months, three months, or even one month after they met?

I think the answer to this question lies in important changes in contemporary culture, changes that seem to require even newly acquainted couples to share information and to open secrets long before they would have done so in an earlier era.

GETTING TO KNOW YOU, GETTING TO KNOW ALL ABOUT YOU

Bill Monsey, thirty-two, and Karen Stillman, thirty-four, came to see me for a few sessions after they had been dating for four months. Neither had been married before, and marriage was not on their current agenda. Each had a good job and a nice apartment, and they were not even considering living together. Nonetheless, they cared for each other a lot and thought there was potential for a committed relationship. They came to see me because, as Bill put it, "We feel like we're stalled. Neither one of us knows how to move this relationship forward. We go out and have fun, but all of our conversations feel superficial."

I asked how they had met and what drew them to each other. Karen laughed, saying, "We met at a singles' dance and spent the evening discussing our prior sexual histories, probably in more detail than we lived them! I liked how honest he was, but it was a little hard to know where to go from there. I'm very close to my mother, and when I told her about this conversation, she said, 'When your father and I first met, we didn't have any sexual history to discuss!' My mother took her cues about building a relationship from her mother. Where am I supposed to go to figure this out?"

Like many new couples today, Bill and Karen were confronting a dilemma. In an age marked by AIDS, herpes, and other sexually transmitted diseases, information regarding prior relationships that might never have been shared—or would have been related in less detail and surely later in the development of a relationship—is now emerging on the first or second date. Long before anything resembling trust is established, intimate secrets of sexuality—not to mention the specter of each other in bed with other people—are part of the conversation. There are no maps from previous generations, no cultural models for relationship building that *begins* with powerful revelation rather than moving toward it.

"It's so strange," Karen said, "because Bill knows my sexual history, but I don't feel like he really knows me. I trusted him with some things about my past that were pretty painful, and yet I had *no* reason to trust him at all. Telling all these things at the very beginning gave us an illusion of closeness. Now when we go out I want to keep things light and on the surface. I'd like our relationship to develop, but it feels like we're frozen."

Neither Karen nor Bill had ever had a sexually transmitted disease. Both knew their present HIV status to be negative. Both had read lots of popular magazine articles about dating in the 1990s. By attempting to be responsible and not keep secrets about their sexual histories, Karen and Bill had placed themselves in a quandary. Karen felt she had shared too much too soon; now she wanted to pull back to what she felt would be a more normal early-dating phase of a relationship. Bill assumed that since they had already told each other such intimate information, there should be no holds barred. "I want to tell Karen everything about my life, but I don't think she wants to hear it and she certainly doesn't want to reciprocate," Bill complained. A relationship that involved secrets told too early had quickly polarized: The more Bill wanted to reveal, the more Karen wanted to conceal.

In our brief work together, I asked Karen and Bill to think about what it meant to be a new couple today in contrast to when each began dating in their teens. We talked about living in a social context that seems to require disclosure of certain secrets long before a relationship has grown sufficiently to hold these revelations. I affirmed the confusion Karen and Bill were feeling. I believe such confusion comes about when deeply personal secrets are told too early, trivializing a relationship rather than strengthening it. Just as in talk show telling, a contemporary myth that highly charged content can be lifted from a connected and empathic relational context underpins the exchange of sexual secrets by virtual strangers. Confusing candor with condoms, many new couples tell each other more than a recently formed relationship can adequately hold.

Karen astutely recognized that telling each other about their sexual histories did not mean that they knew each other quite as much as Bill wanted to believe. I suggested to Karen and Bill that each write the story of their first date and then put these written accounts away in a drawer while they spent time really getting to know each other. Symbolically, they took the secrets that had been opened too soon and temporarily made them "secret" again.

We decided to meet again in six months. When they arrived for the session, they were relaxed and affectionate. They had been enjoying their dates and were beginning to talk about living together. The old struggle over how much to reveal had been replaced by a more natural process of getting to know each other over time. The secrets remained in the drawer.

Karen and Bill and many couples like them are sincerely struggling to make sense of new relationship rules for the 1990s. Newly dating couples come together now in a social context fraught with contradictions where secrecy and openness are concerned. A decade ago stories of former boyfriends and girlfriends were unlikely to have been the topic for newly acquainted couples. But today public-service announcements urging safer sex are sometimes misinterpreted to mean words rather than action.

Surely, it seems, if a person you've just met keeps no secrets about his or her sexual past, this is a person you can trust. Or can you? A genuine desire to be responsible may push you to tell too much too soon, only to find the information used against you.

As you listen to the confessions of a new companion, romantic gullibility may strike your heart while pragmatic cynicism stalks your mind.

Discovering what another person does with our secrets has always been part of building relationships. What parts of yourself you keep to yourself and what parts you choose to share contributes powerfully to any new relationship. Whether your revelations are received gently or harshly, honored, reciprocated, or betrayed tells you an enormous amount about the person you are getting to know. Never before now were revelations so weighted with matters of health, lifelong illness, risks to later fertility, or even death. And never before have the stakes for honesty and dishonesty early in a relationship been higher.

WHEN REVELATIONS TURN DANGEROUS

When Nicole Sondergard came to see me for individual therapy, she was struggling to get her bearings in a relationship in which she was pressured to open secrets.

Nicole was twenty-two when she began living with her twenty-seven-year-old boyfriend, Allan Cermak. The couple had met a year earlier and moved in together six months before I first saw Nicole. Both were living far from their families. They had become engaged shortly before Nicole called for her first appointment with me.

"I thought I knew Allan, but lately he's like someone I don't know at all," Nicole said. "Before we moved in together, Allan said we should discuss our past relationships. I didn't really like the idea, but Allan insisted it was a sign of trust. He said if I wouldn't tell him all about my old boyfriends, it meant I wasn't ready to live with him.

"At first it didn't seem to make any difference, but ever since Allan gave me my engagement ring, all he does is talk about my old boyfriends and ask me questions. Lately he's started to follow me when I go to work or to meet a friend. It's like he's taken what I trusted him with and made it into something ugly," Nicole said sadly.

Nicole went on to tell me that she had had a few boyfriends and sexual relationships before meeting Allan, but that Allan had had only one serious girlfriend, who left him for another man shortly before he met Nicole. Now Allan was using all that Nicole had told him to punish her. He pursued her constantly for more and more details of her prior relationships. When she responded, he got angry. When she refused to respond, he also got angry. I urged Nicole to ask him to come to therapy with her, but he refused.

My work with Nicole centered on the meaning of trust in an intimate relationship. As we got to know each other, it became clear to me that Nicole had had little foundation for placing her trust in Allan before she confided in him. Why had she not relied on her own gut instincts about how much to reveal? "I was raised to defer to men's wishes," Nicole told me. "My father ran our house, my brother got his way. My mother raised me to take orders from men. When I left home I began to question this, but I've never been too good at knowing what I really want. When I started to be with Allan, I just assumed that I wanted what he wanted."

While Nicole and Allan had had a lot of fun together when they first met, she actually knew very little about him before they decided to live together. Some of his comments about women had made her uncomfortable, but he always turned these remarks into a joke and chided Nicole about her lack of humor. They had dated but never spent time with other people. At first Allan's sole focus on her seemed quite romantic. She never questioned his lack of friends. She had no opportunity to discover who Allan might be in relationship to anyone in his family. In short, when Nicole opened secrets to Allan about her sexual history, she took a huge and naive risk that this information would be received well and maintained safely. Her assumption that Allan was trustworthy proved false. Nicole broke her engagement to Allan when he began to threaten her physically.

Despite the claims of popular self-help literature, opening secrets per se does not enhance intimacy. In fact, pressure to reveal stories about your life before you're ready to do so diminishes closeness. If information is pried out rather than freely given, the relationship is born in mistrust. As Nicole painfully discovered, the content of her secrets mattered less than Allan's need to control her. Paradoxically, the more she told him, the less in control he felt and the more he pursued her for petty details. Telling secrets did not lead to closeness and trust, but rather to spying, suspicion, and distrust.

COMMITMENT: A MATRIX FOR SECRETS

I've sat with couples and watched as a secret exploded years of trust that, like Humpty Dumpty, truly could not be repaired. I've seen other couples tell a secret with identical content and go on to experience previously unimagined intimacy and connection.

In all my years as a couples therapist, I've learned that there are few hard and fast rules where secrets are concerned. Secrets between a woman and a man, two women, or two men in a committed relationship can bring them closer, form a nest, and make a boundary. Or such secrets may bind them together in mutual protection, fear, or exploitation.

When one member of a couple keeps a secret from the other, the motive can range from healthy individuation to cynical duplicity. While secrets can certainly be the breeding ground for mistrust, accepting each partner's right to keep particular secrets can also express enormous trust. If you know, for instance, that your diary will never be pried open even if you leave it in plain view, or that your special drawer will never be violated, then you and your mate have discovered how essential secrets contribute to intimacy and reliability. These are the secrets that each of you know the other person keeps, rather than the secrets whose very existence is secret.[1] They define personal territory within a relationship. Such terrain could be trampled on, but many couples agree implicitly or explicitly to respect individual boundaries. From this respect flows enormous confidence that your partner's private memories or secret thoughts will not cause harm to you. Learning to live with such secrets mediates the tension that exists in every intimate relationship between the desire to know all and the acknowledgment that knowing all is never possible.

I've also worked with couples who insist on having no secrets between them, only to discover later that their emphasis on telling all obliterates any sense of individuality.[2] The modern romantic imperative demands no secrets, tempting us with the myth that it's possible to know another person completely. But when members of a couple declare to me they have no secrets, I always feel a bit uneasy. No secrets means no boundaries, no separate self, no private letters or diaries, no place for singular dreams, no mystery. When two "I's" disappear into "we," when thoughts, fantasies, and actions are always plural, the delights of difference disappear. Close individual relationships outside the couple—relationships with extended family or friends that can reinvigorate a couple—are forbidden.

Couples who "have no secrets" often enter therapy because their relationship has become boring and dreary. The injunction against secrets has suffocated individual initiative and the possibility of surprise. Or they arrive at my door because one member has violated the code.

In fact, for many couples, the "no secrets" rule is more mythical than actual. Pretense and inauthenticity stalk the relationship. Not surprising to an outside observer, but often shocking to the "tell-all" couples themselves, is that keeping a secret may become the very route to a new sense of self. But when a couple's implicit or explicit agreement to tell all is unilaterally broken, a marital crisis is provoked, and a good deal of work is required before a new equilibrium emerges.

On the other hand, some couples who come to see me wear a shroud of ten, twenty, thirty years of silence. They are marked by distance, loneliness, and a pervasive sense of being completely unknown by one's life partner. So much has *not* been said for so long, and secrets have become the modus operandi. When I ask each member of such couples what they would like their partner to know, we begin a slow and often scary journey, unpacking years of hidden thoughts, unspoken feelings, and unknown responses.

Power, powerlessness, and struggles for power contribute to many secrets. I've seen couples where one partner's secret constitutes a scornful exercise of power. Entitlement, lies, arrogance, and contempt underpin the high-handed assumption "I know what's best for you to know" in core areas such as sex and money. Gender politics in the wider culture often find expression in such secrets, as husbands assume license to keep business and financial secrets from their wives. Trust, honesty, empathy, and authenticity are sacrificed on the altar of control and dominance.

In other couples, one partner's secret may be a desperate escape from powerlessness. Not surprisingly, women who are beaten or otherwise controlled begin to keep more and more secrets from their spouses.

In less extreme situations, temporary secrets can be the precursor to a new balance of power. For years Selma Alexander directly battled her husband's refusal to tell her how much wealth he had accumulated. In argument after argument, Selma anxiously pursued her husband, Henry, for knowledge about their finances. Time after time he coolly stonewalled and dismissed her, telling her it was his business and, as long as she was taken care of, she didn't need to know specifics. Finally Selma calmly told him that she was going on a trip for a few weeks and that while she would be in touch, she would not tell him precisely where she was going. When she returned, he had set up a meeting with his accountant for her to learn all of the details of their finances. Through a short-lived secret, Selma announced in action that she would no longer beg for information and redefined their relationship as one where she too had the right to keep certain things to herself.

I believe that couples in rich, enlivening, and long-lasting relationships develop a complex repertoire for dealing with secrets. Rather than adhering to one-dimensional rules such as "all secrets are bad" or "don't ever tell . . . ," or "women (men) should keep such-and-such secret from their mate," these couples make room in their relationship both for sharing vulnerabilities and for maintaining personal privacy. They are willing to keep alive the tension between speaking and silence, between individuality and intimacy, giving each its place in the ongoing dance.

EXPLORING SECRETS WITH A PARTNER

Genuine commitment requires you to actively engage secrecy. What do you believe about secrets, and what does your partner believe? What were the rules about and experiences with secrecy in each of your families of origin? Have you talked about this, or is the very topic of secrets off-limits, a secret?

As you and your mate engage with a spirit of exploration, you can reflect on some questions surrounding secrets in an intimate relationship.

- Are there topics I or we should never bring up? How do I know this to be true? Have we agreed through experience that certain areas are off-limits, or am I making assumptions for my partner?
- Do we respect that each of us has some secrets?
- Do we trust that each of us can have secrets that will not cause harm?
- What's the price to our relationship for silence?
- What's the price to our relationship for opening a secret?
- Am I taking responsibility for the impact on my relationship of the secrets that I keep and the secrets that I open?
- What do I expect of myself and my partner where secrets are concerned?
- Where are the boundaries of forgiveness when painful secrets open?

WHEN SECRETS SHOCK
COMMITMENT

Deborah Canaby, thirty-seven, called me for individual therapy. As I attempted to find out a bit about her life, she insisted on speaking only about her forty-five-year-old husband, Jack. For the past eight months, she told me, Jack had seemed remote and unavailable. When he wasn't staying late at the office, he was working out at his health club. Whenever Deborah tried to talk to him about their relationship, he was vague and dismissive. Just before Deborah called me, Jack had missed their son's school play, claiming he was caught in traffic. When I asked Deborah what she thought was happening, she neatly tied all of Jack's behavior together under the popular rubric "midlife crisis."

Deborah was describing almost clichéd behavior for a man having an extramarital affair—distance at home, office parties at which spouses were "not allowed," lots of new clothes, a rash of overnight "business" trips—but when I asked her if she thought Jack was having an affair, she immediately insisted that this could not be so. "Our marriage is very strong," Deborah replied, "and Jack would never do such a thing. You don't know him. He would never lie to me."

But several weeks later, when I invited Jack in for a meeting alone with me, I found that he was indeed lying to Deborah and that he'd been having an affair for many months. Jack had the idea that I would do couples' therapy with him and Deborah while he continued his secret affair. I explained to him that couples' therapy under such circumstances is a sham. Working on a marriage and maintaining a secret affair are incompatible. "Seeing you and Deborah together, while I keep your secret, simply replicates the affair triangle," I told him. I said that I would work with him alone while he sorted out what he wanted to do, but that he would have to ask Deborah if she would be willing to wait while we did some short-term individual therapy.

After six sessions, Jack decided to open the secret of his affair to Deborah. Their marriage went into a predictable crisis as we met to sort out what had happened and what would happen next. Jack ended his affair within a few weeks, but the real work of putting their marriage back together in a new way took over a year.

As I got to know them well, I found two people who had previously hidden every difference, every disagreement. Deborah came from a family where her parents had loud and frightening arguments. Part of what drew her to Jack was his stable and understated approach to life. She was determined to have a marriage marked by peace and harmony at all costs. Jack came from a family where his parents were eternally sad, having lost their first son, Jack's older brother, in a car accident when he was fifteen years old. The accident happened immediately after an argument between Jack's brother and father. Jack was eight when his big brother died, and once the funeral was over, the death and the fight that preceded it were never mentioned again at home. But Jack's parents raised him to believe that nothing was worth arguing over, that life was too fragile and precarious to risk anger.

Issue after issue had gone underground between Jack and Deborah during their sixteen-year marriage. What Deborah assumed was harmony, Jack experienced as hypocrisy. "For years I was lying all the time to Deborah about what made me happy. It didn't take much to move on to a bigger lie when I began my affair."

As often is the case, Jack's affair was profoundly connected to many other secrets. The affair began the year his son turned fifteen, the same age his brother was when he died. His parents' unspoken grief over this loss had made secrecy a way of life. Deborah's denial had equally deep roots. As it emerged, her father had had many affairs. He always left big clues for her mother to discover, leading each time to a huge blowup followed by a dramatic reconciliation but no change in their relationship. "My mother spent her life spying on my father, and he spent his life giving her cause to snoop. Even when it became obvious to me that something was going on with Jack, I just made up my mind to look the other way," Deborah declared.

In our work together, Deborah and Jack constructed a new marriage. An important part of the therapy involved letters they wrote to each other spelling out what each truly wanted and opening many previously hidden thoughts, desires, needs, and feelings. The letters allowed each of them freedom to access what he or she genuinely felt. They were so used to smoothing over differences that I wanted to liberate them from face-to-face conversation, with its constant and constraining verbal and nonverbal responses. Letter writing also allowed each enough time to reflect before responding. Issues that had previously been swept aside began to be negotiated. Lies no longer blanketed their commitment, and spoken differences between them became permissible.

Not all marriages survive affairs and change the way Deborah and Jack's did. A particularly difficult dilemma following the disclosure of an affair is how to allow for essential secrets. Mistrust and suspicion can climb into a couple's bed as permanent bedmates. When couples are unable to resolve an affair, they lose the crucial capacity to draw distinctions between privacy and secrecy. In a paradoxical effort to regain trust, a husband or wife who has had an affair feels compelled to tell every passing thought. At the same time a betrayed spouse, wrapped in wariness and doubt, may engage in snooping and may overinterpret every silence as threat. Some couples, of course, divorce, while others get stuck in the affair and never resolve it or move forward. When I supervised the couples' therapy of Hilda and George Marren, I witnessed a marriage mired in an affair long over.

GETTING BEYOND REVELATION

When Hilda and George first came to couples' therapy, both looked haggard, worn out, and older than their stated years. Hilda spoke about her daily life as "overwhelming," filled with long hours as a school cafeteria worker and raising the couple's three children. George worked as a truck driver and was frequently away from home. When they were together, they often had heated and ferocious arguments.[3] These arguments would begin over some small detail concerning the children, money, in-laws, sex, work, or their nonexistent social life and quickly escalate into what Hilda called "fighting about the past." Bitter, repetitive arguments with no resolution of past or present issues formed the core of this couple's relationship. When their therapist asked what "fighting about the past" meant, George quickly said, "We've had therapy before, my wife and I, and that therapist made us talk about the past, and that made things worse! We quit that therapy. Let's just stick with what's bringing us here now." As he spoke, Hilda silently nodded in agreement.

Hilda and George had put their new therapist in a bind. They tempted her to pursue what sounded like an important secret while simultaneously warning her not to do so. Clearly something had happened in the life of this couple in the past that remained unresolved in the present. Each knew the content of the secret, and each refused to discuss it openly in therapy. They made it clear that whatever "it" was, it had happened long ago and was over. Rather than disrespectfully pursuing Hilda and George about the actual content of their secret, their therapist spent the remainder of the session exploring the secret's meaning and impact. How did whatever happened in the past keep them apart in the present? Who else knew? Did this secret keep them close to anyone else? What were their lives like before this secret? What would their lives and their relationship be like without this haunting secret? If the secret was to go away, what would take its place?

When George and Hilda arrived for their next session, they immediately began to complain again about their arguments, their inability to negotiate, the impossibility of finishing any conflict to their mutual satisfaction, and the place of the old secret in their current fighting. George again repeated, "But we're not going to talk about the past in here."

To their surprise, their therapist agreed. "Tonight," she said, "I thought we'd try to put a boundary around the past—mark it off, put it in its proper place." George and Hilda looked at her quizzically as she handed them each a piece of paper and a pencil and asked if they would be willing to spend a few minutes writing down the past event that was affecting them so profoundly in the present.

At first George hesitated, asking, "How can you write down the past? The past just is, and to me it should never have happened." Hilda asked, "Is this so you'll know that we're both talking about the same thing?" When their therapist replied that she wasn't planning on looking at what they wrote, Hilda and George became more and more curious. Finally George said, "To me the past is everything that's happened since *that time*." Their therapist responded, "*That time*—that's what I want to ask you to write about, if you would."

For several minutes George and Hilda wrote intently. When they finished, their therapist asked them to fold their papers to fit inside a tiny box she had brought to the session. Their painful issue was symbolically made smaller. Then she handed George and Hilda wrapping paper, tape, and ribbon and asked if they would wrap the box. George covered the box and handed it to Hilda to tie on the ribbon. Hilda started to tie a bow, then stopped and looked at her husband. "Oh, no," she said, "I'm not going to put a pretty ribbon on *that thing!*" Whatever had kept this couple angry and distant for so many years was now inside the box, still hidden but now one step removed from their relationship.

Their therapist left the room and returned with a long-handled shovel. "Do you think you'd like to bury this behind the clinic?" she asked. George and Hilda looked quite startled. "It's dark out. It's January," Hilda protested. "You're right—the ground is certainly frozen," their therapist responded, "but I think you two can dig."

George and Hilda were laughing as they went outside and began taking turns digging into the frozen ground. When they buried the box, however, they became quite solemn. With no prompting from their therapist, each murmured an apology to the other.

When they came back inside, their therapist asked George and Hilda if they would be willing to implement one change in their fighting before they saw her again. Would they agree that if, during an argument, either one brought up the past, they would get in their car and drive to where the box was buried to finish the fight? George and Hilda lived about twenty-five minutes from the clinic. Smiling slyly at each other, they agreed to this absurd proposition.

George and Hilda next saw their therapist a month later. They began the session telling her all the things they had done together that month, including visits to in-laws and outings with their children that previously had provoked big arguments. Each looked brighter; they exuded a confidence they had never shown before in therapy. Their therapist asked them how many times they had driven to the clinic. George said, "We weren't over here at all." Hilda remarked, "We had plenty of fights. Good fights. But the moment either one of us would bring up the past, the other one would say, 'Take a trip!' and then we would laugh and settle the *current* argument."

An old, painful, and divisive secret had finally been laid to rest. George and Hilda's secret had defined them as a couple who fought about the past. Words had clearly failed them as they had tried daily for years to talk, shout, and scream away the secret that had engulfed their relationship. Immutable definitions of villain and victim, right and wrong, devil and angel had permeated every conversation. Freed from the same old boring fight that only provoked bitter memories and made remorse, amends, and forgiveness impossible, Hilda and George were now able to begin to solve problems, laugh together, and enjoy each other as they had not done in many years.

GAY AND LESBIAN COUPLES: WHEN ONLY ONE IS "OUT"

Gay and lesbian people must live their lives in a social context marked by homophobia and heterosexism. This context includes state and federal antihomosexual legislation, court decisions that take custody of children away from lesbian mothers, state laws that forbid marriage of and adoption by same-sex couples, and outright gay-bashing. The national military policy "don't ask, don't tell" both promotes hypocrisy at the highest level of government and stands as a metaphor for the secrecy that envelops the daily lives of gay and lesbian people. Such secrecy naturally finds its way into the personal relationships of gay and lesbian couples as they struggle to make sense of living in a time simultaneously marked by new possibilities of openness and realistic requirements of hiddenness and fear.[4]

Unlike many other secrets, the secret of homosexuality is not resolved with one act of telling. Decisions about secrecy and openness must be made at every turn. Can a gay man place a photo of his lover and himself on his desk at work? Can a lesbian woman whose coworkers assume she is a single, heterosexual woman talk about her exciting weekend away at a bed-and-breakfast with her new intimate partner? Can a gay couple who've gone home to one man's family for Christmas embrace each other openly when gifts are exchanged on Christmas morning? And what is the impact on a couple of having to live with a struggle over secrecy springing from the very essence of their relationship?[5]

When Sara-Jean Parkman and Emma Farthing first came to see me, they were ready to end their relationship. A couple in their mid-thirties, Sara-Jean and Emma had met four years earlier, shortly after Sara-Jean's divorce. Emma had identified herself as a lesbian since adolescence, while this was Sara-Jean's first relationship with a woman. Their household included Sara-Jean's eight-year-old son, Danny.

From the time these two women got together they argued over one issue. Emma wanted Sara-Jean to tell her family and friends that she was a lesbian and that they were in a relationship. Sara-Jean absolutely refused. "In the very beginning, I understood that this would take time," Emma said, "but we're four years down the road with no change. Her mother thinks we're roommates. She invites Sara-Jean and Danny over and never includes me. When I want us to have a normal holiday at our house, we can't do it because Sara-Jean has to go to her mother's. I've been out to my family for fifteen years. They accept me and they accept Sara-Jean and Danny. Now Sara-Jean's mother is sick, and her whole extended family expects her to drop everything and take care of her mother because she doesn't have a husband that she needs to take care of. This is the last straw."

While Emma spoke, Sara-Jean looked away. She responded angrily. "I'm so tired of having her tell me how to live and how to relate to my own family. I know my family. I would lose them. My ex-husband would try to get Danny away from me, I'm certain."

Our first meeting was taking place during the same week that a lesbian mother in a southern state had lost custody of her son to her own mother. Whether Sara-Jean's fears were healthy paranoia or unjustified catastrophizing remained to be seen. What was clear, however, was that this couple who loved each other were polarizing bitterly over their ideas about secrecy and openness. Their attacks had become quite personal, and each had completely lost sight of the fact that the origins of their dilemma sprang from a culture that did indeed punish homosexuality.

I asked Emma about her coming out. "Did you go from secrecy to openness all at once," I queried, "or was this an evolutionary process that took place over time?" This question brought Emma back to a time before she ever knew Sara-Jean, a time when deciding to tell people, especially her family, about her lesbianism was frightening. As Emma spoke, Sara-Jean listened to a story she'd never heard, a story that involved difficult decisions, scary expectations, and the fear of losing relationships. As often happens when any couple polarizes on a fundamental issue, complicated stories, doubts, and ambiguities had disappeared from their conversation. Part of my work with them would be to restore complexity where simplistic absolutes now reigned.

While Emma had lots of support from other lesbian women, she'd kept her sexual identity a secret from her family until well into her twenties—far longer than Sara-Jean's four years. Her family was Unitarian and quite open to difference, in contrast to Sara-Jean's strict Christian upbringing. As for all homosexual people, Emma's coming out was not a onetime event, but an ongoing and repeated choice in each new social situation. Even in the present, as she pressured Sara-Jean to come out to her family, Emma allowed that there were places and relationships where her lesbianism remained a secret. I suggested to her that these were locations in her life where she had chosen privacy.

Emma's family had been receptive when she came out to them. Like many families, they had long suspected that Emma was a lesbian but were waiting for her to raise the issue. Their capacity to accept differences enabled them to support Emma. There was never any threat of being cut off. I asked Emma what happened to her "family trait" of accepting differences when it came to Sara-Jean. "I see what you mean," Emma said. "It's just that I've felt it meant she really didn't love me if she wouldn't tell her family about us."

Sara-Jean's own developing lesbian identity, forming as it was in the context of this relationship, had shifted in Emma's eyes from something that Sara-Jean needed to do for herself to a litmus test of their commitment. Accepting Sara-Jean's timing and allowing her the space to think and begin to examine her relationship to her own family was crucial. Sara-Jean, for her part, had become so reactive to Emma's criticism and demands that she'd dug in her heels and could no longer see the positive possibilities of coming out to anyone in her family. Each blamed the other so much and felt so misunderstood that their relationship, once warm and loving, had turned cold and bitter. Both had forgotten that they were responding to each other within the confines of a culture that threatened to reject both of them.

I asked Emma to back off from pressuring Sara-Jean so that she might begin to think through on her own what she truly wanted to do in relationship to her own family. As long as Sara-Jean felt she was losing Emma anyway, she would see no point in risking her family relationships. Gradually Emma began to see that while Sara-Jean's struggle over coming out to her family certainly affected their relationship, the secret belonged to Sara-Jean alone. Only she could do the very difficult work with her family. And she was far more likely to take the risk of openness if she felt supported rather than attacked by Emma.

I also asked both women to think into the future and to imagine their lives both individually and as a couple if Sara-Jean came out to her family—or if she did not. This issue had come to dominate their lives, crowding out anything else. This exercise allowed them to demagnify the secret and enable other parts of their lives to come forward once again. As they imagined both future scenarios, they saw themselves doing many things that didn't hinge on Sara-Jean's coming out to her family: going out together, having friends, taking courses, working at their careers, raising Danny, going on trips. Arguments over when, whether, or how Sara-Jean would tell her family dissolved.

I worked with Sara-Jean and Emma for nearly two years. Over several months, Sara-Jean decided to tell her younger sister, Cathy, who was supportive but didn't think Sara-Jean should tell their mother. Instead of blowing up, as she might have previously, Emma listened to what Cathy had to say, though she differed with her.

Sara-Jean next decided she wanted to tell her best friend, Susan, whom she had known since childhood. Since Susan knew both Sara-Jean's mother and her ex-husband, I suggested she attend one of our meetings to give another point of view. Emma listened closely while Susan described both the rigidity in Sara-Jean's family and the vindictiveness of her ex-husband. There was little doubt that he would try to get custody of Danny if Sara-Jean's lesbianism was known to him. Susan also made it clear that there were many problems between Sara-Jean and her mother that needed to be addressed before there could be any hope that Sara-Jean's secret would be well received.

I coached Sara-Jean to begin to open her relationship with her mother, dealing first with many other issues that had divided them, including her divorce, which had become a taboo subject. While I was working primarily with Sara-Jean, Emma attended all of the meetings. This enabled her to get a much more complex appreciation of Sara-Jean's struggle and to be a supportive ally. By the time Sara-Jean decided to tell her mother, she was clear that she wasn't seeking or expecting her mother's approval. "I told my mother that this was too important to keep secret from her, that I respected her and that I expected her to respect me and my choices in life," Sara-Jean said. "I asked her to honor my privacy where Danny's father was concerned."

Initially Sara-Jean's mother responded with hostility. She refused to see her daughter for several months, but she continued to speak with her on the phone. At first she acted as though she hadn't heard what her daughter had told her. She tried telling

Sara-Jean about places where she might go to meet "a new father for Danny." I reminded Sara-Jean and Emma that her mother was dealing with completely new and unexpected information and that she would need time to integrate a different view of her daughter. "Some secrets," I told them, "need to be opened many times over before they are truly heard."

Sara-Jean was angry and upset in our sessions, but she was able to remain calm toward her mother while at the same time insisting that her mother hear what she had been told. In fact, Sara-Jean's mother never became as accepting as Emma's parents. She stayed connected to her grandson, but she treated the couple with politeness, not warmth, and would not come to their home. Simply because a secret is opened does not mean that all relationship issues will be resolved. As we ended therapy I urged Emma and Sara-Jean to find ways to keep alive those aspects of Sara-Jean's heritage that they found affirming and not drift totally to Emma's family and their ways of doing things because they found more acceptance there.

"I THOUGHT WE REALLY KNEW EACH OTHER": WHEN BI-CULTURAL AND BI-RELIGIOUS COUPLES KEEP SECRETS

When I began my practice as a family therapist, intermarriages were still a rarity. I might see an Irish-American/Italian-American couple who nonetheless shared Catholicism, or a Protestant/Catholic couple, or a Jewish/Christian intermarriage. But today my practice is filled with intermarried couples, including interracial couples, Jewish-American/Arab-American couples, Latino/Irish-American couples, or men and women from working-class families married to people from very wealthy families. These differences in race, ethnicity, religion, and social class are also common among gay and lesbian couples. The time when whom you marry is determined largely by your own family background is certainly gone for many people. And with the exception of very religious families, the time when extended families might make a secret of the very existence of intermarriages has also disappeared.

Initially attracted by difference, many intermarried couples quickly paper over their cultural disparities with a thin veneer of harmony. Arguments with extended family and conflicts with religious institutions over intermarriage often lead these partners to notice only the ways they are alike. Conflicts over religious, ethnic, and social-class differences are like a volcano: simmering beneath the surface, erupting periodically over details of daily life, perhaps blowing up once or twice a year at holiday time before quickly sealing over again, or exploding over how to raise children.

When I first meet intermarried couples in my practice, they frequently attribute their conflicts to everything *except* their cultural and religious differences. Rather, these have become a secret that each knows, but neither acknowledges openly. Combining the myth of the melting pot with the American belief in the individual separate from his or her historical and cultural context, couples may attribute radically different approaches to life purely to personality quirks. Larger cultural connections conveniently disappear.

When Simon and Alexis Kaplan first walked into my office, each appeared extremely angry. Even before I could ask them what was bringing them in, they began to describe and demonstrate a pattern of arguing over nearly every aspect of daily life. While each blamed the other, Alexis insisted that after each long argument Simon's point of view usually prevailed. With a righteous tone but no sense of satisfaction, Simon agreed that most of their "petty fights" ended in his favor.

Married for fourteen years, they had three children—Jon, thirteen, Cara, eleven, and Samuel, seven. While conflict began to stalk their marriage shortly after the birth of Jon, it had turned much more bitter in the last year. "Ever since Jon turned thirteen, we fight about his every activity," said Alexis. "I guess it's true that teenagers make things worse." Simon glowered at his wife as she spoke. Was this couple's war really about becoming a family with an adolescent? I wondered. What else was going on? When I suggested that we slowly reconstruct their relationship, turning first to the time when they met, their well-rehearsed arguments with each other quickly ceased, replaced by a much more genuine tension and sadness.

"We met at Boston College," Simon said. "I was there because I had a scholarship. She was there because it was a Catholic school." This was the first allusion to their religious difference. Alexis went on to tell me of their strong attraction to each other. "He was bright, funny, and very caring—different from the boys I'd dated in high school. My parents sent to me to Boston College so I'd meet a Catholic man to marry. Instead I met a Jewish man and fell so in love that I was certain our religious differences wouldn't matter, and they truly haven't. We worked all that out early, but now we differ about everything else."

When Simon and Alexis decided to marry, both sets of parents warned them of trouble ahead. How would they raise their children? What would they do about traditions and holidays? How would they reconcile their religious beliefs? In an earlier time, one member of such a couple usually converted, but Simon and Alexis married in the 1980s and each felt free to maintain his or her own religious identification. Simon did agree that the children would be raised Catholic. "It was the only way her priest would participate in our wedding ceremony. It seemed like a very small matter at the time," Simon remarked.

Simon and Alexis had a beautiful interfaith ceremony and began their lives together full of hope. "When Jon was born, we started to fight. We went to see a therapist then and he said our fighting was because we had just become parents. He assured us things would straighten out," said Alexis. "But they never have—instead everything's gotten worse."

I asked Simon what it had been like for him to have his son christened. Before he could respond, Alexis assured me that this was no problem for Simon, that their fights were about other things and never about religion. I asked Simon again, and he turned bright red and said, "I gave in on how my children would be raised and I made up my mind that I would never give in on another thing between us." Clearly shocked by his remark, Alexis said, "I never knew. I never knew that's how you felt."

For thirteen years Simon had kept a secret of all his feelings about their religious differences. On Sunday mornings when Alexis took the children to church, Simon busied himself with work. Their arguments were usually worse on Sunday afternoons, but each attributed this to "too much time together." Just prior to Jon's thirteenth birthday, the age of the Jewish bar mitzvah, their fighting escalated. Neither Alexis nor Simon had made this connection.[6]

Our work together focused on the first thorough and open discussion of religious differences that this couple had ever had. Not only were Simon's feelings a secret from Alexis, but religion itself had become a taboo subject between them. They never spoke about Judaism or Catholicism. Each knew very little about the other's beliefs. Since he had told her when they first met that he was a "cultural Jew," Alexis assumed that religion just didn't matter to Simon. She interpreted his absences at any of her religious observances to be his irreligious stance rather than his enormous discomfort.

"When I agreed to raise our children Catholic, I didn't know what it would mean to me. Then I didn't know how to speak about what I was feeling. I had promised, so what good was it to talk about it, anyway? I began to think to myself, you can have an interfaith wedding, but what does an interfaith funeral look like? I felt alone in my own family and I didn't know what to do about it," Simon remarked sadly.

Every week I sent them off with homework designed to open this previously off-limits area of their relationship. They read books, set aside time to talk, and attended religious services with each other for the first time. As Simon's secret opened, their fighting diminished. At one point in our work together, Alexis became quite anxious that Simon would go back on his promise about their children's religious upbringing. "I gave my word fourteen years ago," Simon said, "and I won't renege on that. But I want our children to know what I believe, too." Simon was clear that he wanted his children to know his history and the history of his family over the generations.

Raising religious differences with their children proved to be more difficult than the work Simon and Alexis did to open this taboo area with one another. Their children knew their daddy was something called "Jewish," but they had no idea what this really meant. Only gradually did Alexis realize that she too had participated in maintaining the secret, because it just felt easier than confronting their differences and explaining these to their children. "I so wanted harmony in our family," Alexis commented. "If I couldn't have harmony with Simon on all the things we fought over, at least I was glad that I had harmony where my children's faith was concerned. I guess I looked the other way a lot."

Like many young couples today, Simon and Alexis came together with a strong focus on the present. Their distinctive cultural, religious, and historical backgrounds seemed remote, unimportant except to their parents and clergy. Likewise, any talk about the future that contained religious issues quickly became off-limits. With no access to past or future, they fought over every small detail of daily life. These arguments were both a distraction from and a metaphor for much more crucial but unspoken differences.

Couples living with religious, racial, cultural, and social-class differences need to work hard to ensure that these differences don't become secrets. It's all too easy to treat these differences superficially, as if eating each other's ethnic foods were sufficient—only to discover that your indigestion relates to more profound and unexamined differences. It is particularly tempting to pretend that disparities in power and influence adhering to race, class, and culture in the outside world disappear in a couple's embrace. However, when such inequities are not allowed to be noticed and discussed, they fester, often emerging in seemingly unrelated matters.

WHEN SOCIAL-CLASS DIFFERENCES GO UNDERGROUND

When Janice and Ian Lankton came to see me, they were on the verge of separating. Ian said all of their problems related to the disrespect he felt from Janice's family, who treated him "like a second-class citizen," and from Janice's refusal to support him with her family. Janice insisted that Ian was simply "too sensitive" and that after ten years he should have learned to accommodate her family's sense of humor.

We met on a cold January day shortly after a blowup at Janice's parents' home on Christmas. "Every year it's the same thing," Ian said. "We go to my in-laws' for Christmas. They give beautiful presents to their own children and to their other children's spouses, and I get a piece of junk. This year they gave me a wind-up toy. I felt so humiliated, and I blew my stack."

When I asked Janice what she thought this was about, she looked a bit embarrassed and said it was all a joke. When we talked further, I discovered that they spent every holiday with Janice's family, that her two sisters' husbands' families were always invited, and that Ian's parents and brothers were never included. When I asked why, Janice responded that Ian's parents would be "uncomfortable" at her parents' house, and "anyway, they live too far away." When I tried to unearth the source of this discomfort, both Ian and Janice were silent.

Ian and Janice were both successful lawyers. They had met at a prestigious university. Both were white and Protestant. Only when I asked about their parents' work and background did their profound social-class difference emerge. Janice's father owned a large manufacturing business that he had inherited from his father. Janice grew up in a wealthy and exclusive suburb in Connecticut. She and her sisters went to private schools. They attended lavish debutante balls and were expected to marry the "right" men. When Janice wanted to go to law school, her mother argued that this was unnecessary for the life she would lead, but her father thought she might become the in-house counsel for his business, which she did.

Ian's father was the first high-school graduate in his family. He was an auto worker who eventually became a foreman. Ian's mother worked in a day-care center. Ian grew up in a working-class neighborhood in Cleveland. His two older brothers also became auto workers. All of the family's hopes were pinned on Ian, the youngest, who was the only family member to go to college. When he took out loans to go to law school, his father told him this was the only thing he could imagine that was worth going into debt for.

The American prohibition on conversation about social class coupled with the myth that a college education makes you middle-class allows class differences in a couple to go underground. In fact, the social-class differences between Janice and Ian were enormous. During our meetings Ian heard for the first time that Janice's parents had tried to talk her out of marrying him. "I just thought it would hurt him to know this," Janice said. "And anyway, I stood my ground. I wanted Ian to like my parents and not think they were snobs."

Their wedding was totally planned and executed by Janice's mother. While Ian's family and relatives were invited, they were clearly marginalized. Ian was hurt, but he never said anything to Janice. Following the wedding, the two families never saw each other again. Living in the East and using geographic distance as his excuse, Ian seldom saw his own family. While there are many reasons for family members being cut off, I frequently find that an unacknowledged shift in social class underpins such distance.

When I remarked on their class differences and wondered about the impact of these on their relationship, Janice quickly told me that both she and Ian earned the same amount of money and that he was now the same social class as she was. When I asked how much money each expected to inherit from their respective families, Janice looked away and Ian began to weep. "I'm not crying about money," Ian said. "I'm crying because I've treated my own family so badly in order to be part of Janice's family. It's like I've erased them. I seldom call. I don't visit. I never felt ashamed of my background until I met Janice." While Ian spoke, Janice appeared stunned. This was the first time she heard how her husband felt about their differences and his relationship to his family.

I asked again how their social-class differences affected their relationship. It turned out that Janice often criticized Ian, sometimes in ways that were belittling. She selected all his clothes and warned him about ways to behave when they went out. She had chosen their children's school with no input from him. She planned their vacations and selected their friends. "I know I abdicated," Ian said. "I've just always assumed she knew better because of where she comes from." In large and small ways, social-class differences shaped this couple's relationship while remaining a complete taboo. Janice's unquestioned sense of privilege coupled with Ian's aching and unexamined sense of shame created a relationship in which Ian was perpetually one-down.

Opening the secret of social-class differences, a secret that Janice and Ian and everyone in their social network knew but never spoke about, was just the beginning of our work. For many months together we unpacked all that had been unspoken from the start of their relationship. Janice knew next to nothing about Ian's family. Rather than individuals with a proud history, they had become a subject to be avoided. Ian needed to reconnect with his family. Telling stories about them to Janice was the first step. He followed this with a visit by himself to his parents and his brothers, during which he talked to them about his own disappearance from their lives and expressed his sorrow and his apology.

We spent time talking about where Janice and Ian's core values were similar and where they were different. For example, Ian very much disliked the fact that his children were attending an exclusive private school, but he had never voiced this before. "I don't like that they're getting to know only other wealthy kids. Our neighborhood public school is excellent. Janice has always made it seem like she knows more about education than I do, and I just went along. I want this to change." Changing where their children went to school provoked the first of many confrontations Janice needed to have with her parents. Ultimately Janice told her parents that they absolutely had to treat Ian and his family with the same respect they showed to their other children's spouses. While the two extended families remained fairly distant, Janice and Ian began to alternate holidays at each other's families. While Janice's parents didn't suddenly turn warm toward Ian, their acts of disrespect toward him ceased.

WHEN SWEET SECRETS TURN BITTER: SEPARATION AND DIVORCE

Just as secrets shape couples' relationships when they are together, so do they play a critical role when a couple is coming apart. The discovery of secret betrayals and lies often triggers a separation. A spouse who wants to leave a marriage but has not figured out a way to be direct about it may begin to be sloppy about secret-keeping, so that their mate "discovers" an affair. Even when no outright betrayal is involved, a great silence may descend. Less and less is shared and more and more remains unspoken. I have often witnessed the shock of one partner when the other announces that they've been thinking about leaving for many months or even years but kept this knowledge secret.

Couples make myriad secrets together during the life of their union with the implicit or explicit understanding that these secrets will not be breached without mutual agreement. I've known couples who stayed together long after they probably should have separated, stalked by fear that a profound secret would be violated. During separation and divorce all of the couple's previous promises about keeping secrets may be torn asunder. If the divorce war becomes heated enough, the shared secrets of personal vulnerability and shame become weapons of attack. The content of such secrets may be quite minor, of no particular consequence except as a symbol of the couple's intimacy. Or the substance of the secrets may be enormous, as with secrets about illness, infertility, sexuality, or children's birth origins. Opening these secrets outside the couple announces that a special bond is irreparably broken.

FOR COUPLES FACING SEPARATION OR DIVORCE

While couples who are in the midst of a separation and divorce are seldom their best selves, it's important to slow down and consider the lasting impact of revealing a secret. When your motivation for opening a secret is vindictiveness or revenge, the effects may cast a long shadow and ruin any possibility of future cooperation. It may be helpful to ask yourself a few questions about the reasons behind and consequences of opening a secret.

- Who does this secret belong to? A secret about your spouse's life belongs to him or her. Ask yourself what your former mate would say if you requested permission to tell others. If you imagine permission would be denied, don't open the secret.

- Under what circumstances was this secret made? Try to remember when the secret was formed between you. Was this a pillow-talk secret, a moment of deep shame, a revelation that shaped and contributed to intimacy? Recalling a time of tenderness when a secret was made may challenge your desire to use the secret for revenge.

- What did you originally promise about this secret? If you agreed jointly to keep this confidence, then changing that agreement requires joint discussion, unless the secret puts you or your children or others in danger.

- What is the lasting price for betraying this confidence?

- What are your motives for opening this secret now?

- If you have children to raise together after a separation, how will opening this secret affect your ability to cooperate in their interest?

Information can indeed confer power, but if you use secrets in a power struggle during separation and divorce, you'll likely win a pyrrhic victory.

Each transition in the life of a couple requires new and unrehearsed steps in the dance of secrecy and openness. Intimate partners initially join through revelation, but truly knowing each other through secrets kept and secrets shared is a lifelong process.

Balancing Candor and Caution:
Secrets Between Parents and Young Children

➤

After considerable time, Miranda (age nine) stopped crying, and, while still breathing unevenly, she talked about how isolated she felt. "You want me to tell you everything, but now you won't tell me anything," she charged.

"We've told you," I replied, covering my distress with the measured calmness I affect if I want to appear in control when I am not, "that as soon as we know what is going to happen next, we will tell you."

"That's not what I mean . . . I want to know everything now. I get scared when you don't tell me everything that's going on."

"But nothing is going on," I responded obtusely.

"Then why do you and Daddy talk to each other so much and nobody talks to me?"

—*Kathy Weingarten*

ANDREW AND CATHY BLOOM had come to me for marital therapy three months earlier, but the current session had been dominated by a different problem: Cathy's younger sister, Agnes, had been beaten by her husband, Saul. Cathy had received an emergency telephone call from her sister's doctor the day before. "I couldn't believe what I was hearing," Cathy said sadly. "We knew they were having some difficulties," Andrew added, "but nothing like this has ever happened before." Agnes was now in a local hospital, and extended-family members were flying in from around the country. We had spent most of the session discussing ways for Cathy and Andrew to respond to this crisis when Cathy raised the question of what to tell their children.

Agnes and Saul were very close to Andrew and Cathy's two children, Serena, seven, and Paulette, nine. The girls went on many outings with their aunt and uncle and often spent the night at their apartment. "What do we tell our daughters?" Cathy asked. "Nothing like this has ever happened in our family. This happens on TV, to other families. Our girls love Saul. My mother wants to tell them my sister was in an accident, but that begins a lot of lying and covering up."

Cathy and Andrew were raising their daughters with an intricate combination of honesty and protectiveness. "We always answer their questions," Andrew said, "but we've certainly shielded them from unsavory parts of life. Frankly, I'm often surprised at what they learn in school at such a young age. We turn the TV off a lot, but they come home from friends' houses talking about some afternoon talk show they've seen and asking, 'What's a prostitute?' That's when our policy of honesty really gets stretched. I don't think I'd even heard the word *prostitute* till I was about fifteen."

Andrew's remark reminded me once again just how complicated issues of secrecy and openness have become for parents of young children. I grew up hearing, "Little pitchers have big ears," just before I was shuttled out of the room while the grown-ups talked about mysterious matters. (Of course, I often crept to the top of the stairs and tried to listen in, keeping my own secret about their secrets.) When I ask children today what the expression "Little pitchers have big ears" means, they look at me blankly.

Topics that were taboo in my childhood—sex, reproduction, adoption, serious illness, divorce, drugs, violence—are part of the daily conversational diet of today's children. What was once repressive silence coupled with rigid boundaries between parents and children has now been replaced by its opposite. Today's parents are bombarded with the gospel of "openness," and the popular media are full of cautionary tales detailing the dire consequences of "lack of communication." One young mother I know expressed the dilemma faced by many in her generation: "My children are my friends, but then I wonder—should I tell my ten-year-old what I tell my thirty-five-year-old best friend?" No doubt her own parents would not have described their children as their "friends," and the struggle over what to tell the children would not have been joined.

In workshops I often ask participants, "What secrets did your parents keep from you when you were a child? How does that compare to what you keep secret from your child today?" What moves me most in these discussions is the powerful disorientation parents experience as they struggle with the legacy of silence from their own family of origin and the new cultural imperative of openness at all costs. *They know that protecting children today means informing them, not keeping information from them.* But how and when should they open subjects such as sexual molestation or illegal drugs? Road maps from the past, when children could be easily sheltered from adult realities if a family so chose, are of little use in an age marked by media saturation, increasingly sensational news coverage, and easy Internet access, even by very young children. The confusion today over what children should and should not know is evident in simplistic calls for V-chips and Internet censorship—as if we could return to the mythical era when parents controlled what their children saw and heard. The same confusion underlies the one-size-fits-all solutions provided by some child-rearing experts: What to tell your child at age three, four, five, six, and so on. The key questions go unanswered: Which child in what family? With what emotional tone? In what social circumstances? Simply giving children facts about, for instance, drugs or sex is not the same as providing a much more complex meld of meanings, emotions, values, ethics, and family stories.[1]

Also missing from all of this expert advice is any nuanced discussion of how a given family's social circumstances affect a parent's thoughts, feelings, and actions about secrets and their children. When Andrew and Cathy Bloom left my office that day, they had decided to open the reality of wife battering in their extended family to their young daughters. The Blooms lived in a close-knit community. Their best friends had already urged them not to make a secret. They felt they had lots of support for their parenting. Later that very same day I was confronted with an isolated inner-city mother's absolute determination to keep secrets from her ten-year-old daughter.

A MOTHER WHO KNEW TOO MUCH AND A DAUGHTER WHO KNEW TOO LITTLE

Cleo Robinson, forty-one, had just made her third trip to the emergency room within a month with her ten-year-old daughter, Latesha. For the past year and a half Latesha had been injuring herself in many different ways—cutting her arms and legs, pulling out her eyelashes, breaking her elbow after jumping off a high stoop. An African-American single mother, Cleo lived with Latesha in one of the worst neighborhoods in Brooklyn, where Latesha's lullabies were too often the sounds of gunfire. Crack vials littered their street. In our first meeting Latesha remarked, "There haven't been too many shootings lately," in the same tone that another child might use to tell me about a play date.

The emergency-room staff had referred the family to me both because of their concern for Latesha and because of the intimidation they felt in the face of Cleo's fury. When I first met them, Cleo could barely contain her anger at Latesha. Beneath her anger, I sensed unspoken pain, and I was sure Latesha sensed it, too. But on the surface Cleo was implacable. She accused her daughter repeatedly of "destroying herself." Latesha sat passively as her mother's rage washed over her. Clearly, she had heard it all before. What Latesha had not ever heard, but had certainly felt, was her mother's life story.

I asked Cleo if we might construct her family tree so that I could understand more about the background affecting her and her daughter. She refused. I tried to inquire a bit about her life, and she immediately redirected me to Latesha. When I asked about Latesha's father, Cleo said flatly, "He's out of the picture," and quickly changed the subject. As they got up to leave after our first meeting, I noticed aloud that Cleo was wearing a red AIDS ribbon on her coat. Cleo said, "That's a subject for another day." I left the session thinking that Latesha was a child who knew far too much about the drugs and violence right outside her door and far too little about her own family.

Shortly after the session Cleo called me. "Could we meet alone?" she asked. "There are things I need to tell you, but not in front of Latesha." I was about to become the recipient of Cleo's secrets. I imagined these secrets were relevant to Latesha's problems, but would I be able to help Cleo to see this or would I become an unwitting ally in the silences?

"I was raised by my grandmother, my mother's mother," Cleo began. "Latesha knows that, but she doesn't know why. She's very impressionable and I don't want to give her any ideas." Cleo went on to tell me that her own mother was a heroin addict who had died of an overdose when Cleo was pregnant with Latesha. "My mother destroyed herself. Latesha's only ten and she's well on her way to destroying herself. I'm sure it's only a matter of time before she turns to drugs," Cleo said. "My mother's name was Loretta Mae—I named my baby Latesha Mae, but she doesn't know I named her for my mother. Now I think I shouldn't have done it. She's inherited her weaknesses." I commented that I imagined she named her daughter because she had some good memories of her mother and I wondered if Latesha knew any of these. "We don't talk about my mother," Cleo responded emphatically.

Many other parts of Cleo's life that she didn't talk about with Latesha poured out that afternoon. Latesha had a half-brother who had disappeared at age sixteen, when the little girl was three. "I'm sure she doesn't remember him," Cleo said, "and I've taken down all the pictures." Latesha's father, the only man Cleo ever really loved, left her when she was pregnant with Latesha. Cleo knew he was in the city, but he never called, sent no money, and had never seen Latesha. Since Latesha never asked about her brother or her father, Cleo had convinced herself that these men were of no matter to her daughter. Like many children, Latesha had learned what topics not to raise, what questions not to ask.

A young man whom Cleo helped raise in an informal foster arrangement had died of AIDS a year and a half earlier, shortly before Latesha began to injure herself. Cleo wept as she spoke about him, about her frantic attempts to get him off drugs, about his anonymous death in a city hospital. Then she said, "I'm quite sure Latesha doesn't notice my sadness—I hide it very well." How, I wondered, could I help Cleo to see that Latesha not only noticed her sadness but felt it deeply and had no way to understand it? The enormousness of Cleo's losses colored every moment of her life with Latesha, and yet there were no words spoken to acknowledge these losses. Cleo ended our meeting by insisting that Latesha's self-abuse was ample evidence that she could not handle any of this knowledge.

Cleo's fear that opening her secrets would only make things worse for Latesha is one that many parents share. Keeping a secret from young children most often starts as an act of protection. But keeping a secret to protect a child can backfire. When a secret requires pretense, deception, lies, and evasion, children's radar begins to operate. Growing children who are struggling to make sense of confounding messages from their parents pay a big price, as more and more of their energy and attention gets drawn into responding to mystery. When a mother or father shows intense but unexplained emotion, works hard to hide what he or she is feeling, or unaccountably withdraws, children experience distress. They may become detectives, create elaborate fantasies, blame themselves, or develop painful symptoms.

Latesha witnessed a deeply sad mother every day. And every day Cleo acted as if nothing were wrong. Her mother's words became less and less trustworthy to Latesha. Simultaneously this little girl's sense of her own judgment was constantly challenged. Was she seeing what she thought she was seeing? What was the meaning of her mother's palpable pain? In the face of this confusion, Latesha began to hurt herself. Her self-abuse was a powerful metaphor for all of her mother's unspoken and unacknowledged torment and loss.

When a child's behavior indirectly comments on the presence or content of a secret, parents often respond as Cleo did. In an ever-tightening circle, Latesha's self-harm served as a constant reminder to Cleo of her own mother's drug abuse. I believe Cleo's uncontrolled fury (which had led emergency-room personnel to label her an "unfit mother") was the boiling over of a perplexing stew of misdirected anger and overwhelming fear that Latesha was following a family path of self-destruction. It would be my job to help Cleo untangle these feelings and begin to see her daughter as her ally and not her enemy.

As Cleo and I continued to meet, each session brought forth more stories she had never told anyone. While her mother and father had both been addicted to heroin, they were also talented singers who toured the country in small clubs. When Cleo was fifteen, her father was murdered. The killer was never found. Shortly after that, Cleo became pregnant and her grandmother threw her out. For a short while her mother rallied, stopped using drugs, and took care of Cleo. I spent a lot of time exploring this period with Cleo and hearing about her mother's strengths. No one had ever talked to Cleo about any of her mother's good qualities. She grew up hearing her mother excoriated by her grandmother. "My grandmother told me way too much about my mother when I was very little," Cleo said. "When I was only three or four, my grandmother said, 'Your mother's a drug addict. Your mother's a whore.' I didn't even know what this meant, but I knew it was bad. It made me feel I was bad. I was determined not to do that to Latesha." Here was another piece of the puzzle. Cleo's experience of hearing too much as a young child in a context filled only with anger and blame led her to believe that she should shield Latesha from anything upsetting.

Helping Cleo to arrive at a place where she would even entertain the idea of opening her many painful secrets to Latesha required that we develop a more textured and expansive view of her family's story. Cleo had grown up hearing a very flat and one-sided view of her own mother. There had been good times with her mother, times when she visited and was kind and loving to Cleo, but these were never allowed to be noticed. No one ever discussed the migration of her family from the South, where they had been a closely knit and religious working-class family, to the

North, where the family scattered, became impoverished, and disintegrated. From the self-centered vantage point of any young child, Cleo was left to imagine that her family circumstances were unique and extraordinarily shameful. She firmly believed that keeping all of this from Latesha would spare her this shame. I told Cleo that I believe shame grows in hidden crevices and thrives in silence. "Latesha experiences your shame," I told her, "but right now she has no way to understand what any of it is about."

Together we also looked at her mother's talents and how these lived on in Cleo and in Latesha. Cleo's mother wrote poetry. Latesha had just won a prize at school for a poem. Gradually the secret of Loretta Mae's life, a secret that Cleo had located only in her drug abuse, began to be more complex and, paradoxically, easier to speak of.

I asked Cleo if she would be willing to have a meeting with Latesha in which we would look together at what "surviving" and "self-destructing" meant in individuals and in relationships. I told her I thought both of these qualities existed side by side in her family and in their community. She agreed.

We began the meeting by generating lists of words that defined *surviving* and *self-destructing*. Latesha wrote these on the blackboard. For the first time since I'd met them, mother and daughter were collaborating on a task. I was struck by how Cleo's definitions mirrored her life. Surviving was defined as "hot temper, stubbornness, orneriness," Cleo proclaimed. And indeed, these were qualities that had helped her to survive. Latesha added "strength, caution, courage, and feminism" to the list. They jointly defined *self-destructing* as "addiction, bad habits, and self-harming." Cleo added "whiny." Then Latesha, looking straight at her mother, said, "Put 'sadness' and 'depression' on the list."

I asked if we could talk about people they knew who were "survivors." Latesha began by telling me about a girlfriend of hers who had to live with her grandmother because her mother was a crack addict. Cleo began to weep, and Latesha immediately began to cry, too. When I asked Latesha what was happening, she said, "I'm crying because Mommy's crying." Cleo's long-held belief that Latesha "didn't notice" crumbled. As Cleo cried, Latesha qui-

etly asked, "What's the matter, Mommy?" Through her tears—
and for the very first time—Cleo said, "I'm thinking about my
mother." For the next forty minutes, Cleo began to tell Latesha
about Loretta Mae. This was the first of many such talks, both in
therapy and at home, about Cleo's mother, Latesha's father and
half-brother, Cleo's foster son, and many other family members
and friends. Latesha's self-abuse never occurred again after this
meeting.

Our work together included many ways to deal with secrets.
We made a family tree, and Cleo told many stories about everyone
in the family. Some stories were painful, but many stories were
about hope and courage and perseverance. Cleo took care to make
sure Latesha understood that none of the bad things that happened in her family were Latesha's fault or her responsibility to fix.
We looked at family photographs, including pictures of Latesha's
father and brother that she had never seen. Cleo took Latesha to
the cemetery to see where her mother and father were buried and
to say prayers for them. We talked about some things that might
never be known, such as what had happened to Latesha's half-
brother. I commented to Latesha and Cleo that there were secrets
that life keeps from us and secrets that other people keep from us.
The many losses in Cleo's life became open and available for conversation and healing.

CHILDREN'S SWEET AND
ESSENTIAL SECRETS

"What's the first secret you can remember keeping from
your parents?" I asked my eighty-three-year-old mother. Without
a moment's hesitation, she began telling me about the time she was
five years old and the ice-wagon horse knocked her down. "I
wasn't supposed to go near the ice wagon. But it was just so
tempting. It was a hot Chicago day, and I wanted to pick up the
ice that had fallen on the sidewalk. I bent down in front of the
horse, and he shook his head from side to side and pushed me over
in the street. I knew immediately that I couldn't tell my mother

because she had told me over and over not to go there. The secret didn't last very long—friends of mine went to my house and told her."

As my mother spoke, I remembered hearing this story from my grandmother forty-five years ago. It was part of a collection of stories, a volume that I would now title *Naughty Things My Mother Did*. Missing from my grandmother's version, however, was any reference to my mother's keeping the incident a secret.

While most parents associate secret-keeping with teenagers, children as young as three keep secrets from their parents. When I ask in workshops, "What was the first secret you kept from your parents, and what was that experience like for you?" I most often hear stories about five- and six-year-olds who discovered the heady, slightly liberating, slightly guilty reality of personal thoughts and actions that no one could know unless you chose to tell them. Childhood secrets help us take the measure of our "grown-upness." Can we handle a situation without telling our parents?

My colleague and friend Janine Roberts relates a story from her sixth year: "My father had a large and special box in his work-room in the basement. It was divided into many tiny compart-ments, each holding a different kind of nail or screw. We weren't supposed to go in there, but one day I decided to investigate. It didn't take long before I spilled the entire box all over the base-ment floor. Hundreds of nails and screws! I spent hours carefully sorting and putting everything back. I felt very proud, very grown-up. No one would know. Naturally I made mistakes. When my father came home, he asked who had been in his workroom. I kept my secret, but I felt so disappointed that I hadn't put it all back together correctly. And I was quite sure he knew I had done it." In the space of a few hours, Janine's secret had taken her from six to sixteen and back to six again.

While Freudian thinking has long promoted the idea that children's first secrets are about sexuality, children's early secrets are in fact much more varied. Bringing animals home and hiding them, stealing crayons at school in order to have more colors, taking money out of the wishing well, finding the hidden Christmas gifts in November, trading lunches in first grade, watching forbidden TV shows—the list goes on and on. Often the specific content of the secret is less important than the experience of selfhood it offers. Even secrets that hide misbehavior from parents and contain a touch of guilt also impart a sense of independent decision making. Making and keeping secrets helps young children become aware that they are separate persons with unique thoughts and feelings. As they discover physical and psychological hiding places, they also discover an autonomous self. Fairness and unfairness, justice and injustice, fear and courage, self-justification and guilt all reside in those hiding places as children experiment with secrets.

Secrets with siblings and friends also contribute to our earliest experiences of trust and intimacy. When I was eight I was sent to my room one night without dessert for an infraction I certainly cannot remember. What I will never forget, however, is my fourteen-year-old brother secretly bringing me cookies later that night. Thinking about that incident forty-five years later, I can still recall what it felt like to be understood and cared for by my brother as we jointly put one over on our parents.

Young children make secret pacts, take blood oaths, create codes, and form exclusionary clubs with secret passwords all in the service of discovering how secrets shape relationships and make private worlds without adults. Children's earliest experience of betrayal may arise when such secrets are unilaterally broken. Most of us can recall being on one end or the other of "you promised not to tell."

SIBLING BLACKMAIL

"I sprayed paint on the side of our house when I was seven," Alice Holder, now thirty-five, told me as we prepared for a therapy session with her older brother, Jeff, forty. "Jeff knew I had done it. My father was furious and ready to beat the perpetrator. I kept silent and so did Jeff. But I paid a price. Jeff called me his 'slave' and said I needed to do whatever he wanted or he would tell. I remember that incident because it speaks volumes about our relationship. Throughout our lives, I've let Jeff protect me from our parents' wrath, and in return he's exploited me for his benefit."

Through secrets, children learn that information can equal illicit power in the politics of family life. Parents are often amazed at the intrigue and manipulation among siblings where secrets are concerned. Unchecked, a brother or a sister's sly threats about a sibling's secret can result in what one woman called "sibling torture."

STRETCHING THE LIMITS OF LOYALTY

"Do I do what my family wants me to do or do I follow my own beliefs?" This question—which fills many a therapy hour for adults—arises in infant form when children keep secrets that violate family norms. Young children need to learn that different families are in fact different cultures, each with its own customs, practices, and beliefs about right and wrong. The budding capacity to have differences with your family, to challenge the family program, often emerges in secrets.

When I was ten I was not allowed to ride the elevated train in Chicago without my parents. My best friend, Geena, was eleven. Able to go around the city at will, she saw absolutely no reason why I couldn't ride the train with her. We plotted for several days to make a trip to downtown without my mother knowing. While I had no name for it at the time, clearly the pains in my chest were my first experience with anxiety.

The night before our undercover journey, I stayed at Geena's house. I couldn't sleep and I couldn't eat. How could I have a secret with Geena that broke my parents' rule? Another secret welled up inside of me. How could I keep from my best friend that I was too scared to go? The conflict was enormous and just a bit more than my ten-year-old psyche could handle. Just before the train arrived at the station, I burst into tears and ran and called my mother. While loyalty to my family won out and Geena never forgave me, I think of this incident now as a ten-year-old's first attempt at differentiation. This is my earliest recollection of even imagining a major challenge to what my parents told me to do outside our home. For most of us, such glimpses of revolution start in childhood secrets.

Sometimes a secret allows a young child to balance complex and competing loyalties—to family, to friends, to self. In 1944 Kathrine was a ten-year-old Swiss child growing up in the uneasy neutrality of World War II. The oldest of four children, Kathrine faced twin anxieties at home: her mother's extremely difficult pregnancy with her fifth child and her father's volunteer work as an air-raid warden. In the midst of this day-to-day confrontation with life and death, Kathrine discovered an island of tranquility and delight.

"I remember fleeing our house often to spend time with my best friend, Maria," Kathrine told me. "She lived quite nearby in a beautiful three-story house with her German paternal grandmother, her Czech mother, and her Swiss father. Maria was my dear friend, and I was attracted to her family and to the way they lived, so different from my own. They sat at lunch for hours, eating Austrian and Czech food, which I loved. They talked and talked. And they were musical. They had a piano in the dining room, and after lunch one or another family member would play classical music and the others would sing. No one in my family was making any music at that time in our lives."

But this joyous, seemingly perfect family scene had a profound fracture. Maria's father and grandmother supported Hitler openly. When they listened to the war news on the radio, Kathrine realized that they wanted Germany to swallow up Switzerland. Kathrine's family shouted angrily and booed whenever Hitler was on the radio; Maria's family cheered. "I loved my friend," Kathrine said, "and I loved the art and food and music in her home. I felt for sure that if my family knew their politics, that would be the end of my friendship and my visits. So I kept the secret to myself. Somehow I divided the two worlds quite neatly in my heart."

When the war ended, the secret opened. During the Swiss de-Nazification program, Maria's father was brought in for questioning. He admitted his Nazi sympathies but blamed them on his loyalty to his German mother. Kathrine and her parents read his story in the local newspaper. Her parents told Kathrine that they were not surprised. They had suspected his leanings all along but wanted their daughter to differentiate between Maria and her father and grandmother. "Even though my parents gave permission, I somehow couldn't stay friends with Maria once the secret was out," Kathrine said.

Maintaining the secret had allowed Kathrine to inhabit and appreciate two disparate worlds. Loyalty to her friend was possible only as long as Kathrine did not bring home Maria's family's political convictions, which flew in the face of everything her own family believed. When the secret became public, however, Kathrine could no longer juggle and balance such pivotal and heartrending differences. Now her continued friendship with Maria could be seen and judged as disloyalty, both to her family and to her larger community, which had sacrificed so much to stand against Hitler and the Nazis.

Many secrets that young children create and maintain—and perhaps eventually reveal—contribute to their developing sense of self. Through them, children gain an early understanding of boundaries in relationships, of predicaments involving loyalties and obligations to others, and of the complexities of lying and honesty among family and friends. Such secrets teach children to reach inside themselves and struggle with dilemmas in ways that no parental lecture or school curriculum ever can. But not all secrets are this benign. Some children's secrets weigh them down, limit their choices, and shrink their souls.

CHILDREN'S SECRETS, CHILDREN'S BURDENS

"I was taking a shortcut through an empty lot to my friend Arthur's house," Kirk Brownley recalled. "Suddenly a woman I had never seen before ran up to me and began beating me with her cane. She kept yelling that I was disrespectful. I finally got away, but not before she had bloodied me pretty badly. I was eleven at the time. I just knew I couldn't go home and tell my father and mother what happened. I lied and said I fell and that was the end of it. Even now, telling you, I can feel again how scared I was and how alone."

Kirk was forty-seven when he told me that story in therapy. He was struggling with his inability to trust anyone or to rely on even those closest to him. When I asked him to recall an early secret, he immediately remembered this incident. "Why do you think you decided not to tell either of your parents?" I asked. "I just thought I deserved whatever happened. I grew up hearing that I was bad. If I got in any trouble at school, even if it wasn't my fault, my parents would punish me again at home. Even though I couldn't figure out what I had done, if this lady was hitting me, I must have done something. It took me twenty years to figure out that she must have been crazy and that I hadn't done anything wrong," Kirk said.

Kirk's story hints at the enormous pain carried by some children's secrets. Kirk's father was an alcoholic who capriciously turned on his children. One moment he could be sweet and loving, and the next moment he could be full of rage. Kirk's mother had little energy for him and his younger sister. Kirk learned far too early that his parents were unreliable. In Kirk's world, adults were not safe confidants or trustworthy protectors. Absent any sheltering adult, Kirk kept many secrets as a young child. With no one to take his side, correct his perceptions, or offer an alternative view, these secrets reinforced his sense of himself as "bad," adults as unreliable, and the world as dangerous. Thirty-five years and many failed relationships later, we began to challenge these beliefs in therapy. For the first time in Kirk's life, sharing secrets felt possible.

Children keep toxic and dangerous secrets for many reasons. Some, like Kirk, learn quickly that their parents are unreliable. Some children keep secrets because they realize that their parents are extremely vulnerable due to mental illness, addiction, or acute emotional distress. In family therapy I have often seen parents who mistake their children's silence and seemingly high level of functioning for maturity, when in fact these children are straining beyond their years and their capacity to take care of their parents. I've talked to six- and seven-year-olds who are terrified by their father's unemployment or by their mother's daily withdrawal into her bedroom, and yet show their parents only perfect behavior at home and at school. Having learned to keep their thoughts, questions, feelings, and observations silent, they show up in my office with inexplicable stomachaches, headaches, or insomnia.

Some children keep secrets because they fear disappointing their parents. Expectations that are beyond a young child's capabilities breed guilty secrets. If a youngster is cheating on tests, altering grades, hiding misbehavior, or inflating achievements, I take this as a signal that the parents need to reevaluate what they are expecting from their child.

Nine-year-old Stevie Fortuna sat with his head down, his hands over his face, and his legs drawn up to his chest. His mother, Eva, began the meeting by telling me how upset she had been when she discovered two days earlier that all of the weekly newspapers Stevie was to have delivered were in the garbage can in her garage. Stevie was the oldest of three children. His father had left the family a year and a half earlier to live with his girlfriend. When Eva described Stevie as her "little man," I watched as he curled up further, practically disappearing in the corner of my couch.

Stevie was an excellent student, a good athlete, a fine big brother to his two little sisters, and a constant source of pride to his mother. When Eva suggested he try a paper route, there was no question of his not taking it on. Now Eva was frightened, angry, and disappointed. "What does this mean?" Eva implored. "Is this the beginning of his becoming irresponsible like his father?" Stevie remained silent during his mother's tirade.

I spent some time with Eva alone that day in order to calm her down and hear more of her current life story. During the day she worked in a day-care center, enabling her two little girls to attend for free. She received no child support.

After supper she took nursing courses at the local community college. A young teenager came in to watch the children, but it was clear to me that she relied on Stevie to care for the girls. Acting far beyond his nine years, he gave his sisters snacks, put them to bed, and read to them. After doing his homework, he waited up for his mother. What indeed would cause this responsible young boy to act so uncharacteristically?

I told Eva that it seemed to me that Stevie wanted her to know he couldn't handle the paper route, but he couldn't tell her directly. "He left the papers in the garage where you would find them," I said. "When children talk to us without words, I think it's often because they want our help with something."

When Stevie rejoined us, I asked him if he would be willing to draw his paper route for me. As Eva and I sat quietly nearby, Stevie drew apartment buildings and houses, carefully putting in the street names and numbers, coloring the rooftops, decorating the gardens. When he came to one house, he stopped and sat still for quite a while. Then Stevie took up a crayon and drew a ferocious-looking dog with long white fangs.

"That's dog's larger than any of the people you drew," his mother commented thoughtfully. At that point this stoic little boy crumbled. Through his tears, he told his mother that this dog had been growling and snapping at him every time he came by with the newspaper. Eva's "little man" was suddenly and appropriately nine years old. Stevie had been so terrified of being attacked by the dog that he simply stopped delivering the papers. At the same time, he was so worried about disappointing his mother that he kept his fears a secret. With a child's unique logic, Stevie threw the papers in the garbage at home, where his mother was sure to find them. "I figured if you got mad at me, I could just quit the route and never tell you I was afraid of that dog," Stevie said.

While opening Stevie's secret solved the initial mystery of his behavior, this was only the beginning of our work. Stevie's secret pointed the way to lots of issues for Eva and her family. Stevie needed to be nine years old and not nineteen or thirty-nine. After telling his mother about his secret fear of the dog, Stevie was also able to reveal other fears—normal fears for a nine-year-old whose father had precipitously left the family. Eva's expectations of Stevie became more realistic. Stevie grew able to make mistakes and not feel he had to hide them from his mother. He remained a very responsible human being, but with responsibilities appropriate to his age. Eva's own strengths became more and more visible. I frequently challenged ideas that Eva heard from her extended family and from the popular media that single parents can't raise healthy children, especially sons. We worked together for several months, during which time Eva took her husband to court and began receiving the child support that was due her.

WHEN CHILDREN KEEP DANGEROUS SECRETS

Ellen Padulla was twenty-seven years old when she first consulted me. "I can't keep friendships, my relationships with men never last beyond three dates, I sleep poorly, and you can obviously see that I weigh too much," Ellen poured out to me in the opening moments of our first meeting. And then she turned silent. My gentle questions were met with nods or shrugs. Ellen reminded me of so many women and a few men I've known over the years: chronically depressed; enormously anxious; harming themselves with alcohol, drugs, food, and self-abuse; and struggling through life with little joy. Ellen and I would spend eleven sessions before she even hinted at the secret of sexual abuse in her childhood, a secret she had never before revealed to anyone.

In recent years we have discovered that far too many children keep secrets driven by fear and intimidation.[2] Secrets of physical and sexual abuse are secrets shaped and maintained by adults' exploitation of their power over children. In these circumstances, adults feel entitled to demand secrecy, while children feel required to keep such secrets. Abusive parents assume a right to conceal, while abused children fear the consequences of revelation.[3] These consequences may include further punishment, violence toward other family members or pets, destruction of personal belongings, or dissolution of the family.

Very young children who are sexually abused absorb complicated messages about secrecy. One message is usually some version of "You have to keep this secret because you are special to me and telling will ruin this specialness." This is placed side by side with "You have to keep this secret because it is your fault that this is happening and if anyone finds out you will be punished." The secret thus preserves a warped sense of privilege alongside a distorted sense of personal shame.

While coercion and threat may play a critical role in children's secret-keeping, these same children often feel a strong pull to protect their abuser. Love and hate, tenderness and violation, loyalty and unreliability, refuge and harm may all exist in the complex mix. At the end of a therapy session, one little girl drew a picture of her abusive father. Under the picture, she wrote: "I love him. I am so angry for what he did to me."[4]

I've worked with adult women in therapy who were sexually abused as young children and who were never explicitly told to keep this secret, yet they knew they had to do so. For some, the abusing adult is also the only adult supporting the family. For others, the nonabusing parent is emotionally unavailable. For still others, the abuser is the only person in their lives who offers any attention.

"I just knew it was bad," Ellen finally told me. Her uncle had begun abusing her when she was five, and continued until she was eleven. "My mother sat two rooms away reading the paper. Did she know? I don't know. But then I remember thinking, what would be the point in telling her? My father had already left us. I think I knew she couldn't really protect me or take much care of me."

Ellen's uncle was also providing financial support for the family. Ellen knew that if she told anyone what was happening, what was left of her family would break apart.

Young children keep dangerous secrets from nonabusing parents whom they experience as vulnerable or unreliable. When it is obvious that others know that they are being sexually or physically abused and do nothing to stop it, children quickly discern that there is little point in opening the secret. No one will protect them. Worse, they may be told that they are imagining things or lying.

When young children open a dangerous secret, they need to be able to connect with trustworthy adults. The first concern must be to stop the abuse and provide physical safety. But this is only the beginning of a much longer journey toward emotional safety and relationship reliability. Therapy and other caretaking with children who have disclosed the secret of incest need to validate the child's experience and respect his or her sense of timing in talking about what happened. Children need to know that caring adults in their lives will allow them the space to explore and express *all* of their contradictory feelings and beliefs, or they will simply shut down and make new secrets about those emotions that they sense no one wants to hear.[5]

SECRETS, YOUNG CHILDREN, AND DIVORCE

Splits in the family provoked by separation and divorce are a breeding ground for secrets on both sides of the generational divide.

When a marriage is on the verge of collapsing, parents must struggle with what to tell their children. During my twenty-five years as a family therapist, I have seen damage done both by extreme secrecy and by excessive openness.

Some parents tell their children far too little, requiring them to live in an obviously emotionally charged and negative atmosphere with no overt discussion of what's happening in the family. Often these parents have not been able to admit to themselves what's happening, and so telling the children feels impossible. Nonetheless, even very young children know when their parents are coming apart. Many parents have brought their children for therapy, concerned about symptoms that are actually a response to mystification about Mom and Dad's marriage. As one mother told me, "Our son is only three, but when we fight, which is every day now, he runs over and stands between my husband and me and yells, 'Stop, stop!' We tell him everything's okay, which of course it isn't. And then he pulls us together and says, 'Hug!' We don't want to even touch each other, and then my son has a tantrum." In families where icy distance has replaced the heat of battle, children often take it upon themselves to pull their parents toward each other by misbehaving. Telling children everything is okay when they can see for themselves that this is not true or refusing to tell them anything while domestic war is breaking out around them only adds to their distress.

Other parents tell their children far too much. They confide adult marital problems, tell children their plans to leave before telling their spouse, disparage each other, and demand one-sided loyalty. Paradoxically, such openness overload by parents leads children to keep more secrets about their authentic feelings. As one woman told me, "My earliest secret? I was four and I told my mother I hated my father, who had left us. But I never hated him—I loved him. She hated him, and it was what she wanted to hear."

During the process of separation and divorce, parents must walk a tightrope between secrecy and openness where their children are concerned. Parents who pretend good feelings between each other while they are seething with rage only confuse children: If Mom and Dad feel so good about each other, why are they splitting up? Parents who use their children as confidants, telling them each and every detail of the breakup and expecting them to take sides, put children in an untenable loyalty bind. While they will see their parents' pain, children need to be told many times it's not their responsibility to heal it. They need straight information that emphasizes what's going to happen to them. They need to know where each parent will live and where they will live. They need to know when they will be with each parent. Whenever possible, they need regular and reliable schedules. Changes in income, housing, holidays, and so forth should be discussed in terms that young children can understand. When both parents are able to talk to their children jointly about what is happening in the family, the possibility of secret alliances between a parent and children against the other parent is lessened.[6]

Children want to know why their parents are getting divorced. The opportunities for blame and self-justification are legion in the invitation or demand by children to explain the circumstances. This is a time to go slowly and to reflect on the future consequences for the former spouse and for parent-child relationships. Telling children information as a strategy in struggles between ex-mates will contribute to deteriorating postdivorce relationships.

Divorce is an event, but, more important, it is also a process. As family relationships shift and transform during and after divorce, decisions about what to tell children will necessarily change. Two people who are ending an adult relationship no doubt have different perspectives on what happened. Very young children have little if any capacity for understanding the complexities and nuances involved in a marriage and its breakdown. Sorting out what information belongs to children and what belongs only to the adults is a thorny process that does not yield to simple prescriptions. Among ten couples, for instance, I might see nine who have no reason ever to tell their children about the extramarital affair that contributed to their divorce. In one of those ten families, however, the children may have seen many clues, and they will be far more distressed by not hearing the truth than by having their reality confirmed.

When parents are able to cooperate for the well-being of their children, I work with them in therapy to determine what information regarding the causes of a divorce should be shared with their children. We consider this as a process taking place over time.

- What information do children need to know now?
- What may be kept secret temporarily and opened at a later time when a child is older?
- What is permanently private and never to be discussed with children?

When parents can come to some agreements on what and when to tell their children, they are far less likely to pull children into inappropriate and harmful side-taking. While children may not like being told that some things are off-limits, they can be helped to understand the difference between secrecy and privacy. And once a topic is firmly off the table, most children are able to leave it to the grown-ups with a certain sense of relief.

CASUALTIES IN THE DIVORCE WARS

When I first met eight-year-old Jessie Bonhart, she had just started stuttering. Her parents, Paul and Sally, had divorced two years earlier. They were referred to me after a psychological evaluation of Jessie showed her to be extremely anxious. Jessie lived with her mother and visited with her father every other weekend. In our first meeting, the hot tension between her parents was palpable; each contradicted nearly every statement the other made. Nonetheless Jessie, their only child, seemed to have adjusted well—until she began stuttering. What, I wondered, was changing in this little girl's world?

When I met separately with Paul and Sally I was deluged with each one's enormous blame and anger. Each insisted that they kept these feelings away from Jessie and supported her relationship with the other parent. "Has anything changed recently?" I asked Paul. "Yes, I suppose so," Paul said. "I've stopped hiding my girlfriend, Anne, from Jessie. I know I agreed when Sally and I divorced that I wouldn't involve Anne in Jessie's life, but this is two years later and it's ridiculous. Anne and I are living together now, but I've told Jessie not to say anything to her mother because I don't want the hassle."

When I met with Sally, I discovered the other side of this equation. After every weekend visit, Sally quizzed Jessie: "What did you do? Where did you go? Who did you see? Who was with Daddy?" Sally was still hurt and furious that Paul had begun seeing Anne during their breakup. During their divorce mediation, Sally demanded and Paul agreed that Anne stay out of Jessie's life. No time limit was put on this agreement, and no mechanism was put in place to revisit the issue. Sally felt certain Paul would break his word. In effect, she made Jessie her spy. This eight-year-old girl was hearing Daddy say, "Don't tell Mommy," and hearing Mommy say, "Tell me what Daddy's doing."

I brought Paul and Sally together and told them that Jessie's stuttering was a perfect metaphor for her experience. She was a young child being asked simultaneously to speak and not to speak by the two people she loved the most in the world. Only they could release her from this bind by coming to some new agreements between them.

We initially worked together for three months, first focusing on some issues remaining from their divorce and then looking at where they were two years postdivorce. Each was devoted to Jessie's well-being, which made getting her out of the middle easier than it would have been with some divorced couples. Paul agreed he would make no more secrets with Jessie, while Sally agreed not to pump her daughter for information after every visit. As they put this into practice, Jessie's stuttering ceased.

I also worked some with Sally alone to help her accept the reality of Paul's relationship with Anne. I asked her what she was doing on the weekends when Jessie was at her dad's. Mostly she visited with her own mother, who in fact was fanning the flames and encouraging Sally to cross-examine Jessie. This, it turned out, was a repeat of Sally's childhood after her own parents' divorce. We worked on ways to back her mother off. Sally wanted Paul to spend more time with Jessie, and we negotiated a weekly evening visit that coincided with a course Sally wanted to take. When our intensive work was done, we met every three months for two years in order to maintain open negotiations between the adults and to keep Jessie out of the middle.

EIGHT PRINCIPLES FOR DIVORCING PARENTS

- Separate your thoughts and feelings about your ex-spouse from your child's thoughts and feelings about his or her parent. During divorce, parents often feel threatened that they will lose their children's loyalty and affection, and so they demand that children express only one point of view. If you allow your children to think and feel only the way you do, they will make secrets of their genuine ideas and emotions.

- Take time to consider what you want your children to know about the causes of the divorce. The acute crisis of divorce often promotes reckless telling that cannot be retracted. Life is long, and you and your ex-spouse are likely to share graduations, weddings, and grandchildren's birthday parties.

- Don't keep an earlier marriage and divorce a secret from your children. They will find out at some point and experience enormous mistrust. Integrate this knowledge into conversations when your children are young.

- Don't make your child your confidant. Find another adult—a good friend, close relative, or a therapist—for this necessary role. Children in divorced families do best when they can remain children and not become the recipients of their parents' anguish.

- Help your children to understand the differences between privacy and secrecy in divorce. Many issues belong only between the adults.

- Don't keep the better times in your marriage a secret from your children after divorce. Many family stories go underground when a marriage disintegrates, leaving children with a warped sense of adult relationships. Children need to know their parents' early love story when there was one. Hearing what each parent once cared for and respected in the other helps children stay connected to both parents whenever that's possible.

- Don't keep genuine safety concerns a secret from your children. If your ex-spouse has problems with alcohol or drugs, your children need to know how to respond.

- Establish pre- and post-transition rituals when children go from home to home. When parents and children are separated for a day, a weekend, a week or longer, they need ways to catch up with each other that do not violate boundaries of privacy. Establish some agreed-upon ways to tell each other stories of your time apart. Your children are just as curious about what you've been doing as you are about what they've been up to, but take care not to pry about your former spouse.

ILLNESS IN THE FAMILY

Six-year-old Ramona Baez came for her weekly play therapy with a psychology intern. As she did at every visit, Ramona went immediately to the toy box and took out the play stethoscope and put it around her therapist's neck. "You are the doctor," Ramona announced emphatically. "The baby is very sick. Where is the medicine? The baby is worse." Soon Ramona got angry at the "doctor." She began to yell, "You're not a good doctor. You don't help the baby." And soon after that she dissolved in tears. Ramona's mother has AIDS. Supposedly her diagnosis is a secret.

Like many families in which someone has a life-threatening illness, Ramona's family thought they could keep this information from her. Their motives for secrecy were complex. They wanted to protect her. They felt uncertain about her capacity to keep the secret from others outside the family. And Ramona's mother was afraid of her little girl's questions. "Will she ask how I got it? Will she ask if I'm going to die?" her mother wondered.

While children are usually the last to be told about a serious illness, they most often know well before the telling. Children show their burdensome knowledge in repetitive play. Ramona's intensity in her "doctor game" rose and fell depending on the state of her mother's health that week. Other children paint the information in their pictures. One little boy "didn't know" that his father had spinal cancer. When he was asked to draw his house, he drew a gravestone in the front yard. Asked to explain, he said, "My dog is very sick and he might die soon." The family had no dog. Living daily with the unspeakable illness of a parent, grandparent, or sibling, some children experience physical pain. One little girl who hadn't been told that her mother had breast cancer showed up every day in the school nurse's office with "pain in my chest." And children demonstrate their struggle with knowing what they're not supposed to know through angry outbursts, often at friends or teachers. One boy who was sitting in the principal's office after striking another child was asked, "Is it easier to be angry or scared?" The boy—whose father had not yet revealed his AIDS diagnosis—replied, "Angry, of course."

When illness strikes, many parents are simply at a loss for words to explain what's happening. TV movies may introduce us to the illnesses of the week, but they are about somebody else's family. Only a generation ago, the names of many illnesses either were not spoken aloud or were mentioned only in hushed tones when children were out of the room. Parents today must struggle with a paradox: The media saturates us with talk about cancer, heart disease, Alzheimer's, diabetes, stroke, and HIV/AIDS, but we have little direct experience with how to talk to children about these illnesses in our own families. Wrapping an illness in euphemisms seems to keep it at a distance. Naming an illness, first to yourself and then to your children, makes it more real.

As with many painful secrets, adults need to do their own emotional work before they open illness secrets with their children. They often have to deal with stigma, shame, and self-blame. And they need to prepare for children's probing questions. Often the question behind their questions is, "What will happen to me?" When a life-threatening illness is kept secret, this crucial question remains ignored, denied, and unaddressed. Today many programs working with people with HIV/AIDS coach parents on how to open the secret of their illness with their children. This both alleviates the stress of such profound secret-keeping and enables the parents to plan for their children's care as they become sicker.

Opening an illness secret to young children raises another dilemma: Who else can and should know? Even very young children sometimes struggle with this issue. Seven-year-old Kevin told a psychiatric resident, "My mother takes AZT." "What do you think that is?" the trainee asked. The youngster thought for a moment and replied, "Animal, zoo, toy." "Why does she take it?" "She has AIDS, but I'm not supposed to know, so don't tell," he said.

If open knowledge of an illness is going to threaten a family's housing, jobs, friendships, or a child's school placement, then young children will need help carrying the burden of privacy. While talking about what needs to stay in the family is important, children also need a safe place, such as in therapy or with a trusted adult friend, to talk about what is happening to them and to their family.

Children have a right to know if they or someone in the family has a serious illness. Children with life-threatening conditions know their situation. They quickly intuit the meaning of hospitalizations, of trips to the doctor, of medications they must take, and the obvious but unspoken sadness of family members. When illness is kept a secret from children, they feel mistrustful of adults at the very point when they need them most.[7]

WHEN CHILDREN HAVE A RIGHT TO KNOW

Some secrets should never be kept from children. Information about biological heritage, adoption, third-party conception, and family composition, such as the existence of half-siblings who live elsewhere, *belong* to children. Parents who deal successfully with these issues recognize that they are never dispatched in one or two conversations, but rather are part of the ongoing dialogue in their family's life.

Many parents tell themselves that when their child reaches a certain age, they'll open a secret about adoption or parentage, only to find that this age comes and goes with no revelation. As the secret becomes harder and harder to open, it grows larger and larger. If, on the other hand, an infant is told that she's adopted from the first moment she's held by her new parents, there will never be cause to struggle with opening that particular secret. There will never be a time when her adoption was not known to her. The subject will never be a taboo. Specific information—the facts of her adoption, the complex thoughts and feelings of all concerned—can be talked about as part of an ongoing family conversation, geared to a child's readiness over time.[8]

DECIDING TO CONCEAL, DECIDING TO REVEAL

Parenting young children is filled with many complicated choices about concealing and revealing. Knowing our own motives and making decisions is sometimes a tricky business.

- When are you protecting your children from more than they can handle?

- When are you protecting yourself from their penetrating and uncomfortable questions?

- Is opening a particular secret more about your own need to tell than it is about your children's need to hear?

- Are you opening a secret so your child can take care of you? Children often think the content of toxic secrets is their responsibility to fix. They need to be reassured that no matter the topic and its ramifications, it is neither their fault nor their job to resolve it.

- Will opening a secret outside your family put your family in jeopardy? If so, then very young children who have not yet developed the capacity to understand family privacy, boundaries, or the difference between inside and outside should not be told

specifics. Asking a toddler or kindergartner not to
tell a secret outside the house is asking something
that the child cannot understand. At the same time,
since even small children absorb obvious family distress and become very disoriented when this is
denied, find ways to acknowledge sadness or anger
while at the same time reassuring children that you
will handle it.

· Are the issues strictly adult matters? If so, then you
need to open the secret with another adult—your
spouse, a good friend, a therapist—and resolve your
own distress. Our children watch us carefully. When
they see us taking care of business, they return to
their own lives.

Opening secrets with children requires a repertoire of skills
and strategies. Storybooks, photographs, movies, or joint activities
can provide natural openings. Gentle, planful telling that occurs
when time is available is vital. Moving from what is hidden to
what is open usually takes many conversations.

Children don't hear the way adults hear. Often parents have
told me that sensitive information they were keeping secret didn't
seem to matter to their child. "I told him his father and I were
separating, and he just went out and played," one mother complained to me. Every child takes in new and potentially loaded
information in his or her own unique way. Questions often come
later, disconnected to the initial telling.

Children are constantly growing and changing. A decision to
keep a secret from young children is never final. And the act of
opening a secret to children is only Act One. As we'll see in the
next chapter, concealing and revealing reappears in novel and chal-
lenging forms and with new opportunities for relationship change
when children become adolescents.

10

Private Investigations:
Secrets Between Teens and Parents

◄——

Adolescence is a time for . . . psychological cogitations to take place, cogitations that rarely become public or publicized. The results of adolescent thought experiments, like the thought experiments themselves, typically remain secret. It all makes for a great deal of work, it makes for a difficult time, it makes for a seemingly totally self-preoccupied soul. . . . So the secret-keeping adolescent learns much about the structure of language, thought, and action almost as a by-product of his or her thought experiments and psychological twistings and untwistings.

—Thomas J. Cottle

THE GIRL WHO COULDN'T KEEP SECRETS

Andrea sat on the couch in my office with her legs tucked under her, looking far younger than her sixteen years. Her mother, Rachel, exhausted, settled only a few inches from Andrea.

Their proximity contradicted the obvious tension and anger between them. In tears, Rachel complained, "She did it again. She came home smelling of beer, and in a car driven by one of her friends, even though I've told her and told her to call me for a ride home. How many times do we have to go through this? I really just want to give up." Turning her head away from her mother, Andrea whispered, "Why do you have to know everything I do? I can't even keep a thought to myself."

I had known Andrea and her mother, a single parent, for a few months. Each session seemed remarkably similar. Andrea would do something to break the rules, and her mother would be intensely angry, hurt, and disappointed. One week it would be violating curfew, the next week cutting a class, the following week drinking, and the week after that pamphlets about birth control left where her mother would find them. With what seemed like clumsy provocation, Andrea would speak on the phone to her friends loudly enough for her mother to hear every plan. She'd often leave her diary open and available to her mother's watchful eye.

Much of what went on between Andrea and her mother seemed, at first glance, to be banal parent-teen struggles. But these flare-ups differed from the ordinary. Andrea seemed determined to brief her mother on every aspect of her life, all the while denouncing her mother for being intrusive. She lacked any capacity for commonplace adolescent guile. When she tested any limit, she seemed unable to keep this from her mother for more than thirty seconds. In turn, Rachel responded to Andrea's tiniest steps toward autonomy, such as going shopping without telling her, with amplified fear, agitation, and despair. What was going on here?

Since Rachel agreed that Andrea had a fairly nice group of friends, I asked Andrea to compare how much her mother knew about her life, her innermost thoughts, her daily actions, with what her friends' parents knew about them.

"Are you kidding? My friends are always telling me that I tell my mother way too much. My friends can keep secrets from their parents and nobody gets freaked out. Anytime I even try to keep something from my mother, I just start to feel so awful, and then I *have* to tell her. I think it means we're close, but I'd like to be a little less close once in a while."

Rachel responded that there were times when she wished she knew a bit less about everything her daughter was up to, that her own life might be a little calmer, but that whenever she tried to back off, Andrea would find a way to let her know about a recent or upcoming escapade. She also allowed that if she didn't know what Andrea was doing or thinking, she became terribly anxious. When I tried to suggest that there might be other ways for a mother and a daughter to be close, Rachel quickly and anxiously changed the subject and once again began to berate Andrea.

I interjected, "Most teens I know manage to keep certain things to themselves, to have some 'sweet secrets.' It's a way to begin to be a little bit separate from your family—kind of a dress rehearsal for when you become an adult. Where," I wondered aloud, "does the idea come from in this family that a sixteen-year-old needs to tell her mother everything?"

The mood in the room shifted immediately and profoundly. Rachel began to weep. Rather than the frustrated tears I was used to seeing, I felt I was witnessing deep grief. Andrea moved swiftly to reassure her mother, but I gently stopped her. "Give your mom a little room," I said. After several minutes Rachel began to speak.

"I grew up hearing, 'You have to tell us everything. Please don't keep any secrets from us. If we'd known where Anna was that day, she'd have made it out with us—not telling us is what killed your aunt Anna. We had no choice, we had to leave.' My parents are Holocaust survivors. They fled and hid as the Gestapo was rounding people up. My aunt Anna, my mother's older sister, was a headstrong teen at the time. They fought with her all the time, but she always kept secrets about where she was going, who she was with. That last day they had to leave without her—they didn't know where she was. No one ever saw her again. Andrea is named for her, you know. My mother says they're a lot alike, but I tell her all the time not to worry, that Andrea tells me everything."

As her mother spoke, Andrea appeared surprised and shocked. "I never knew about any aunt Anna. Why didn't you tell me?" Listening to all of the family stories over the years about her grandparents' experiences as survivors of the Holocaust, Andrea had assumed that the whole family escaped. The secrets behind the rule of "no secrets," a secret that had remained mired in guilt and anguish for thirty-five years, was now out. As is so often true, it was a secret located both in the history of a culture and in the specific experiences of one family.

Rachel explained that she had grown up hearing so much about Aunt Anna and being so frightened by the stories that she determined not to tell Andrea. She made her own mother promise to keep silent, convincing her that Andrea was less likely to follow in Anna's footsteps if she didn't know anything about her. Rather, Andrea grew up in an environment that was permeated by a fear-laden but mysterious requirement to "tell all" that had been interrupting the normal steps toward developing a separate self.

Adolescence is a time of life in America that is typically marked by tentative steps away from the family. In many other cultures, the transition from childhood to adolescence and young adulthood is facilitated by rituals. Very often, such rituals include culturally agreed-upon acts of secret-keeping, whereby the young person is temporarily taken to a remote place where secret knowledge of adult life is imparted. Sharing this knowledge with small children is forbidden. Essential secrecy is woven into the life cycle. Our culture lacks such rites of passage, yet secret-keeping is still crucial to adolescent development. As teens experiment with behavior that is kept secret from parents, a new boundary among family members is created, along with an adolescent's emerging sense of self.

With no capacity for making and keeping secrets as a teen, Andrea remained fused with her mother, locked in a relationship that disallowed separateness or even temporary distance. Learning to rely on anyone outside the family was forbidden by the unspoken edict to have no secrets. A critical element of successful teenage life—practicing autonomy with a safety net—was unavailable. In a family where secrets had come to carry the meaning of disappearance and death, Rachel kept a core secret from her daughter in a misguided attempt to protect her. Such are the paradoxes of secrets.

ESSENTIAL SECRETS OR DANGEROUS SECRETS?

Teenagers of the 1990s live in a very different landscape in which to make secrets than their parents or grandparents did. The essential adolescent secrets of a generation or two ago, such as smoking cigarettes and frantically airing out the house before parents came home, or sneaking a taste of alcohol and refilling the bottle with water, now seem quaintly antique in an era where 50 percent of all high-school students report getting drunk at least every two weeks. And baby boomers who shocked their own parents by smoking marijuana and having "liberated" sex must now struggle with their teenagers' engaging in the very same behavior but with far more dangerous consequences. In an age of sexually transmitted diseases and increasingly toxic drugs, some secrets kept by teens can indeed be deadly.

The parents I talk to are often confused about how much privacy their teen can safely have and frightened about the meaning of secrets in their children's lives. Their bewilderment often manifests as a perplexing oscillation between intrusion in unnecessary areas in their teen's life, such as their taste in clothes or hair styles, and disengagement in those areas that are critical for parental involvement, including sex education, birth control, and alcohol or drug use.

The line between essential secrets and dangerous secrets has become exceedingly thin in an age when many teens keep such physically lethal or emotionally harmful secrets from their parents as severe alcohol and drug abuse, date rape, suicide attempts, and violent attacks by peers or strangers. According to police estimates, 60 percent of teens don't tell their parents when they are mugged on urban streets or in suburban shopping malls. These are not secrets that will be told jokingly around the dining room table twenty years hence.

Simultaneously parents have become more afraid to ask their teens what's going on in areas where it can be extremely dangerous to maintain silence. Distortion of the normal need for secrecy in adolescence, in a culture where the connections between teens and parents are often frayed, results in a pattern of mutual distancing and no conversation on topics that require greater openness.

Developing a thoughtful, creative position and a competent range of responses to teens and their secrets today involves a complex stew. A given family's current social and economic terrain, the values and beliefs embedded in ethnicity, social class, and specific history, and each parent's biography as a secret-keeping adolescent intertwine to inform actions.

ADOLESCENT SECRETS— YESTERDAY AND TODAY

Take a moment to reflect on your own adolescence:

- As an adolescent, were you able to keep secrets from your parents?
- What were the secrets you kept?
- How did your parents respond if they discovered one of your secrets?
- Were there differences in the kinds of secrets that you kept from your mother and the ones kept from your father? What accounted for the difference?
- What was the relationship like with your closest confidant?
- Did you keep secrets with or from your siblings?
- How would you compare the secrets you kept with the ones you imagine your teen keeps from you now?
- How would you compare the secrets your parents kept from you with the ones you keep now from your teen?

SECRET BURDENS: THE HIGH PRICE OF LOYALTY

Gregory Richards was fifteen when his father lost his prestigious job as a bank executive due to his increasing problems with alcohol. While Gregory knew of his father's drinking, the job loss was initially kept a secret from him. Acutely ashamed and humiliated by his sudden loss of status and income, Mr. Richards begged his wife not to tell their children or anyone else that he had been fired and was now driving a taxi. Every morning Mr. Richards dressed for the corporate world and left the house as if he were going to his office. Instead, he drove to the cab company, where he would change out of his suit and tie and spend the day driving a cab. Gregory sensed enormous tension between his parents but was afraid to ask what was going on until one day when he spotted his father sitting in the taxi. With bewilderment, he confronted his mother for information. She told him about his father's job loss but, as was standard in this family, did not discuss his father's drinking problem. Sensing his mother's enormous shame, Gregory didn't inquire about the financial impact on the family or press for any other details.

Now he was in on the secret, but his parents enjoined him from telling the younger children, his friends, or anyone in the extended family. As Gregory learned that family loyalty required duplicity and betrayal, his own behavior began to deteriorate.

The extremes of the pretense required were visible one night when Gregory was out with his friends in town. They hailed a taxi that turned out to be driven by his father. Gregory's father pretended not to know him and signaled Gregory to respond similarly. Following this bizarre incident, Gregory began to cut classes and verbally berate his father, calling him a liar and a quitter. These verbal assaults quickly deteriorated to physical fights between Gregory and his father. All the while, Gregory kept the secret, and the family's attention turned from the core issues—Mr. Richards's alcoholism, finances, and employment problems—to a focus on what they called "Gregory's violent outbursts."[1]

Adolescents are fully capable of understanding boundaries and the need, at times, for secrets that maintain privacy or protect the family from unwarranted intrusions. But no teen should be asked to keep secrets that require deception and evasion on a daily basis or that cut the child off from a parent, siblings, extended family, or friends. When an adolescent is required to sacrifice his or her own development and devote a lot of energy that should be going into friendships, schoolwork, and activities to the maintaining of a family secret, then an adult is asking too much of that child.

Sometimes a parent makes a teen his or her confidant. They

tell emotionally powerful secrets that are far beyond an adolescent's capacity to handle. Particularly toxic are secrets that one parent tells a teen that must be kept from the other parent. Secrets that require teens to betray some family members in order to stay loyal to others twist the meaning of trust in relationships. "How," an adolescent wonders, "can I be simultaneously trustworthy and untrustworthy with the people who are supposed to mean the most to me? If I keep Dad's affair a secret, what does that say about my relationship with Mom? If I tell Mom, what does that do to my relationship with Dad?" Some teens take a third way out: engaging in behavior that points to the content of the secret but does so with ambiguity.

Sara Morrison, seventeen, was a model student, vice president of her class, and headed for college—until her father confided that he was having an affair, but that Sara must not tell her mother. Not only did her father tell her details of the affair, but he complained bitterly about his marriage and his poor sex life with Sara's mother. He also indicated that this was one of many affairs he had kept secret from Sara's mother over the years.

In short order Sara's grades plummeted. She broke up with her steady boyfriend and began staying out late and spending time with boys who were dropouts. She provocatively let both parents know that not only was she sexually active, but she was sleeping with several different boys. In a misguided attempt to let her mother know her father's secret without breaking her word to him, Sara sacrificed her own well-being.

MAKING A SECRET WITH MOM OR DAD

As we've seen, when a parent begins the secret-making process, the result can be a terrible loyalty bind for a teenager. But what about when a child comes to a mother with a secret and says, "Please don't tell Dad"?

Here, as usual, there is no one right answer. The specific content of the secret, family patterns through time, the parent's own experience as a secret-making adolescent, and the impact on current family relationships and individual well-being must all be factored into a commitment to keep a secret. For instance, if a mother keeps a secret about her daughter's abortion, how will that affect her relationship with her husband? How will it affect his relationship with his daughter? What about the mother's relationship with her daughter? In one family, a mother's refusal to keep this secret risks that the daughter will be beaten by her father. In another family, agreeing to keep this secret may rob a daughter of a father's supportive response. Or suppose a son tells his father that all of his friends are drinking at parties but adds, "Don't tell Mom, because we know how she gets." Is there a long-standing family pattern of keeping critical information from Mom? Is she labeled as "the hysterical one," when, in fact, she is responding with such intensity precisely because she is kept out of the information loop? Or is the son just asking for some temporary support while he figures out a way to stay out of trouble?

Sometimes a teenager will tell a parent an important confidence without requesting that the other parent not be told. Here a parent should think carefully before suggesting or insisting on secrecy. What messages about shame and a young woman's sexuality are sent when a mother tells her eighteen-year-old daughter that her father mustn't know that she's sexually active because "it would break his heart"? What pressure does a father put on his son if he tells him his low SAT scores must be kept a secret from his mother while he takes the test again?

Once a parent promises to keep a secret with a teen, it is crucial that it be kept—or renegotiated directly with the child. Violating a confidence with an adolescent sends a strong message that a parent cannot be trusted just at a time when relationship reliability and accountability is most needed. Such a broken promise is often coupled with a secret about breaking the secret that ultimately promotes paralysis in family relationships. When fourteen-year-old Ellen Downey was caught shoplifting with her friends, she begged her mother not to tell her father. She adored her father and feared both his anger and his disappointment. Within hours her mother told her father and made him promise not to tell Ellen that he knew. In this ever-tightening knot of silence, no adequate response to Ellen's shoplifting was possible.

TO MAKE A SECRET OR NOT

A request for secrecy from your teenager requires careful reflection.

- Does keeping this secret put my child in any danger? Secrets such as bulimia, drug use, or thoughts of suicide are secrets that you cannot promise to keep without jeopardizing your child's safety and cutting you and your family off from needed resources.
- Does keeping this secret support family patterns that are problematic or ineffective? For instance, if you and your daughter habitually keep your wife from knowing critical information, any given secret between the two of you may simply be another version of this triangle.
- Think back to when you were an adolescent. What were your parents' responses when you shared your secrets? Do you want to act similarly or differently?
- Think ahead. What will the impact of this secret be on various family relationships over time?
- Is this a temporary secret that can enable you to help your youngster figure something out in an atmosphere of safety? For instance, many teens want to share secrets regarding their emerging sexuality. When a parent can receive such information calmly and commit to temporary secrecy, an atmosphere of thoughtful questioning and support can be created.

"NONE OF YOUR BUSINESS": TEENS AND PRIVACY

"She's driving me crazy. She reads my mail, wants to know where I've been, asks for every detail of a date I've had, listens to my phone calls." This litany of complaints came not from a sixteen-year-old, as you might imagine, but from her single mother. Karen Bolling, an only child, had lived alone with her mother, Ellen, for fifteen years. In many ways, they lived more like sisters than mother and daughter. Karen had the mistaken notion that every aspect of her mother's life was her concern.

Adolescence in our culture is a time when the zone of personal privacy expands. The particulars of this expansion vary from family to family, often depending on the family's ethnic background, social class, and specific beliefs about privacy. Upper-middle-class families can usually afford to give a teenager his or her own room. In less affluent families, privacy may be defined by a dresser, a single drawer, or a shoe box full of confidential data. Diary writing is often a central symbol of adolescent privacy, as teens begin to have thoughts that they want to keep entirely to themselves. In my experience, few actions by parents upset teens more than reading their diary without permission.

Many parents grow anxious as their teen becomes more private. "What's he hiding?" they wonder. It's important to talk about privacy and to come to some agreements about what an adolescent can count on remaining private. For instance, are bedrooms off-limits? What about opening closed drawers or closets? Diaries? Letters from friends? Telephone calls? Similarly, it helps if parents are clear about what they consider to be private in their own lives. Many teens have the notion that as their right to privacy increases, their parents' decreases, and that part of growing up is to know all about what's going on in adults' lives.

When I work with parents and their adolescents, I often hear intense arguments centering on the lines between privacy and secrecy. An outraged fifteen-year-old's exclamation, "How dare you go through my drawers?" is met by an equally exercised parent's response, "This is my house, and I'll look anywhere I want." After calming down the heat, I try to shed some light on important differences between secrecy and privacy, reminding teens and their parents that truly private matters on both sides of the generational divide neither block access to the knowledge required to live one's life nor pose threats to safety.

Secrets that teens keep that their parents need to know are those that involve potential danger. Shouts of "It's none of your business" should not be allowed to back parents off from secrets about drug and alcohol abuse, violence, victimization, or suicidal thoughts and plans. And while fear quickly converts to blame and accusations, adolescents are far more likely to hear their parents if the atmosphere is marked by concern.

Adolescents sometimes ask me, "Why should I tell my parents things about my life? They keep secrets from me about what's going on in their lives." Just as a parent needs to know if their teenager is keeping a dangerous secret from them, an adolescent needs to know the content of a secret that directly affects his or her life. Normal struggles of adolescence may find expression in the recesses of family taboos. For instance, in research done with Latina adolescents who had attempted suicide, every girl's mother had also attempted suicide as a teen and had kept this a secret from her daughter.[2] As in these families, the appearance of psychological and behavioral symptoms in a teen both point to and distract from central family secrets.

WHEN SECRETS KEPT FROM TEENS CAUSE DANGER

Adolescence is a time in family life when parents need to rethink and renegotiate the secrets they may have kept from children when they were younger. Most parents keep shameful events in their family background a secret from children. Certainly young children should not be expected to cope with stories of suicide, murder, or severe abuse in their own family's history. They may respond with terror or with pseudo-mature caretaking of their parents. But adolescents require an expanding encyclopedia of family stories in order to sort out their own developing self. When such stories cannot be woven into the fabric of family life, instead remaining secret, they assume a power out of proportion to the entire sweep of a family's history. Paradoxically, the dangerous family secret that is *kept* from an adolescent, that is not open for examination, is the secret most likely to be reenacted in the adolescent's life.

The telephone call from Cora Jankowski's mother was filled with tears and anguish. "My daughter's run away. This is the third time. Her father wants to call the police—I don't know what to do." As I sat later with Cora's parents, I heard the details of her disappearances. Unlike some runaway teens who go to friends or relatives, each time Cora ran away she put herself in danger. The first time, she was found by the police after she had been beaten by a new boyfriend. During the most recent episode, she had ended up in a homeless shelter. What could be going on in this seemingly solid middle-class family to provoke such desperate behavior?

As I listened, I became aware of bitter anger and deep divisions between the parents, extending well beyond their current dilemma with Cora. "I left last year for a while," Cora's mother told me, "but we told the kids I had gone on a trip. I just needed some time out to think. Cora asked me if it was a separation, but I told her it wasn't." The parents were on the verge of another separation when Cora began her running away.

I became curious about how this family used distance to solve problems. Was Cora simply adopting a family tactic? "This seems like a family where people 'run away'—who else has run away?" Mr. Jankowski looked startled and chuckled uncomfortably. Story after story then emerged of people running away on both sides of the extended family. Often family members stopped speaking for years. Mr. Jankowski's father left the family and was never heard from again. Mrs. Jankowski's grandfather ran away from the army in Poland and came to America. Grown sisters and brothers put as much geographic and emotional distance between each other as possible. Relatives never gathered for holidays and were unavailable for any support. "How much does Cora know about these stories?" I asked. Mr. Jankowski related that since they never saw members of their extended family, they also never spoke about them. They hadn't told Cora or their four other children any of these stories. Family history itself was a taboo subject. This family lived in a constant state of "running away."

We met for two and a half hours that afternoon and began unpacking what had remained hidden for so long in this family. By the end of this first meeting, both parents' anger and frustration with their daughter began to mellow. Mrs. Jankowski remarked, "When I reflect on what's happened in both of our families, Cora's running away makes a different kind of sense. It's been our only strategy for dealing with difficult times—I guess she knew that somehow, even if we never said it." When I saw Mr. and Mrs. Jankowski two days later, they told me that Cora had started to phone them. I asked them to tell her during the next phone call that she was not the only family member who had ever run away—that it was, indeed, a "family trait." After their next conversation, Cora said she would meet them at my office to arrange returning home. At that point we were able to begin our work together to develop other ways to cope.

OPENING SECRETS AFTER SEPARATIONS

Forty-year-old Una Parker and her three adolescent children, Arthur, eighteen, Tamara, sixteen, and Edward, fifteen, came to see me in family therapy because Tamara's guidance counselor had grown worried about her irregular school attendance. When I met them in the waiting room, I immediately saw a worn-out mother accompanied by three teens, each plugged into a separate headset. As I was soon to learn, these earphones were a vivid metaphor for separation and aloneness in this family.

In our first meeting, Una looked very sad and spoke to me with bewilderment. "My children won't obey me. I don't know where Tamara goes when she's not at school. They won't go to church with me. They don't come home on time." As Una spoke, all three children appeared bored and disinterested. What made this family different from many other families with teens who break the rules was their recent reunion after many years of separation. The three teens had arrived in Brooklyn fourteen months earlier from Jamaica to rejoin their mother, who had been in New York alone for eleven years. During that time, Una had seen her children twice for brief visits. The last visit had been five years ago.

Tamara was the first of the children to speak up. She sharply let me know that she believed her mother had no right to make rules for her. "She thinks I'm still a little child, 'cause I was when she left. I don't have to listen now," Tamara said. As she spoke, Una began to cry, and her two sons quickly moved their chairs over to her, one on each side. Edward put his arm protectively around his mother's shoulder. Tamara now sat alone and glowered at her mother and brothers. "He wants to leave and go back to Jamaica," Tamara said, pointing at Arthur, "but every time he says so, Mommy cries and that's the end of it." Tamara in effect volunteered to be the family "truth teller." Everyone else appeared tense as she spoke. Ms. Parker tried to redirect me to Tamara's school problems, but it was clear to me that before we could deal effectively with Tamara's cutting her classes or Arthur's future plans, we needed to create a place where their very different stories of Una's migration, their eleven-year separation, and their reunion could be told.[3]

When children are separated at a young age from their parents and reunited in adolescence, many secrets have accumulated. Ghosts take up residence during the reunion: the untold stories about why a parent originally left or, conversely, why a child was sent away; the deep feelings engendered by the parting; and what has gone on in each one's life during the separation. Therapy with teens and parents who have been separated by migration, long-distance moves following divorce, being cut off after divorce, foster care, or residential treatment needs to focus first on opening all that the family members have missed in one another's lives.

I began my work with Una and her family by asking if we might construct a genogram. This visual family tree allows a family to show me quick snapshots of their development over time—marriages, births, separations, deaths—and all of the crucial entrances and exits in their lives. As often happens, the teens were extremely interested in their previously unspoken family history.

Their father had left for Miami shortly after Edward was born. He reappeared briefly, left again, and started a new family. All three children were silent and attentive while their mother recounted her desperate and unsuccessful attempts to keep her former husband connected to his children. This was one of many stories they had never heard.

In 1982, with little money and absolutely no hope for work in Jamaica, Una decided to come to New York, as her three brothers had done. Like many immigrant women in her situation, she planned for her stay to be brief. "I thought two years maximum," Una said, "and then I would go back." Placing her seven-, five-, and four-year-old children with her mother, Una left and came to the States as an undocumented immigrant. She worked as a home health aide and sent as much money as she could back to Jamaica to support her children. Shaking his head, Arthur said, "Grandma complained about how much we cost her. We never knew you sent any money. We just thought you were having a good time in New York." Just as her children had not heard true accounts of her life away from them, so Una had not heard their often difficult experiences living with her mother. Our work together required that we build a safe enough place to hold intense and previously unacknowledged feelings, contradictions, split loyalties, and distressing experiences.

Painfully Una spoke of how much she missed her children. Assurances by her mother that they were fine, coupled with a familiar pattern of grandmothers raising grandchildren in Jamaica that went back to slavery times, when parents were often separated from their children by white masters, supported Una's new decision to take the time needed to get her green card and bring her children to New York. "I imagined it would be one or two more years," Una said. "Instead it took seven years to get my green card and another year to save the money to get a bigger apartment and bring them up."

Throughout this conversation, Arthur, Tamara, and Edward were learning new things about their mother, about her struggles in New York, her terrible working conditions for low pay in the homes of sick, elderly people, her perseverance and courage on their behalf. Twice in eleven years Una had risked going home to Jamaica and reentering the United States without documentation. Her children had had no idea what this entailed and were angry that she didn't come more often. The visits were a confusing mix of agitation and distance. When Una finally brought her children to New York, she anticipated reconnecting with children who were thirteen, eleven, and ten years old, their ages when she had last seen them. Instead, three adolescents who had never been out of the countryside in Jamaica entered a two-bedroom apartment in a West Indian and Orthodox Jewish neighborhood in Brooklyn.

Una, Arthur, Tamara, and Edward were trying to negotiate two unanticipated and contradictory family life-cycle transitions at once. They were coming together to build a family just at the time in the childrens' lives when they wanted and needed more autonomy. Una, for her part, regarded them as much younger than they were. On the other hand, her rules were made for a sometimes dangerous life in Brooklyn, while Arthur, Tamara, and Edward were used to safety out in the country. Their adolescent rebellion was complicated by their anger at her leaving them years earlier and at their sudden uprooting from Jamaica. "We had no control when you left," Arthur said, "and we had no control when you brought us here." Una had long anticipated that her children would feel the same way she felt about their reunion, and so there was no place upon their arrival to express all of their feelings of loss and dislocation. Only when Una began to reveal how she had felt when she first came to New York did her children feel they had permission to show their sadness.

Our work together went on for six months. Much of the therapy was spent with each family member telling stories of their time apart, unearthing secrets, and sharing long-hidden feelings that mother and children had kept from each other for eleven years. The teens' feelings of abandonment and Una's painful guilt were spoken aloud for the first time. Many sessions were spent poring over photographs, each telling the stories behind the pictures. They exchanged humorous incidents of Una's life in New York and funny stories from the childrens' lives in Jamaica for the first time. Not only had the painful experiences gone underground before our work together, but none had dared tell about any happy times, either. Una thought her children would think she didn't care about them if they heard about any good times she had away from them. The children, for their part, imagined their mother would think they didn't need her if she thought they were having fun without her. While recounting the separate good times was bittersweet for each family member, I suggested that these stories held resources for building their lives together now.

As mother and children's separate pasts intertwined to weave a contemporary and multifaceted story of migration, separation, and reunion, the Parkers' individual lives and their relationships with one another changed profoundly. By the close of therapy, Tamara was attending school regularly. Arthur had agreed to postpone his decision about returning to Jamaica until he completed a two-year computer technician training course. Una grew into her role as the mother of teenagers, holding fast to a few necessary rules while also helping her children learn to negotiate the sometimes confusing terrain of their inner-city neighborhood. The children's anger at their mother dissolved, replaced by a sense of family solidarity. With her children's support, Una went back to school at night to become a licensed vocational nurse. Arthur and Edward alternated meeting their mother after class to accompany her on the subway ride back home.

While the Parkers had a long separation and many experiences that had become secret or taboo, even much shorter disjunctures between parents and teens can breed a sense of alienation, a feeling of not knowing how to catch up with one another's lives. A taciturn adolescent who sees his father and stepmother once a year for two weeks, a fourteen-year-old girl who visits home once a month from a residential treatment center, or a worried teen whose mother has been hospitalized for two months for depression all need mutual storytelling time with the adults in their lives. Left to their own devices, most adolescents will not initiate this process. Parents who haven't seen their teens for a while and who ask directly, "What's been happening in your life?" will probably be met with shrugs or very short answers. On the other hand, parents who casually open the stories of what's been happening in *their* lives during a separation and remain open to hearing what life is like for their teen will likely generate an easy give-and-take.

WHEN TEENS KNOW TOO LITTLE: RESOLVING SECRETS OF IDENTITY

In popular parlance, "adolescence" refers to a stage in an individual's life. In my own experience, adolescence is also a powerful season in family relationships. As a child moves closer to the doorway of adulthood, tension abounds in any family—how much freedom to give a teen, how much responsibility, how many more chances there are to get it "right." Celebrations of each step toward grown-up competence alternate with regrets over lost opportunities. And if secrets have been kept that directly affect an adolescent's capacity to know him- or herself, pressure will be building in the family. The time before a child leaves home is rapidly running out, while the time that a secret has been kept from a child has grown longer and longer.

Powerful countervailing forces toward burying a central secret ever deeper or finally opening it sometimes appear in the guise of severe adolescent and family crises. The behavior and emotional turmoil shown by a teen can be a distorted mirror of the content of a secret. This provides a rationale to frightened parents to keep the secret, out of the belief that to open it would provoke even greater upset.

The teen years are often the last chance for parents to open a secret that goes to the heart of a child's identity—adoption, parentage, missing family members, or cultural and ethnic background—especially if they wish to do so under their own guidance, protection, and control. Revelation of a long-standing secret whose essence belongs to a child will have reverberations across all family relationships.

Kaye and Bob Keeler requested to see me with their son, Josh, sixteen, and their daughter, Brianna, eleven. When we met in the waiting room, anger and defensiveness between parents and son were palpable. As Josh sat appearing sullen and unhappy, his father told me, "Josh is in trouble again." When I asked what he meant by "again," Bob told me that Josh got into trouble every autumn, shortly after school started. This time the trouble was bigger. Josh had stolen money off a teacher's desk. He had sworn and brandished his fist at her when she confronted him. He'd been suspended from school. And, despite eyewitnesses, he continued to deny his responsibility for the incident.

The timing of Josh's troubles intrigued me. When I asked for more details, I learned that "autumn" meant mid- to late October. "He ruins Halloween for me every year," Brianna complained. When I tried to find out what else might be going on in the family in October, Kaye adamantly stated her belief that each year school pressures became too much for Josh. She and Bob also told me they believed that when November rolled around, Josh always pulled himself together because Christmas was coming and he wanted good gifts. This year, however, his behavior was simply intolerable and waiting for him to settle down on his own was unacceptable to the parents and to the school. Bob insisted that the only problem in the family was "Josh's behavior. We're here about Josh, and I'm just fed up."

It's certainly not unusual for any family with a troublesome teen to express anger and frustration. As I talked with the Keelers, however, I noticed that any attempt on my part to find out other family information or to talk about anything besides Josh's behavior was immediately blocked. All family anxiety was centered on Josh. In contrast, Bob described Brianna as "a wonderful girl who never gives us a drop of trouble." As her father praised her, Brianna smiled at me sweetly, and Josh pulled his cap down over his eyes.

Between our first and second meetings, Josh came home drunk several times, adding a new problem and keeping the focus on himself. Just as with the stealing, he denied drinking despite obvious hangovers. Kaye and Bob responded to Josh's drinking with an odd mixture of fury and concern. "First they yell at me," Josh complained, "and the next minute they're trying to hug me. I just feel so confused by them. But you know, that's nothing new." When I tried to ask Josh a bit more about his feelings of confusion, he shrugged and said, "I'm tired of talking. Ask them."

The combination of Kaye and Bob's absolute refusal to allow me to explore issues other than Josh's behavior, the emergence of a new problem right after we began our work, and Josh's habitual "October surprises" made me begin to wonder about secrets. I have often found that when a family can speak about only one topic, there is an underlying fear that broader talk will lead us to areas that are off-limits. It is not unusual for a family member, especially an adolescent, to "cooperate" with the family's unspoken need to avoid new conversational territory. While some teens act in ways that tear open family secrets, others, like Josh, seem to collude with the secrecy by distracting everyone. In addition, upsetting behavior that recurs seemingly on schedule often both points to and diverts attention from some unspeakable anniversary, most often one of loss.

At our third meeting Kaye and Bob showed up at my door alone. I've learned that when parents arrive for a therapy session without the children who were expected to attend, secrets are often on the agenda. So I prodded gently and asked if there was anything in the family's history that they thought it would be helpful for me to know. Hesitating and looking at Bob for reassurance that it was okay to speak, Kaye began. "I'm not sure if this is of any importance, but Bob is not Josh's father. He's Brianna's father. Bob adopted Josh when he was ten months old. He was just a baby, you know, and everyone thought it would be better if he didn't know."

As the story slowly unfolded, I learned that Kaye had been briefly married to Jerry, an exciting but irresponsible man who died drunk in a car crash sixteen years earlier on October 19, when Josh was three months old. Kaye's parents, especially her mother, advised her to get on with her life. When she met and married Bob, everyone agreed that the life and death of Jerry should remain a secret.

I asked Kaye and Bob if they had thought about when they would tell Josh about his biological father. Bob said he didn't think they would ever tell him, and reiterated that he was Josh's father. Kaye responded softly that she thought about this question frequently. She felt that when Josh had a serious relationship with a woman, she would want him to know. Bob had had no idea that she was considering ever telling Josh. As is often the case, thoughts and feelings about the secret had also become secret.

Their secret was one that did not simply reside between them. Many family members and friends knew the actual story. Kaye and Bob lived in a small community. The local newspaper had published accounts of the car crash. "Who do you think will tell Josh if you don't?" I asked. "How do you think he'll respond if he learns the story from other people?"

We were at the beginning of a process that would take many months. While Josh was no doubt responding to the presence of this core secret about his origins, I felt there was no need to rush. The usual pattern was for Josh to erupt in misbehavior every October and then settle down. We could take our time to consider all of the ramifications of opening this secret. Premature disclosure of a central family secret can often cause harm for individual family members and relationships. When a secret poses no immediate danger to a teen, it is better to proceed slowly, building a relationship safety net of sufficient strength. As I discovered, I needed to help Kaye dissolve enormous shame and address both parents' fears before they could move forward with telling Josh.

Part of what drove this secret had begun well before Jerry's death. Kaye and Jerry's relationship had started in high school. Jerry came from a working-class family, while Kaye's family was upper-middle-class. Her parents forbade her to date Jerry. The young couple sneaked around to be together, which no doubt added to the excitement of their relationship. In short order, Kaye became pregnant with Josh. Both Kaye's parents and Jerry's parents heaped great shame on Kaye and insisted that they marry. Kaye's own parents denounced her for becoming pregnant and insisted on a small wedding with no reception afterward. When Jerry was killed, his parents blamed Kaye and cut off their relationship with her. They hadn't seen Josh since he was an infant, but Kaye lived in fear that they would one day knock at her door.

As we grew to know each other, Kaye spoke poignantly about feeling sad every October. "It's not that I'm still in love with Jerry," she explained to Bob, "but he was my husband and the pain is still there." In fact, Kaye withdrew every October, uncharacteristically spending a lot of time by herself. When she said she was sure no one noticed, Bob commented that he had indeed noticed but was afraid to ask what was troubling her. Again, the secret was underpinned by more secrets.

It was now a small leap to begin to wonder about the impact on Josh of his mother's annual deep sadness. Like many children who see their parents sad but sense they should not ask why, Josh went on a yearly campaign to distract his mother. He succeeded brilliantly. In short order his mother was mad, not sad, and the whole family became busy dealing with Josh. Over the years, however, Josh's behavior had changed from the diversionary antics of a small child to actions, such as stealing and drinking, that reminded his mother more and more of his biological father. Kaye remarked, "My mother said if Josh doesn't know about Jerry, then he won't follow in his footsteps. He'll turn out like Bob and be responsible and clear-headed. I don't understand it, but I guess she was wrong."

When there is a secret about a child's origins, parents become hypervigilant at the first sign of negative behavior that is reminiscent of the biological parent. As parents anxiously over-react, a child often responds with more of the same behavior. A vicious cycle is set in motion. Because there is a secret, a more balanced view of the missing parent is impossible to elaborate. The child gradually becomes the parents' worst nightmare, with whispered explanations of "It must be in his genes."

As Kaye and Bob began to connect Josh's behavior with the core secret, they became convinced that they wanted to tell him. At this juncture, I asked them to think about the impact of opening the secret to other people in the family. Telling a secret regarding another person's identity is never so uncomplicated as simply telling that one person. In the Keeler family, discussions were needed first with Kaye's parents and Bob's parents. This was done not to ask their permission, but to enable Kaye and Bob to inform them respectfully of their decision and to deal with any anxiety up front. A broad climate of family support was being created. We talked about why Brianna also needed to be told the secret. Not to do so would create a new secret and separate Josh from his half-sister just at a time when strong relationships were most essential.

Finally we made plans for Kaye to reconnect with Jerry's parents. They were important both as Josh's grandparents and as people who could offer him a more complete view of his father.

I asked Kaye and Bob whether they wanted to open the secret with Josh at home or in a family therapy session. "What would you advise?" Kaye asked me. I told them that most often opening secrets to teens is best done at home, in their natural setting, unless the secret involves danger, which was certainly not the situation here. "Telling Josh at home will make it easier to sort out all of the stories of your lives together again and again," I told them.

When Kaye and Bob opened the secret with Josh, he was, at first, understandably angry that this had been kept from him. Kaye talked with him about her own pain and confusion when his father died and her deep wish to protect him from any hurt. Over several months, she told Josh both positive and troubling stories about his dad, helping him to appreciate that people are complex. We worked in therapy to help Josh integrate this profound new knowledge about himself and his family. At home, Josh pored over photographs he had never seen. He learned where his eyes and nose and chin came from. Josh had never before seen his early baby pictures. He particularly wanted me to see a picture of Jerry holding him shortly after his birth. He met his paternal grandparents, who welcomed him and gave him books his father had especially loved. Kaye and Bob took him to the cemetery where his father was buried, enabling Josh and his mom to mourn openly and together for the first time.

As the secret opened, relationships began to change. Josh and Brianna began to have fun with each other, replacing their previous anger and distance. Brianna's "perfect child" role dissipated, and we spent a session focused on some homework she hadn't turned in. Much to Bob's surprise, Josh approached him more, not less. And Kaye and Bob began to integrate the reality of her first marriage into their relationship. Jerry had been a taboo topic. The couple had lived for years with the pretense that Kaye had never been married before. A critical part of her biography had gone underground, buried in shame. Bob, in turn, had lived with a mystery, for while he knew that Kaye had been married before and that

Jerry had been killed, he was unable to ask his wife what her life was like before he met her. "I lived with assumptions. I lived wondering how she felt about him, how that compared to how she felt about me," Bob said. In turn, Bob had never felt comfortable telling Kaye about his life before she met him. The central family secret had prevented this couple from living one of the most important aspects of an intimate relationship, sharing earlier history and retelling yourself to someone who loves you.

The Keelers initially came to see me in October. By January they opened a secret that had been kept from Josh and contaminated all family relationships for fifteen years. The following September, after much work and many changes, they gathered all three sets of grandparents and held a moving ceremony in which Bob and Josh openly "adopted" each other.

Located deep in a family's history and originally made with good intentions to protect a young child, many secrets gather velocity during adolescence. When a teen is experiencing difficulties that seem to make no sense and that do not resolve despite a parent's best efforts, it is likely that a secret underpins the painful puzzle. Secrets that require deception, lying, hiding, or betrayal make clear and meaningful conversation impossible just at a time in family relationships when communication is crucial. The normal unfolding of life that teens require is choked in families where there is a central secret.

While every secret is its own special conundrum, conceived and brought forth in each family's unique history and culture, opening painful secrets with any adolescent requires strikingly similar dimensions—thoughtful timing, an atmosphere of safety and support, and a connected, empathic relationship in which to live out the aftermath.

Teens and secrets forge a profound paradox. Developing a separate, knowable, reliable self requires keeping some secrets. And nothing can derail a teen's sense of selfhood so much as when core secrets are kept from them. Unresolved family secrets follow us like uninvited shadows as we take our tentative steps away from home. But as we'll see in the last chapter, it's never too late to make new decisions about the secrets in our lives.

Chapter

II

It's Never Too Late:
Resolving Long-Held Secrets Among Parents, Grown Children, and Adult Siblings

—◆—

Tell them about how you're never really a whole person if you remain silent, because there's always that one little piece inside you that wants to be spoken out, and if you keep ignoring it, it gets madder and madder and hotter and hotter, and if you don't speak it out, one day it will just up and punch you in the mouth from the inside.

—*Audre Lorde*

ON A COLD MARCH DAY in 1985, I opened my office door to meet seventy-four-year-old Carrie Allenby and her seventy-five-year-old husband, George. Rather than sitting next to each other, in the way my consulting-room chairs are normally arranged, both quickly moved their chairs to sit on opposite sides of the room. Carrie's silver hair was pulled tightly into a bun. Although the room was warm, she kept her coat on, and I noticed that she wore little white cotton gloves, which were unusual for the wintertime. George sat rigidly in his seat, never taking his eyes off his wife. "We've been told to see you by Carrie's doctor," George began. "She's in the hospital, but they sent us over here to talk to you—I don't exactly know why. We've tried everything. Carrie's been given antidepressants, tranquilizers, lots of therapy. Nothing works."[1]

UNTYING A FIFTY-YEAR-OLD KNOT

Carrie had been hospitalized for unrelenting anxiety three weeks earlier. This was her fourth hospitalization in as many years. "My husband doesn't understand," Carrie said. "I just have these fears and I have to wash my hands." Carrie went on to tell me that she was terrified of germs. She spent hours each day washing her hands and weeping. For over a decade, she had not touched another human being, including her husband, her two grown daughters, Catherine, forty-nine, and Ellen, forty-eight, and her young-adult grandson and granddaughter. Earlier in her life Carrie had been a piano teacher. Now she would not touch her beloved piano—she believed the keys were covered with germs. Nor would she shop, handle money, play cards, travel, visit friends and family, or let anyone into her home. Lurking germs held both Carrie and George hostage. Their only joint outings at this point were to see myriad doctors and therapists. Carrie's fear of germs and constant hand-washing were now the only allowable topics of conversation in the family.

At our first meeting George and Carrie insisted that the only conflict they'd ever had was over Carrie's hand-washing. When I asked about other problems during their half-century-long marriage, George replied, "I don't remember having any." A sensible and logical man, George felt certain he could talk Carrie out of her fears. When he failed to persuade her, they would argue. Following each argument, they would go to separate corners of their home, where each remained sad, lonely, and angry until the next fight a few hours later.

While all manner of individual therapies had been tried with Carrie, no one had ever worked with George, Carrie, and their grown daughters. I suggested that we all meet the next day. Shortly after that session began, I realized that what Carrie called her "phobia" was now the tune to which everyone in the family danced. Ellen and Catherine fought with each other over who would "save" their parents and who would "cure" their mother. They competed to come up with new approaches: acupuncture, hypnosis, biofeedback. They argued over "who had it worse," their mom or their dad. Both daughters seemed mired in unexplainable guilt and spent most of their free time worrying about their parents.

By our third meeting Carrie had left the hospital. All of the family members were downhearted that Carrie was no better. At that juncture, I asked to see Ellen and Catherine once without their parents.

During that meeting each told me that their mother and father, separately and secretly, complained bitterly about each other. When the daughters tried to raise these grievances in joint conversations, each parent denied having made such complaints. Ellen implored me to see her parents separately in order to hear their secret dissatisfactions about one another. I declined, knowing that if I did so, I would simply become "one of the kids."

At the end of my session with the daughters Catherine gave me a clue to the dilemma of our work together. "My parents don't like outsiders, including professional helpers and anyone else outside the immediate family." Outsiders, she explained, were to be treated with polite distance and diplomacy. Genuine conversations with outsiders, certainly including me, were doomed.

I asked Ellen and Catherine if they would be willing to have a session with their parents in which they raised their concerns in front of me. I told them I would do whatever I could to keep the conversation going but that they would truly lead the meeting. With some hesitation, they agreed.

The family entered for our fifth session. The daughters took their now-familiar seats between their parents. With great trepidation, Catherine and Ellen each began to speak about problems in their parents' marriage. The first of many taboos was broken. At first George and Carrie continued to insist that their only problem was Carrie's fear of germs and incessant hand-washing. Rather than back down, as they usually did, Ellen and Catherine held their ground. Bit by bit George and Carrie began to acknowledge other conflicts between them. George said he wanted to travel and felt resentful that Carrie refused. Carrie, in turn, said she felt George criticized her unfairly. Their conversation took baby steps away from the overwhelming focus on Carrie's "phobia." None-theless, their differences seemed quite ordinary. They argued over what television show to watch or what to eat for dinner. When their daughters tried to raise questions about their relationship over time, George and Carrie once again insisted that they had been getting along fine until "Carrie's problem." Then Catherine began to push: "I remember there was lots of distance between you when we were little—why was that?" The silent tension grew unbearable. Ellen suddenly insisted that we stop, protesting, "My father has a heart condition. I don't think we should go any further with this." George and Carrie nodded in agreement.

What, I wondered, had happened in this family to tie every-one up in protective knots? Our meeting had certainly challenged the myth that the only problem was Carrie's "phobia," but when Catherine asked about the past, walls of concrete seemed to go up.

I wrote George and Carrie a letter after this difficult meeting and asked them to consider if they wanted to continue in therapy. I told them that Ellen seemed to be saying that they needed to be protected, and I wondered if they agreed. I assured them that if they chose to go forward and open what appeared to be some old and very painful wounds, I would provide a safe place to do so. I received no reply.

Three weeks later Catherine came to see me alone. "After our meeting with you, we all went back to my sister's apartment. It was the first time my mother had been there in years. We had the first open family argument that I can ever remember. My father was especially angry at Ellen for suggesting that his heart condition meant he couldn't handle things. He seemed determined to let us know that he could handle things just fine." The content of their argument seemed far less important to Catherine than the fact that things were beginning to come onto the table. During the heated discussion, Ellen, who until then had presented herself to the family as a single woman, revealed that she had been secretly living with a boyfriend for five years. She went on to tell them that she was struggling with a drinking problem and had just begun to seek help. For the first time in many years, the family was attending to matters besides Carrie's "phobia."

Catherine asked if she might continue to see me by herself in order to become "less involved" in her parents' troubles. I agreed. She said she doubted that her parents would be back to see me.

Three months later my phone rang. It was Carrie. "I think we need to come see you," she said. Carrie never had phoned me before, since the telephone harbored germs. I offered to meet them two days later.

When I went to the waiting room to greet them, I was struck by how different they looked. They seemed lighter somehow; they were dressed in bright colors for the first time since I'd known them. And while Carrie still kept her gloves on, she had taken off her coat. Our conversation began humorously—another change. Carrie told me a story about washing George's face in bed forty years earlier. "Was it fun?" I asked. "Well, he sure didn't mind," Carrie said, laughing. "Do you still wash his face in bed?" I teased. "We sleep in separate bedrooms now," George replied sadly, abruptly changing the mood. Then the long-shut door swung open. For the next hour and a half, we reconstructed the painful story of this couple's life together. Secret after secret spilled forth: Carrie's enormous fears about becoming pregnant again after the birth of two babies within two years; a doctor who refused to give her birth-control information, telling her to go home and have more children; ferocious arguments between George and Carrie about sex; George becoming impotent following a medical treatment in his forties; separate bedrooms; unresolved fights about sex conveniently replaced with arguments about hand-washing. "We had far more conflicts over sex than we've ever had over my hand-washing," Carrie said.

Slowly the room filled with the power of the unspoken, the unvoiced, the untold. Then Carrie, her voice shaking, her eyes filling with tears, told me a secret she had kept for fifty years. "Catherine was born before we got married," Carrie said, her head bowed in shame. A secret that would probably never be created in today's world had shaped and limited this family's relationships for half a century.

When Carrie's parents discovered the pregnancy in 1935, they quickly sent her to a relative in a neighboring state. George went after her, telling his family only that he had found work—explanation enough during the Depression. Shortly after Catherine's birth, George's mother discovered the truth from a friend. Rather than deal with her son, she wrote Carrie a brutal, excoriating letter, blaming her for the out-of-wedlock birth—a letter that Carrie had never told George about until that day in my office. She wept as if the letter had arrived yesterday—tears she had hidden from George for nearly fifty years.

Shortly after Catherine's birth, George, earning forty cents an hour, saved up enough money for a marriage license. The couple were married by a justice of the peace, with no family or friends in attendance, no celebration, and a heavy burden of shame.

"Do your daughters know this story?" I asked. "We never speak about it," Carrie replied, "but I know they know. They must know because my whole family and George's family know. We look at wedding pictures together from Catherine's marriage. But they've never asked to see our wedding pictures. It's because they know and they don't want us to know they know—I'm sure of it."

Carrie had hidden their marriage license in the bottom of an old trunk in the basement. George and Carrie never openly celebrated their wedding anniversary. Their daughters' birthdays went unmarked. And no one ever asked why.

I heard and held their secret tenderly. In the weeks that followed, this unexpected experience catalyzed rapid change. The rigid boundary that this secret had erected between the family and the outside world, so eloquently expressed in Carrie's overwhelming fear of germs, had been breached. Carrie began to play the piano again. She also asked me if I could arrange for her to meet with a "germ expert." Clearly she was ready to come out of the corner into which her "phobia" had painted her. I arranged a meeting with a family physician who replied honestly and respectfully to all of her questions. "How long can a germ live in a shoe?" Carrie asked. "Not long," came the reply. Carrie laughed and cried, and then she turned to George: "Let's go shopping."

Their new openness allowed them to spend time apart as well. George went on a fishing trip, and Carrie spent the night at her sister's home for the first time in many years.

I suggested we make a video of their story to show their daughters, but I was at least ten steps behind them. George, a previous master of circuitous conversation, looked at me and declared, "No, that's too indirect—let's just bring them in for a meeting and tell them."

The first thing I noticed when they walked in was Carrie's hands. They were uncovered for the first time since I had met her. Carrie began the meeting, her voice choked with fear and anguish. She took their marriage license out of her purse and laid it on the table before Catherine. "We've always feared that since you were born before we married, you would hold it against us," she told her elder daughter. "We've both known for as long as I can remember," Catherine said sadly. "But we never felt we could talk to you about it."

The session took many unexpected turns. George spoke at length about what that time in their lives had been like. Movingly he told his daughters how much he had loved Carrie and wanted to be with her when her family sent her away. Among the many family secrets that had been hidden from Catherine and Ellen was their parents' love story and the difficult beginning of their life together. While it was the Depression and no one they knew had money, George still had felt it was his personal fault that they were poor. They lived bereft of support from either family. They hid from former friends. Finally, after Ellen's birth, they moved back home, where more and more conversations went underground lest they touch upon this secret.

Later in the session Catherine became angry, and a new story emerged. "Why did you treat me so badly when I became pregnant before my wedding?" A secret untold had simply repeated itself in the next generation. While George and Carrie did attend Catherine's wedding, she had been made to leave their house in shame. Twenty-seven years after the fact, George and Carrie apologized and asked Catherine to forgive them. "We did exactly what was done to us, and it was wrong both times," Carrie said.

Toward the end of the meeting, Ellen said vehemently, "This has to be a turning point. You have to promise us—no more secrets. No more Mom telling me something and then saying I can't tell Dad or Dad telling me something and saying I can't tell Mom or Catherine." George and Carrie agreed.

As they stood to leave, Carrie walked over to me, took my two hands in hers, and thanked me. I was honored to be the first person she had touched in many years.

Opening this central secret was only the beginning. Months of work followed. Together we looked back a half century at the cultural values and pressures that had shaped their families' harsh response to Catherine's birth. At the time when Catherine was born, a birth out of wedlock was loaded with unspeakable shame. Premarital sex was condemned, and women took the brunt of the social punishment for it. "I remember hearing," Carrie said, "that boys just couldn't help themselves, that it was up to girls to stop them. I was already a young woman and I thought that whatever happened was certainly my fault." Reexamining these beliefs in the context of the more liberal 1980s allowed George and Carrie to challenge them—and ultimately to forgive their own parents.

We also explored how the painful secret had been repeated for three generations. Carrie, Catherine, and most recently Catherine's daughter had all become pregnant before marriage. Perhaps these pregnancies were indicators of misguided family loyalty; perhaps they were an awkward attempt to open the original secret; or perhaps they were a sign that that it is impossible to learn from experiences that nobody admits have happened.

As we completed our work together I was struck by the enormous changes in Carrie, George, Catherine, and Ellen and in their relationships with one another. No longer was Carrie's life handicapped by a debilitating psychiatric symptom. She shopped and traveled and entertained in her home again. Her white cotton gloves went to the scrap heap. When Carrie and George walked into my office, his arm was gently around her shoulder. Catherine and Ellen no longer spent their time and energy focused on their mother, her problems, or their parents' marriage. Family loyalty could now be expressed in words and actions rather than by silence. Catherine and Ellen made a sweet secret, giving their parents a surprise anniversary party, the first in their half-century marriage. Carrie said good-bye to me, this "outsider" whom they had allowed into their lives, by bringing me a homemade rhubarb pie.

COMPLEX LIVES, COMPLEX SOLUTIONS

Carrie—and her entire family—had become prisoners of her many diagnoses and treatments. Terms like "obsessive-compulsive," "anxiety disorder," and "phobic" filled her charts, oversimplifying and totalizing her complex life story. An entire textbook's worth of psychiatric interventions had been tried with Carrie— individual psychodynamic therapy, cognitive-behavioral therapy, antianxiety medication, antidepressant medication, hospitalizations. During one hospitalization, in an effort to "desensitize" her, she was made to pick up other people's dirty laundry. In another, a microbiologist lectured her for forty-five minutes about germs. The psychiatric resident who first asked me to meet Carrie had told me that the hospital staff was recommending that she go to a nursing home. "Is she physically ill?" I asked. "Not at all," came the reply. "The staff just feels her husband needs a break." Carrie was regarded by the mental-health professionals working with her as "resistant," "unworkable," "a crazy old lady." She met with a psychiatrist every six weeks simply to get her prescriptions renewed. When her life turned around after the central secret opened, she told me that she didn't want to see the psychiatrist anymore, and that she wanted help to stop all of her medications. "When I ask him the side effects of my medications, he tells me not to worry myself about such things. And anyway, he's such a downer," she told me. "He's always talking about nursing homes. I don't need a nursing home." Indeed she didn't.

I feel enormous concern about all the other Carries whose therapy ignores the likely presence of painful secrets, instead applying intervention after intervention and ultimately blaming the client for not changing. In today's managed-care environment, it's ever more likely that biochemical interventions will be the first approach chosen, perhaps coupled with very brief, one-size-fits-all therapy. Unearthing deeply buried secrets and working effectively with their tangled consequences takes time, trust, safety, and commitment. And every such therapy must be unique and tailor-made.

RISKING OPENNESS

My experience with Carrie and her family has been replicated over and over in my work with older parents and their adult children, and with grown siblings. When a call comes to me for such therapy, I can be almost certain that we will be dealing with decades of pain and alienation, confusion and misunderstanding, secrets and lies.

Motivations for starting this work are complex, and the range of initial issues is enormous. A long and bitter parental marriage has finally dissolved in divorce, catching grown siblings in a torrent of loyalty pulls; an elderly parent has recently died, leaving a will that omits one child; a problem or crisis in the grandchild generation—drugs, alcohol, trauma—activates the entire extended family; a sister fails in work and begins to borrow money from a more successful brother, while demanding this be kept secret from her husband and children; an aging parent's Alzheimer's disease raises questions about a secret child who died as a toddler; a brother is given the opportunity to buy the family homestead at a price that cheats the other siblings of their financial legacy; an elderly parent's looming death forces a family to deal with a sister who has been mentally ill since adolescence and sheltered in the family home.

Most often, one adult sibling starts the ball rolling, inviting others to begin this work. I've sat with one remaining parent and an only adult son or daughter. I've also met with twelve or fifteen people—elderly parents, middle-aged siblings, their spouses, and young-adult grandchildren—all coming together to take the risk of opening what has stayed shut tight for too many years.

Each time I meet with a new family, I'm impressed all over again by the ways that certain long-standing secrets prevent people from deeply touching each other, create inauthentic and unreliable relationships, and constrain genuine expression. When secrets are maintained for decades, all family relationships become skewed by covert alliances and the mysterious cutting off of certain individuals. Family members are "missing in action," physically present but emotionally absent. Seemingly meaningless feuds have often kept them separate and distant. Individuals have been forced into narrow roles, their personal development thwarted. Key life choices have been made without sufficient knowledge. And each time I finish a first meeting—usually three or four hours long, because of the geographic and psychological distance that people travel to begin this work—I'm moved once again by the courage people bring to this endeavor, and by the human desire to heal and to connect.

"SURELY I KILLED HIM": RESOLVING A SEVENTEEN-YEAR SECRET

On a dark December afternoon I made my way to the psychiatric emergency room for my weekly supervision session with beginning psychiatric residents who were learning family therapy. When I arrived, I met Alan Franco, thirty-three, who had been brought to the psychiatric emergency room by his parents, Eva, sixty, and Jack, sixty-one. For the past several weeks Alan, who lived with his parents, had been increasingly agitated. The previous night he had brandished a baseball bat at his mother. "Every winter we go through this," Alan's father said quietly. "This year it seems worse than ever."

As I sat behind the one-way mirror, providing consultation over the telephone to the young therapist who sat with the Francos, I wondered what could have happened in this family's life to bring them to this point. Eva and Jack looked utterly drained, their faces almost gray. Alan was highly agitated. Looking disheveled, he could barely sit in his seat.

Suddenly Alan began shouting, "The story of Michael, the

story of Michael, we have to discuss the story of Michael." Looking very pained, Jack leaned over and quietly said, "We're not here about Michael—we're here about you." Gently the therapist asked, "Who's Michael?" "Michael's gone," Eva said as her eyes flooded with tears. "He was our eldest son, Alan's older brother. He's gone over seventeen years now."

Michael had been a star student and athlete who died suddenly of a cerebral aneurysm when he was twenty and Alan was seventeen. He had married shortly before his death, leaving a pregnant wife, Sandy. In the aftermath of Michael's death, Sandy and the Francos had fought bitterly. When her now seventeen-year-old son was born, she denied the Francos any opportunity to be with him.

Their losses were so painful and overwhelming that each family member had simply stopped talking about Michael, his life, or his death. I suggested to the therapist that she inquire about how each family member had mourned this terrible loss.

"I go to my church alone every week. I light a candle, and then I sit in the back by myself," Eva said tearfully. No one in the family had known she did this. "I visit the cemetery. I go to Michael's grave alone two or three times a month," Jack said haltingly. "I've never told Eva or Alan that I go." Alan remained silent while his parents spoke, and then refused to add his own response to the therapist's question. While not a secret per se Michael's death had become a taboo subject, constantly on each one's mind and never mentioned.

How, I wondered, had Michael's death frozen Alan in his own development? It was as if time had stopped for him in late adolescence. He had never finished high school. He didn't work. He had no outside relationships. For most of the year he spent his days and nights in front of the television set. His parents never confronted him, never insisted that he find work or contribute to their household. Eva said, "Frankly, I'm afraid of him. I leave him alone. We live around each other, and that usually works, except when he gets like this."

Alan "got like this" every year shortly before Christmas. While it was not the anniversary of Michael's death, Christmas seemed especially loaded with memories that the Francos wanted to escape. The family's celebration of Christmas had been rigidly identical for the past seventeen years. Eva said she decorated the house in order to "pretend that we're happy and that we're just like other families." And Alan behaved strangely, menacingly, sending another powerful though covert message: "We're not happy, we're not like other families."

"Each year I put out a little crèche that Michael made when he was twelve," Eva said. This particular decoration seemed to signal Alan to become more outrageous, distracting his mother from her obvious pain. "I make a nice dinner on Christmas," Eva said sadly, "but Alan won't come to the table. My husband and I wish we could visit our relatives, but Alan threatens that he'll wreck the apartment if we go. One year a therapist he was seeing told us we should go anyway. When we returned, Alan had trashed his room."

Alan had seen eight different therapists since Michael's death and had spent considerable time in a psychiatric day-treatment program. He had also gone through several different courses of antidepressant medication. But in seventeen years no one had ever suggested that Alan and his family should be seen together. Only the immediate threat of violence had brought them to our emergency room.

Toward the end of the first session, Jack commented, "We just have to get through Christmas, and then Alan will settle down again." But the strategy of "let's just get through Christmas" was no longer working. Something had to change to allow this family to grieve openly and begin to move on.

The Francos used few words with each other. It seemed to me that it would do little good to urge them or even invite them to talk at more length about Michael, his death, or the loss of their grandson to them. Instead, during a short break before the family left that day, I called the therapist to come behind the one-way mirror and suggested to her that she ask each of them to bring a symbol to the next meeting—something that would show who Michael was to them. I thought that through sharing these symbols during the therapy session, they might be able to shift their pattern of isolated grieving and connect more openly with one another. I had no idea that this ceremony would also bring forth a secret Alan had been harboring for seventeen years.

When the family came for their second meeting, they all appeared more calm, less anxious and upset. The therapist quietly asked them to share their symbols of Michael. Slowly Eva began. "I brought a poem about a mother's love for her son. I found this in a book shortly after Michael died, and I copied it and put it in my wallet. I've never shown it to them." As she softly read the poem to them, she began to weep. Jack reached over and took her hand. Alan sat perfectly still as his eyes flooded. Jack brought out Michael's high-school class ring. In a soft voice he revealed that he had carried it in his pocket every day since Michael's funeral. Finally Alan took out a photograph of two handsome boys. The photo had been taken at Michael's high-school graduation. It showed Michael and Alan with their arms around each other's shoulders as Michael tossed his graduation cap in the air.

I suggested to the therapist that each family member hand his or her symbol to the others, tangibly connecting them in their previously solitary grief. Spontaneously each began to tell stories about Michael for the first time. In sharp contrast to the first session, when Alan had fidgeted and shouted, he listened attentively to his mother and father. Eva and Jack's long-hidden hopes and dreams about Michael came pouring forth. Then it was Alan's turn to speak.

"We played baseball together all the time," Alan said. He hung his head and sat speechless for three or four very long minutes. The therapist remained silent, respecting Alan's struggle to speak. "Two years before Michael died, I hit him in the head with a baseball. It was an accident. Surely I killed him," Alan sobbed. The very air in the room seemed to disappear for a moment as each took in the magnitude of what Alan had just said. Then Eva reached over and silently took Alan's hand in hers. "It wasn't like that," Jack finally said through his tears. "It wasn't your fault, it was never your fault. I never knew you thought that."

For seventeen years Alan had harbored his enormous secret guilt. When Michael died, the family was in such shock that no one had ever told Alan the medical explanation for his brother's death. And he had never asked. Later Alan took his sister-in-law's cutting herself and her son off from the family as further confirmation of his culpability. Not once in all of the therapy Alan sat through had he even mentioned his belief about his part in his brother's death. If anything, individual therapy had only reinforced the family silence, their protective and isolated style of mourning. Note after note in Alan's thick psychiatric file spoke of "dysfunction," "clinical depression," "unresolved mourning," "personality disorder," and so on. But the meaning of Alan's unremitting pain remained as secret and unexplored as his unexpressed guilt and anguish. As the family left that day Alan turned to the therapist and asked if she would help him find some good vocational training. Eva said quietly, "We need to write Sandy."

The Francos were just at the beginning of the longer work that would be needed for Alan to become a fully functioning adult and for them to reconnect with their daughter-in-law and grandson. But they had already begun to shift the patterns of silence and distance that had pervaded their family for so many years.

Their loss of Michael had been so shocking and profound that words were simply insufficient. Unable to talk together about the tragedy in their family, the Francos, like many families, grew disconnected in other areas of life. Separation and mutual silence became the fertile soil for Alan's self-condemning secret.

We live in a time when talking is often seen as the *only* mode for people to connect and express themselves. When speech becomes impossible, other human resources—affection, writing, symbols, rituals—need to be used to promote healing and to alter encrusted taboos and secrets.

A PILGRIMAGE TO THE WALL: OPENING THE SECRETS OF VIETNAM

"I want to reconnect with my children—I was told you were somebody who could help me with that. Can you or not?" Wally

Sims asked me in our initial telephone conversation. There was an edge of anger and impatience in his voice. I replied that there was a lot I needed to know, and invited him in for a consultation.

At our first meeting, Wally, forty-eight years old, walked quickly from the waiting room into my office. Before I could ask a question, he identified himself as divorced for nine years and with no current contact with his grown son, Frankie, twenty-six, and daughter, Eloise, twenty-five, their spouses, or his four young grandchildren. "They don't want anything to do with me," Wally said, "and I don't really blame them. I wasn't much of a father." Wally went on to tell me of years of alcoholism, intermittent unemployment, and uncontrollable bouts of anger leading to abuse of his wife and son. He spoke with remorse, sadness, and confusion that his life had come to a place where he had lost his entire family.

When I met Wally, he had been sober for three years. He attended Alcoholics Anonymous. Since there was no history of alcoholism in his family, I wondered why he had turned to alcohol for so many years and how he had decided to go into recovery. "It's a long story," Wally sighed. And clearly, it was a story I was not about to hear in our first meeting. He spoke frantically about his intense wish to see his children and grandchildren. But he became silent whenever I reached for the causes of the cutoff relationships. Throughout the session, Wally seemed like a frightened and caged creature to me. At moments he stood up and walked around the office. At other moments he sat looking at me, wordless, seemingly unresponsive.

At the end of the session I told him I needed to understand what he thought had happened between him and his children before we could plan some ways to contact them and invite them to a session. "I'll call you," Wally said. "I have to think about this."

Nearly three months went by before I heard from Wally again. Messages on his machine went unanswered, and I finally concluded that he didn't want to come back. Then came the call: "I need to see you. Can I see you?"

In our second meeting, Wally began tentatively, "When I

was twenty-one, I went to Vietnam—infantry. I doubt you'll understand. I never talk about this. No one who wasn't there can understand." There ensued a two-hour meeting, full of fits and starts, as Wally struggled for words to tell me about the events of a quarter century ago that were still shaping his life.

Like thousands of Vietnam veterans, Wally had lived in utter silence about his war experience. When he returned from the war, the unaccepting culture around him promoted his secret-keeping. While the full extent of any trauma can seldom be held by words, the anti–Vietnam War sentiments created a context ripe for pervasive concealment. Wally was unable to explore where it might be safe to speak and where it was not. He had never spoken of the war to his wife, whom he married after he returned. During their fifteen years together she was awakened repeatedly by his screaming nightmares, but he would simply tell her it was nothing and to go back to sleep. His children knew he had served in Vietnam but knew nothing of his experience.

"Only guys who were there understand," Wally said. "The guys in my group at the VA all say the same thing—that we just need to talk to each other." I told them that perhaps he was right, that fully comprehending what he had experienced might be beyond me, but that I would do my best to listen with care. I realized that much of my early work with Wally would involve bearing witness to his pain.

Over many sessions Wally told me his story, a story previously kept within the boundaries of groups of other veterans but secret from everyone else. Wally had loved a Vietnamese woman and had a daughter with her. He had planned to marry and bring his wife and little girl to the United States, even though he knew his parents would disapprove. But when he came to find them one day, he discovered that both had disappeared. No one could tell him whether they were alive or dead. For a long time after his return to the States he tried to forget about them. "Drinking helped," he told me. But from time to time his strategies to block them out failed. At those times he would stop drinking for a few weeks and secretly try to find out information about them. Bureaucratic roadblocks made his search impossible. Furtive and full of guilt, he became unavailable to his wife and children, who had no idea what was going on. After each unsuccessful attempt, Wally fell into depression and more drinking.

I worked with Wally alone for many months. He began to write letters to the missing woman and their daughter that he read to me in therapy. Gradually he concluded that he would never know what happened to them. Rather than trying to deny his grief and loss, as he had for so many years, only to have it unexpectedly attack his heart and soul, Wally permitted himself to keep their memories alive. Only now was he ready to deal with his other children. As we discovered, however, Wally's readiness to meet with Frankie and Eloise did not mean they were ready to meet with him.

Wally's calls to his children went unanswered. A letter to Frankie was returned unopened. He then wrote Eloise about his therapy with me, and she called and asked to see me alone. Following this meeting, Frankie joined her. Both children wanted to see their father, but their hurt and anger were enormous. Working with everyone's permission, I served at first as a shuttle diplomat. Wally's story was his own to tell, but preparing Eloise and Frankie to listen was my job. It was clear to me that Wally would first need to hear and acknowledge his children's pain. Only then would we be able to fill in all that was missing in their knowledge of their father. Wally's story needed to stand on its own, not serve as any kind of justification for what he had done to his children. Once Wally took responsibility for his actions toward his children, I believed they would be able to receive their father with empathy.

Our first sessions together were extremely difficult. Frankie was filled with rage at his father for years of physical abuse. Eloise cried, remembering times when Wally would get close, seem interested in her life, and then mysteriously push her away. I had prepared Wally to listen and not defend himself or justify his behavior in any way. His sorrow at what had happened to his children was deep and sincere. After Wally apologized for all the hurt he had caused, I suggested that we take a break for a month. During that time Wally visited each child's home and began to get to know his grandchildren. He also wrote to his ex-wife to tell her what was happening between him and their children, and to tell her how sorry he was for all the harm he caused her. She never replied, but she also didn't stand in the way of Wally and his children reconciling.

When we next met together, Wally looked at Eloise and Frankie and started by saying, "I still can't talk to you about what I need to talk about. I don't know what to do. The words won't come." Sobbing, Wally looked at me and said, "I'm sorry—I can't do this." Eloise and Frankie were bewildered. What did their father need to tell them that he couldn't or wouldn't speak of?

Wally and I had talked previously about the Vietnam War Memorial in Washington, D.C. He had spent years assiduously avoiding anything to do with the wall. He threw out magazines that mentioned it. He turned off the TV when it was shown. Seven months before he called me for the first time, he had finally gone to the wall with a buddy from his old unit. "It's what it made it possible for me to call you in the first place," he told me later.

I asked Eloise and Frankie if I might talk to their father alone briefly. "Would it help if you took them to the wall?" I asked. "Your children would get a glimpse of what happened to you, of what it means. You wouldn't have to talk, you know, unless you find that you want to."

And so Wally, Eloise, and Frankie went together to Washington to visit the wall. Wally showed them the names of the men he knew personally who had died. Later that day, as they sat together in Wally's hotel room, he began to open some of the secrets he had held for so long, including the story of his first love and his first daughter.

When they returned to see me, Frankie and Eloise each spoke about how their lives made a different kind of sense now. "I always felt like I was carrying some kind of shame," Eloise said, "and I never understood it. I used to think it was because my father drank, but that never fully explained it for me. I see now that it was my father's shame at not being able to protect his first family. I can put it down now and not pass it on to my children." Frankie went on to say that knowing he had a half-sister he would most likely never meet—indeed, he would never even know if she was still alive—made him feel very sad. "I think I have some sense now of what my father's turmoil had been about," Frankie said.

"Have you told us everything?" Frankie wanted to know. Wally replied, "There are still parts of this I haven't said. There are atrocities I can't speak about. Trust me that they happened. The wall holds them. It's enough."

As in many families where long-held secrets open between parents and adult children, Frankie and Eloise had to reinterpret their lives and reshape their relationships in the light of new and startling information. Their long-held view of their father as a complete and utter villain softened. In its place, they began to build a more complex tableau, one of a man who could love, suffer, cause pain, be frightened and selfish and confused—and ultimately do the work that was necessary to receive true forgiveness.

FINDING OUR VOICES

Ella Jackson, thirty-eight, called me in the midst of a terrible crisis. She had just discovered that her mentally handicapped sixteen-year-old daughter, Kay, had been repeatedly raped by two janitors at her school. Kay had kept this violent abuse a secret for four months, afraid, she said, of "getting anyone into trouble" and especially concerned that she might upset her mother. While she kept the secret, however, Kay began to show profound personality changes, becoming intensely hostile and angry toward family members, in contrast to her usual sweet and quiet nature. Finally, during a visit to a local public clinic, Kay found out she was pregnant. It was then that she revealed to her mother the terrible secret of the rapes.

Ella's initial request was for a meeting that would include several elders from her church. The clinic nurse who had delivered the news of Kay's pregnancy had also told Ella cavalierly that she would arrange an abortion. Since abortion was outside the bounds of her religion, Ella took Kay and fled. "I want to know that you'll respect and understand our faith," Ella explained. At our meeting, the church elders seemed primarily concerned to find out who I was and what I might offer to the family. Following their lead, I did not even mention the subject of abortion. Later, I learned, they held their own meeting and decided that because of the extraordinary circumstances of Kay's pregnancy and her disabilities, an abortion was both permissible and wise.

Two days after my meeting with the elders, we began our family therapy. When I first met this African-American family, which included Ella's husband, Samuel, forty-five, and her son, Emmett, nineteen, I was struck with just how overwhelmed they were. They reminded me of what I've witnessed in families that have just experienced a sudden and unexpected death. Since finding out about the rapes, no one in the family was performing the tasks that any family requires—cooking, laundry, opening the mail, paying the bills. Emmett had stopped going to his college classes because he was so worried about his sister and mother. Our initial work would have to be getting everyone back on their feet.

I spent a lot of time in our first family meeting attending to Kay. She seemed very frightened and confused. The word *rape* had not even been in her vocabulary. The janitors had initially lured her to the boiler room with promises of treats. After that they threatened her and insisted that she come with them. She told me she began yelling at everybody at home, but no one, including Kay herself, understood her call for help. I asked her if she was continuing to yell now. "Since they found out about it," Kay responded, looking around the room at her family, "that's when all my anger went away." With utter simplicity and clarity, this handicapped youngster captured the transformation that accompanies opening a coerced secret.

During this first meeting, Kay spoke in a whisper. I wondered to myself if this was her response to being raped or if she was frightened of me. As she left that day, Ella pulled me aside and told me that this was the way Kay always spoke. I wondered why, but tucked that away for later.

As I began to know the family that day, I was struck by an obvious paradox. Everyone proclaimed Ella as extremely strong and invincible. She had raised both of her children alone from their births until three years earlier, when she married Samuel. At the same time, the family seemed to treat her as if she was quite vulnerable. I felt confused, but I needed to attend to their obvious crisis first.

By our second session a few days later, Kay had transferred to another school. The family tried to bring criminal charges against the men who had assaulted her. Quickly they discovered that the district attorney would not press charges, stating that this was the word of two men—who, of course, denied the charges—against that of one mentally handicapped girl. The district attorney's office did not consider Kay a credible witness in her own behalf. The family was distraught. Samuel and Emmett told me they wanted to take matters into their own hands. I was able to convince them that this was a course of action that would put them at great risk. Nonetheless, the family desperately needed justice. They discovered that the janitorial company that leased these men's services to the school system knew of and had ignored other allegations of molestation. The family filed a civil suit. Two years after we concluded our work together, the suit was settled in their favor.

Ella had seen Kay through her abortion and worked closely with me to get her into rape crisis counseling, but now Ella seemed to be falling apart. Always the strong center of her entire family, she simply couldn't function. "I need to send Kay to my mother's for a while," Ella said in tears. "I can't help her. I don't know what to do." Samuel looked at me and said, "She won't eat, she can't sleep, she doesn't go to work. I've never seen her like this. What's happening?" At that moment Ella exclaimed, "Look what's happened to Kay—she'll never be able to learn to recognize danger." Ella seemed frantic. She repeated over and over, "She'll never be able to learn to recognize danger." I tried to recruit Ella's problem-solving skills; could she help Kay to learn to recognize danger? It was to no avail. "Recognizing danger" clearly had some deeper meaning that we would need to discover. "Would you like to see me by yourself next time?" I asked Ella. The rest of the family nodded with relief as Ella replied, "Most definitely."

Ella arrived alone, and before I could even ask how she was, she began to speak. "I was raped when I was a young girl. This was by a family member. I stopped thinking of it long ago. I said this'll never happen again. And now it's happened to Kay." After this revelation Ella fell silent. We sat quietly together for a few minutes. Then I gently asked Ella whom she had told when this happened to her. Rather than reply, she abruptly changed the subject. I tried to bring her back to where she had started, but it was if she had never spoken. Clearly she had told me a long-held secret and immediately felt tremendously unsafe. I would need to work with her to build a nest strong enough to hold the enormity of her experience. I thought we might approach it through other family history, so I invited Ella to tell me more about her upbringing and her extended family.

Ella was the oldest of four children. Her father died when she was seven years old, just a year after the birth of her youngest sister. Her mother, Bernice, had no skills and no income. After a year on welfare, Bernice sent Ella from their cramped apartment in the Bronx to live in Georgia with Bernice's older sister and brother-in-law. They were successful; they lived on a big parcel of land and had no children. "Why, of all the children, were you the one who was sent away?" I asked. "I have no idea," Ella replied diffidently.

Ella had been sent into a nightmare. She endured years of terrible physical and emotional abuse by her aunt. She was beaten capriciously; she was forced to do work far beyond the capacities of a young child; letters from her mother were kept from her. "Other children came to live there, too, but I was the only one she beat," Ella told me. Again I asked why she thought this was so, and again Ella shrugged and said, "I have no idea."

"I saved up enough money from baby-sitting, and when I was fifteen I ran away, going back to New York on a bus. I had no idea where my family was. I got pregnant with Emmett and the man left me. The same with Kay. I found my church—they took me in. Little by little I found my family," Ella told me. By her early twenties, never having finished high school, Ella had become the strong hub of her entire extended family. With two toddlers in tow, she went back to school and got a scholarship to a state university, supporting her young family on welfare until she graduated and got a good job. She never told her family about anything that happened to her in Georgia, and no one ever asked.

"What's been the impact of race and racism in your life?" I asked her. At that moment Ella drew in a deep breath. "Earlier you asked me why I thought I was the one they sent away, and I said to you I don't know. And earlier you asked me why I thought I was the one my aunt beat, and I said to you I didn't know. I know. It's because I am the darkest one in my family. I never said that to another soul."

Something profound had shifted between Ella and me. Something had made it possible for her to tell me, her white therapist, this painful secret. We talked for a long time about what it meant to her. Ella had done a lot of thinking about skin color, about the history of African-Americans in this country, about the effects of racism on her own family and in her daily life, but she had never spoken about it to anyone. I took her openness now as a sign that I had her permission to revisit the question she had run from early in our meeting.

"I want to go back to where we began this afternoon," I started. "Yes, I can do it now," Ella said. Two teenaged cousins had come regularly to work at her aunt and uncle's place. They quickly saw this nine-year-old girl as easy prey and started what became years of intimidation and sexual abuse. Each time they came, Ella would try to hide. But it was her job to bring them cold drinks, and they would taunt her through the window until she came out. Ella tried once to tell her aunt, but her aunt angrily refused to believe her. "In any case," her aunt declared, "if anything happened, it must be your fault. You must be leading them on." That was the last Ella ever spoke of it for twenty-six years.

Then in her early teens her uncle began to show a predatory sexual interest in her. Ella would come out of the shower to find him lurking. Finding her alone at breakfast, he would make unwelcome comments about her breasts. "There were guns in the house. I decided I would shoot him if he touched me. But then I knew I'd go to jail," Ella said. It was at that point that she ran away. It was a much more complex story than she had been able to tell me even an hour and a half earlier.

"How did you survive?" I asked. "Great literature saved my life," Ella replied. "I had a library card and I took out novels and plays and read them, and I saw that other people lived differently than I lived. And I knew that someday I would live differently, too."

I knew now what drove Ella's despairing cry that Kay would never be able to learn to recognize danger. I asked what she thought the differences were between her situation as a child and what had happened to her daughter. Ella thought the only difference in what happened to her and what happened to Kay was that she had the cognitive capacity to make sense of her situation and ultimately escape. I pointed out that there was a more important difference: "Kay is in a relationship with you, in a trusting, loving relationship. You hear her pain, you believe her. When this happened to you, no one believed you, and you were silenced."

When Ella got up to leave that day, she hugged me and said, "For the first time I don't feel ashamed, I don't feel guilty. As a matter of fact, I feel like I felt when I got on that bus leaving Georgia—I feel lighter, a bit lighter."

When Ella returned for the next meeting, she came with Samuel. I was uncertain whether she had told him about our meeting, but I felt clear that the secret she had shared with me had transformed into something private. Ella might determine that she wanted to open it to others, but no one else had a right to her story. It was quickly apparent that she had not yet told her husband of our conversation, but there was obviously a new spirit in her and in the entire family. She brought Kay back home, telling me that she realized sending her away was too reminiscent of having been sent away herself. Samuel told me, "Kay is so happy to be home. Emmett walks her to the bus so she can get to her new school. He's returned to college. And I'm just so glad to see Ella sleeping soundly at night." "I feel stronger," Ella said. "What's helped you to feel stronger?" I asked. "I think our talking the last time," Ella replied obliquely. "I see now she *can* recognize danger."

When I next met with Ella alone, I talked with her about my own belief that there might be others to whom she'd want to tell her story. I never assume that people who have been traumatized need years and years of therapy, nor that they will never recover. Rather, I want to form an alliance with a person's resilience and courage, of which Ella had plenty. And I want to promote further healing through family relationships and friendships. Generosity, empathy, and witnessing by others *outside* of therapy are the resources of lasting change.

"I want to talk all of this over with my own mother," Ella told me. "I don't want to blame her or make her feel guilty, but I've realized this was a critical thing that happened to me—she needs to know." Ella decided to go to her mother's apartment to talk. When she next saw me she told me that her mother had wept and held her as she told her terrible story. As often happens, after Ella told her mother this painful secret, her mother opened a secret from her own life. "After I finished speaking, she began to cry more and told me about being raped by a white man in the South when she was eighteen." Ella lifted her head and threw back her shoulders. "This is it, Evan," she declared. "This is at least three generations of women in my family who have been sexually abused and *silenced*. We will be silent no more."

Our next meeting included Kay. I hadn't seen her for several weeks, and I was struck that she now spoke in a normal tone of voice. Kay had given up her whisper. She hadn't yet heard her mother's secret, yet she somehow knew that speaking up was a good thing and that she could do it. I felt sure that she saw a new confidence in her mother, one that told her she could feel more confident. Kay told me all of the ways she knew to stay safe and that she had taught these to her girlfriend. She went on to complain that her school was getting jobs for the students, but that the special-education students were being paid less than the regular students for the same jobs. "It's unfair," Kay proclaimed. "I agree," I told her. "What do you want to do about it?" "I want to complain to the principal." We practiced a bit in the session. The next day she went to school, complained to the principal, and got the whole situation changed.

By now Ella had decided to tell her story to her younger sister, Dawn. Their relationship was a stormy one, as Dawn was quite jealous of Ella. Ella asked if she might bring Dawn to a session with me. Once again Ella had an opportunity to tell her story and receive support, furthering her own healing with each telling. "I wish I'd known," Dawn said. "All these years I thought you were the lucky one to be sent to Georgia. I thought you were comfortable while we were struggling. I resented you, and I was mad at Momma."

After her talk with Dawn, Ella gathered her mother and siblings at her mother's apartment to talk about skin color, breaking this terrible taboo that underpinned many relationships in the family. "I told them we can't pretend about this anymore," Ella told me after the meeting with her family. "It's all very complicated, and I think this conversation was just the beginning."

Finally, near the end of our eleven months of work together, Ella felt ready to tell the story of her sexual abuse to her husband and children. She had planned to do this in a family therapy meeting, but one day she arrived home in the middle of an argument between her husband and her children. They turned on her when she walked in the apartment, each insisting that she take their side. Tired of being seen as invincible by her husband and children, and wanting, finally, to share the load, Ella said, "Sit down. I have something to tell you." With that, she told them all her story. Then she firmly announced: "You cannot simply turn to me to solve problems in this family. We have to solve problems together."

Secrets of terror, intimidation, abuse, and dominance had robbed generations of women of their full voices in the Jackson family. Despite this, their strength remained. When Kay's terrible secret poured forth, Ella nearly collapsed, caught up in the tornado of memories of her own abuse. But soon she found her voice, first in the safety of the therapy room and our relationship, and then, most important, with her family. As Ella led the way, Kay gained courage to speak, and her mother opened a half-century-old secret. As with so many families that I've been honored to know, speaking one's own truth, with love and concern for others, brought forth more authentic lives and deeper, more reliable relationships.

AFTERWORD
SECRETS TODAY AND TOMORROW

~

In 1997, as I finished this book, newspapers, magazines, and talk radio were filled with the quandary of doctor-assisted suicide. A taboo issue ten years ago, assisting the suicide of a terminally ill person has in the last five years become an openly debatable concern. New technology capable of prolonging life in the face of terminal illness had brought with it new and painful dilemmas. At the same time, patient activism, especially among people with AIDS, has brought forth the notion that terminally ill people have the right to make decisions about how much suffering they can tolerate. And while lawyers, ethicists, doctors, and pundits put forth their pros and cons, the practice goes on in secret: A physician gives a dying patient a prescription, lecturing and warning him for twenty minutes on all of the wrong ways to use this medication that can result in his death. Without words, each knows the meaning of this conversation and the secret that will soon go to the grave. A doctor secretly helps a suffering cancer patient to die and then risks writing about it in a medical journal. A family splits in two when a grown son takes his mother to court to prevent her secret plan to visit Dr. Jack Kevorkian with her husband, who is affected with Alzheimer's disease. In a repeating macabre dance, Dr. Kevorkian acts out the secret of assisted suicide, followed by an intense media focus opening the secret.

In the summer of 1997, the Supreme Court of the United States ruled on the legality of doctor-assisted suicide. The Court decided to uphold the ban. Secrets attached to an illegal activity, one that is nonetheless practiced by at least one fifth of doctors and nurses today, remain. Misunderstandings about what terminally ill people are truly requesting continue in an atmosphere marked by mystification and indirection. Should a later Court rule that assisted suicide is a protected right, then there will be new secrets about people who end their lives too easily in a context of family or managed-care coercion. A new set of secrets is on the table, and we must deal with them.

When our parents were growing up, they and their parents didn't have to cope with secrets about assisted suicide. They dealt instead with other secrets. In 1998, or 2000, or 2050, new topics for secrets will surely appear. And like our parents and grandparents and great-grandparents, we and our children and grandchildren will continue to struggle with deceit, lies, safety, protection, searching for justice in relationships, and the burdens and joys of revelation as we create ourselves and each other through making, keeping, and opening secrets.

NOTES

CHAPTER 1 · LIVING THE DILEMMAS

1. For a thoughtful and informative discussion of privacy in the arenas of abortion and AIDS, see A. Brill, *Nobody's Business: The Paradoxes of Privacy* (New York: Addison-Wesley, 1990).

CHAPTER 2 · THE SCULPTURE OF FAMILY SECRETS

1. Peggy Papp, A.C.S.W., was the family therapist with this family. I worked as her consultant behind the one-way mirror.

2. This story is from the work of Janine Roberts, Ed.D. See her "On Trainees and Training: Safety, Secrets and Revelation," in E. Imber-Black (ed.), *Secrets in Families and Family Therapy* (New York: W.W. Norton and Co., 1993), for a discussion of this case in relationship to location. See E. Imber-Black and J. Roberts, *Rituals for Our Times: Celebrating, Healing and Changing Our Lives and Our Relationships* (New York: HarperCollins Publishers, 1992), for a discussion of using rituals to resolve and heal long-held secrets.

3. See Imber-Black and Roberts, *Rituals for Our Times,* for a thorough discussion of the relationship between rituals and healing of losses, and for the ways rituals enable life-cycle passages.

CHAPTER 3 · THE SECRET SOCIETY

1. L. Gruson, "Black Politicians Discover AIDS Issue," *The New York Times*, March 9, 1992, p. 7.

2. See L. W. Black, "AIDS, Secrets and African-American and African Caribbean Families," *HCSSW Update*, Spring 1994, for a discussion of this critical connection.

3. N. Boyd-Franklin, "Racism, Secret-Keeping, and African-

American Families," in E. Imber-Black (ed.), *Secrets in Families and Family Therapy* (New York: W.W. Norton and Company, 1993). This chapter is an excellent resource regarding secrets in African-American families as these are shaped and maintained by racism. It contains several examples of effective family therapy to address such secrets.

4.   E. Barkley-Brown, "African-American Women's Quilting: A Framework for Conceptualizing and Teaching African-American Women's History," *Signs: Journal of Women in Culture and Society* 14, (1989), pp. 921–29.

5.   N. Boyd-Franklin, *Black Families in Therapy: A Multi-systems Approach* (New York: Guilford Press, 1989).

6.   See Shirlee Taylor Haizlip's moving memoir *The Sweeter the Juice: A Family Memoir in Black and White* (New York: Simon and Schuster, 1994) for a powerful example of the effects of skin color secrets.

7.   P. Shenon, "Bitter Aborigines Sue for Stolen Childhoods," *The New York Times*, July 20, 1995, p. A4.

8.   D. M. Gitlitz, *Secrecy and Deceit: The Religion of the Crypto-Jews* (Philadelphia: Jewish Publication Society, 1996).

9.   R. Bragg, "Defending Smith, Stepfather Says He Also Bears Blame," *The New York Times*, July 28, 1995, p. A10.

10.   P. Druckerman, "Domestic Violence Gets More Attention Since Simpson Case," *Sentinel Magazine*, August 4, 1994, pp. 11, 14.

11.   See H. G. Lerner, *The Dance of Deception* for a discussion of women who fake orgasm. Lerner notes that a generation ago gynecological texts instructed doctors to encourage women in such secret pretense in order to "please" their husbands.

12.   See T. M. Phelps and H. Winternitz, *Capitol Games* (New York: Hyperion, 1992), for a complete discussion of what happened to Anita Hill when she tried to open this secret and what effect this episode had on the secret of sexual harassment in the workplace.

13.   P. Orenstein, "Looking for a Donor to Call Dad," *The New York Times Magazine*, June 18, 1995, pp. 28–35, 42, 50, 58.

14.   See N. King, *Speaking Our Truth* (New York: Harper Perennial, 1995) for a beautiful and moving collection of narratives by men who were sexually abused as children.

CHAPTER 4 • "WE KNOW WHAT'S BEST FOR YOU TO KNOW"

1. J. H. Jones, *Bad Blood: The Tuskegee Syphilis Experiment* (New York: Free Press, 1993), pp. 5–6.

2. Ibid., p. 219.

3. A lawsuit was filed on behalf of the men and their heirs and settled out of court, with the government agreeing to pay $10 million. This money was to be divided into $37,500 cash payments to subjects who were still living in 1973, $15,000 to the heirs of the deceased, $16,000 to living members of the control group in the study, and $5,000 to the heirs of the control group. Fewer than 120 subjects were still alive. Finding the heirs of the deceased proved to be extremely difficult. Any money not claimed after three years reverted to the U.S. government.

4. M. Lee and B. Shlam, *Acid Dreams: The C.I.A., LSD and the Sixties Rebellion* (New York: Grove Press, 1985).

5. In the 1960s research began to show that the acceptance of difference in adoptive families is highly associated with successful adoption. See D. Kirk, *Shared Fate: A Theory of Adoption and Mental Health* (New York: Free Press, 1964). This research was largely ignored by adoption professionals. For further discussion of this issue, see A. Hartman, "Secrecy in Adoption," in E. Imber-Black (ed.), *Secrets in Families and Family Therapy* (New York: W.W. Norton and Co., 1993).

6. While this belief may have been supported in earlier times when women were shamed for out-of-wedlock births, this is often no longer the case. Yet many who support closed adoption today still insist on this position. In fact, current research supports the opposite: 35 to 45 percent of birth parents decline to follow through on giving their baby up for adoption under conditions of closed adoption, while only 6 to 15 percent change their minds in open adoption. See B. M. Rappaport, *The Open Book: A Guide to Adoption Without Tears* (New York: Macmillan, 1992).

7. An earlier principle in adoption held that birth mothers would not relinquish their children unless they were guaranteed confidentiality. Clearly, this belief was rooted in the stigma heaped on these women. Evidence now points to a different position held by

most birth mothers. Since 1980 Michigan has given birth mothers an opportunity to choose whether or not to have identifying information about them made available to their children over eighteen. Ninety-eight percent have chosen to make this information available.

8. See K. D. Fishman, "Problem Adoptions," *The Atlantic*, September 1992, pp. 37–69, for an excellent discussion of the difficulties in special-needs adoptions, including cases illustrative of the ways critical information is withheld by agencies.

9. To view the multiple levels of lies and secrets, and the tragic psychological and social effects of these abductions, see the 1985 Academy Award–winning film *The Official Story*.

10. E. Rohter, "El Salvador's Stolen Children Face a War's Darkest Secret," *The New York Times*, July 30, 1996, pp. AI, A6.

11. Ibid.

12. In another example of secrecy in adoption resulting in evil and exploitation supported by a government, thousands of Australian Aborigine children were kidnapped and placed with white families or put in orphanages. Between 1918 and 1960, these children were stolen from their families by a government that believed they were "rescuing" children from dark-skinned people, who they believed were incapable of raising children. Some were kidnapped immediately after birth while their mothers recovered from their delivery. Of special interest were mixed-race children. Many of the children of what is now called the "Stolen Generation" were either not told they were adopted or were told they were Fijian, Samoan, or Polynesian. P. Shenon, "Bitter Aborigines Sue for Stolen Childhoods," *The New York Times*, July 20, 1995, p. A4.

13. In fact, success rates for live births vary widely from program to program. In 1994 Mount Sinai Hospital Center of New York City, considered a premier fertility center, had to pay $4 million to hundreds of childless infertility patients to settle a suit over false success-rate claims. Mount Sinai claimed a 20 percent success rate when, in fact, the true rate was far lower, between 10.9 percent and 13.7 percent. Some clinics artificially boost their success rates by counting pregnancies rather than live births, despite a very high miscarriage rate when using reproductive technologies.

14. P. Orenstein, "Looking for a Donor to Call Dad," *The New York Times Magazine*, June 18, 1995, p. 35.

15. R. D. Nachtigall, "Secrecy: An Unresolved Issue in Donor Insemination," *American Journal of Obstetrics and Gynecology* 168, no. 6 (1993), pp. 1846–51.

16. Orenstein, "Looking for a Donor to Call Dad," pp. 42, 50, 58.

17. S. Chartrand, "Parents Recall Ordeal of Prosecuting an Artificial Insemination Fraud Case," *The New York Times*, March 15, 1992, p. A16.

18. G. Cowley, A. Murr, and K. Springen, "Ethics and Embryos," *Newsweek*, June 12, 1995, pp. 66–67. Also, for a firsthand story by one of Asch's patients whose embryos were stolen, see D. Challender (as told to Susan Litwin), *Redbook*, December 1995, pp. 84–87, 116–18.

19. Cowley, Murr, and Springen, "Ethics and Embryos," p. 66.

20. A. Easley, "University of California at Irvine Settles," *Business Wire*, July 18, 1997.

21. For a description of many cases that emerged in the 1980s and 1990s, see E. Burkett and F. Bruni, *A Gospel of Shame: Children, Sexual Abuse, and the Catholic Church* (New York: Viking Press, 1993).

22. Cheryl Swenson, one of dozens of children abused by Father James Porter, and witness to the abuse of other children, tried to tell Father Armando Annunziato, who screamed at her and shut the door in her face. When she tried to tell a nun, she was made to stand up in front of her class and apologize for saying such a thing about Father Porter. Ibid., pp. 9–10.

23. CNN Special, "Fall from Grace, Part Four: Alleged Victims Band Together," November 14, 1993. Transcript from Journal Graphics, p. 4.

24. *Long Beach Press Telegram.* "New Law Gives Hope to Victims." July 10, 1996, p. B8.

25. K. Murray, *Reuter.* "Texas Catholic Church Must Pay $120 Million." July 24, 1997.

26. A *New York Times* computer analysis of the death rates for infants of normal weight born at public hospitals in New York City

showed a substantially higher death rate than for infants born at private hospitals. Serious birth injuries were also substantially higher. Such information has been kept secret from the general public. *The New York Times*, March 5, 1995, pp. AI, B2.

27.   See S. Woolhandler and D. U. Himmelstein, "Extreme Risk—The New Corporate Proposition for Physicians," *The New England Journal of Medicine*, December 21, 1995, pp. 1706–7.

28.   P. Gray, "Gagging the Doctors," *Time*, January 8, 1996, p. 50.

29.   R. Pear, "Doctors Say H.M.O.'s Limit What They Can Tell Patients," *The New York Times*, December 21, 1995, p. BI3.

30.   T. Lewin, "Questions of Privacy Roil Arena of Psychotherapy," *The New York Times*, May 22, 1996, pp. AI, D20.

31.   In 1996–97 I had the opportunity in my capacity as president of the American Family Therapy Academy to participate in a coalition of all of the presidents of the major mental-health organizations to create a bill of rights in response to managed-care erosions of patient confidentiality and other issues of secrecy and health-care policy and practice. This coalition was historic, as it was the first time that all of these organizations were willing to put aside their own turf protection and guild issues to address a common concern.

CHAPTER 5 • TALK SHOW TELLING VERSUS AUTHENTIC TELLING

1.   For a complete discussion of the history of talk television and the wider context in which it is embedded, see J. A. Heaton and N. L. Wilson, *Tuning In Trouble: Talk TV's Destructive Impact on Mental Health* (San Francisco: Jossey-Bass, 1995).

2.   J. Whitney, "Why I Simply Had to Shut Up," *New York Daily News*, June 11, 1995, p. 6.

3.   Talk television is extremely profitable. A typical show costs about $200,000 a week to produce, compared to an average $1 million a week for a drama. In 1992, for instance, Oprah Winfrey's show earned $157 million, Phil Donahue's show $90 million, and Sally Jessy Raphael's show $60 million (Heaton and Wilson, *Tuning In Trouble*).

4. *Newsweek*, March 20, 1995, p. 30; *The New York Times*, March 12, 1995, p. A22, and March 14, 1995, pp. A1, A10.

5. The tragedy attached to this particular show distracts our attention from an important dimension of many of these programs, which is that they commonly pander to feelings of homophobia, racism, and sexism. See Heaton and Wilson, *Tuning In Trouble*, for a full discussion of this issue.

6. Whitney, "Why I Simply Had to Shut Up."

7. J. A. Heaton, and N. L. Wilson, "Tuning In to Trouble," *MS. Magazine*, September/October 1995 V. 6, # 2, pp. 45–48.

8. See R. Cialdini, *Influence: How and Why People Agree to Things* (New York: William Morrow, 1984), for a discussion regarding studies on compliance showing that once people agree to participate in something, they often go along with much more than they originally intended.

9. See L. Armstrong, *Rocking the Cradle of Sexual Politics* (New York: Addison-Wesley, 1994), for a thoughtful discussion of the impact of such "experts" on talk television when the topic is incest. According to Armstrong, such a structure diminishes the issue, reducing it from one with crucial political implications to simply a matter of personal opinion.

10. Jamie Diamond, "Life After Oprah," *Self*, August 1994, pp. 122–25, 162; also see Heaton and Wilson, *Tuning In Trouble*, for a thoughtful critique of the questionable quality of such "aftercare."

11. *Sally Jessy Raphael Show*, November 29, 1994, "We Want Mom to Leave Her Cheating Husband"; transcript by Journal Graphics.

CHAPTER 6 • CONCEALING AND REVEALING

1. For an insightful discussion of AIDS and secrets, see L. W. Black, "AIDS and Secrets," in E. Imber-Black (ed.), *Secrets in Families and Family Therapy* (New York: W.W. Norton and Co., 1993). Black's work highlights the multileveled secret of HIV and AIDS, examining culture, community, institutions, and family.

2. See M. Mason, "Shame: Reservoir for Family Secrets," in E. Imber-Black (ed.), *Secrets in Families and Family Therapy* (New York: W.W. Norton and Co., 1993).

3. For a moving example of a secret of parentage, adoption, and skin color emerging at a funeral, see N. Boyd-Franklin, "Racism, Secret-Keeping, and African-American Families," in E. Imber-Black (ed.), *Secrets in Families and Family Therapy* (New York: W.W. Norton and Co., 1993).

4. J. Katz, "The Tales They Tell in Cyberspace Are a Whole Other Story," *The New York Times*, January 23, 1994, section two, pp. I, 30.

5. T. Gabriel, "Some On-Line Discoveries Give Gay Youths a Path to Themselves," *The New York Times*, July 2, 1995, pp. AI, AI6.

6. From a description of the Adoptees Mailing List, America Online.

7. G. Kolata, "When Patients' Records Are Commodities for Sale," *The New York Times*, November 15, 1995, pp. AI, CI4.

8. J. W. Roberts, "Health Care Bill Sacrifices Our Privacy," *The New York Times*, August 7, 1996, p. AI6.

9. For an excellent discussion of the paradoxes of "outing," see A. Sullivan, *Virtually Normal: An Argument About Homosexuality* (New York: Alfred A. Knopf, 1995). Sullivan argues that outing is promoted as a process to diminish stigma and secrecy, but since it is based on shock, terror, and shame, it actually promotes it.

CHAPTER 7 • SELF-SECRETS

I. While much is made of the cost of illegal immigrants to the United States and to individual states, the government services provided to undocumented immigrants is more than offset by the taxes they pay. According to the Urban Institute, a nonpartisan research organization, documented and undocumented immigrants pay $70.3 billion a year in taxes, while receiving $42.9 billion in services. That such information is not widely known by the public contributes to an atmosphere where secrecy is driven by prejudice. See R. Rayner, "What Immigration Crisis?" *The New York Times Magazine*, January 7, 1996, pp. 26–31, 40, 46, 50, 56, for a carefully researched and beautifully written article detailing the ways that undocumented immigration has been framed as a political issue exploiting racism and xenophobia.

2. See C. Siebert, "The DNA We've Been Dealt," *The New York Times Magazine*, September 17, 1995, for a personal and moving discussion of one man's struggle to decide about genetic testing for an incurable heart condition that killed his own father. Through interviews with geneticists, members of a large extended family facing an inherited illness, and thoughtful reflections on his own situation, Siebert helps us ponder the question of when to keep a secret from ourselves.

3. This story is adapted from G. L. Sanders, "The Love That Dares to Speak Its Name: From Secrecy to Openness in Gay and Lesbian Affiliations," in E. Imber-Black (ed.), *Secrets in Families and Family Therapy* (New York: W.W. Norton and Co., 1993).

4. For an excellent and thorough discussion of eating disorders and secrecy, see L. G. Roberto, "Eating Disorders as Family Secrets," in E. Imber-Black, (ed.), *Secrets in Families and Family Therapy* (New York: W.W. Norton and Co., 1993).

5. These figures are from *All Things Considered*, National Public Radio, "Illinois Legislature Set to Debate Mandatory AIDS Testing," March 7, 1995.

6. J. Purnick, "When AIDS Testing Collides with Confidentiality," *The New York Times*, May 18, 1995, p. B4.

CHAPTER 8 • MAKING AND BREAKING COMMITMENTS

1. S. S. Hendrick, "A Generic Measure of Relationship Satisfaction," *The Journal of Marriage and the Family* 50 (1988), pp. 93–98. In this study, secrets that partners knew were being kept were correlated with relationship satisfaction, while secrets that partners did not know about were correlated with relationship dissatisfaction.

2. See Rosmarie Welter-Enderlin's wonderful chapter, "Secrets of Couples and Couples' Therapy," in E. Imber-Black (ed.), *Secrets in Families and Family Therapy* (New York: W.W. Norton and Co., 1993), pp. 47–65, for a discussion of the ways that "telling all" in couples, in fact, leads to secrets. Welter-Enderlin brings both an American perspective and a European one to her work with couples' secrets.

3. I originally described this therapy in "We've Got A Secret!

A Non-marital Marital Therapy," in A. Gurman (ed.), *Casebook of Marital Therapy* (New York: Guilford Press, 1985).

4. Cheryl Muzio, "Lesbians Choosing Children: Creating Families, Creating Narratives," *Journal of Feminist Family Therapy* 7, nos. 3–4 (1995), pp. 33–45, describes the painful process of a lesbian couple's adoption of a child. Since many adoption agencies refuse to work with lesbian couples, the secrecy required led each member of the couple to become more and more critical of the other, lest any hint of their lesbianism appear. The couple rearranged their home and their clothing and expunged any sign of affection between them.

5. In the National Lesbian Health Care Survey of nearly two thousand lesbian women, only 27 percent were out to all of their family members, while 88 percent were out to their gay and lesbian friends, and just 17 percent were out to coworkers. C. Alexander, "The State of Lesbian Mental Health," *In The Family* 1, no. 3 (1996), p. 6.

6. See E. Imber-Black and J. Roberts, *Rituals for Our Times: Celebrating, Healing and Changing Our Lives and Our Relationships* (New York: HarperCollins, 1992), for a discussion of the critical importance of rituals in expressing beliefs and shaping identity.

CHAPTER 9 • BALANCING CANDOR AND CAUTION

1. See A. C. Bernstein, *Flight of the Stork: What Children Think (and When) about Sex and Family Building* (Indianapolis: Perspectives Press, 1994), for some wonderful examples of how young children make sense of information about sex and reproduction. Bernstein's work helps parents understand the cognitive and emotional processes of very young children without oversimplification.

2. According to a careful study, 16 percent of women had been sexually abused by a relative before age eighteen, 4.5 percent by their own fathers. See D. E. Russell, *The Secret Trauma: Incest in the Lives of Girls and Women* (New York: Basic Books, 1986).

3. See D. Miller, *Women Who Hurt Themselves: A Book of Hope and Understanding* (New York: Basic Books, 1994), for an extended discussion of the deleterious effects on children of secret-keeping when they are being abused by parents or other caretakers.

4. M. Sheinberg, F. True, and P. Fraenkel, "Treating the

Sexually Abused Child: A Recursive, Multimodal Program," *Family Process* 33, no. 3 (1994), p. 265.

5. The work of Marcia Sheinberg, M.S.W., and her colleagues in the consortium "Making Families Safe for Children," sponsored by the Ackerman Institute in New York City, pays special attention to the needs of abused children to gain a sense of their own power and agency after the sexual abuse has been discovered. In a therapy model using individual, group, and family therapy, care is taken to help children to decide who they want to talk with about the abuse. See Sheinberg, True, and Fraenkel, "Treating the Sexually Abused Child: A Recursive, Multimodal Program."

6. See C. Ahrons, *The Good Divorce: Keeping Your Family Together When Your Marriage Comes Apart* (New York: HarperCollins, 1994), for an excellent research-based popular book that addresses age-appropriate needs of children in divorced families.

7. See M. Tasker, *How Can I Tell You: Secrecy and Disclosure with Children When a Family Member Has AIDS* (Bethesda, MD: Association for the Care of Children's Health, 1992), for an extended essay dealing with disclosing HIV/AIDS to children. The book is filled with many moving and courageous stories, and includes transcripts of conversations.

8. See L. R. Melina, *Making Sense of Adoption: A Parent's Guide* (New York: Harper and Row, 1989), for many fine strategies and activities that parents can implement to keep adoption and third-party conception open topics with their children.

CHAPTER 10 • PRIVATE INVESTIGATIONS

1. This story is from the work of Peggy Papp, reported on in "Secrets Between Parents and Children," in E. Imber-Black (ed.), *Secrets in Families and Family Therapy* (New York: W.W. Norton and Co., 1993).

2. This finding is from a preliminary qualitative clinical research study at North Central Bronx Hospital conducted by Judy Cobb, Ph.D., Eliana Korin, Psy. Lic., and Barbara Iwler, M.S.W.

3. My thanks to Judy Cobb, Ph.D., Helen Quinones, Ph.D., Charles Soule, Ph.D., Rosa Ramirez, Ph.D., and Rosemarie Alonzo-

Chatterton, M.S., for their wonderful work with Dominican families in the Bronx, New York, which focused my attention on the critical issues of untold stories that must be told when teens and parents have been separated.

CHAPTER 11 • IT'S NEVER TOO LATE

1. For an academic discussion of this family's therapy, see E. Imber-Black, "Secrets in Families and Family Therapy: An Overview," in E. Imber-Black (ed.), *Secrets in Families and Family Therapy* (New York: W.W. Norton and Co., 1993), pp. 4–28, and E. Imber-Black, "Ghosts in the Therapy Room," *The Family Therapy Networker*, May–June 1995, pp. 19–29. Working with this family altered much of my prior thinking about families and secrets and helped me to challenge prevailing orthodoxies in the family-therapy field. I have discussed their impact on my thinking in E. Imber-Black, "Odysseys of a Learner," in D. Efron (ed.), *Journeys: Expansion of the Strategic-Systemic Therapies* (New York: Brunner-Mazel, 1986), pp. 3–29.

INDEX

ABOUT THE AUTHOR

Evan Imber-Black, Ph.D., is Director of Program Development at the Ackerman Institute for the Family in New York City and Professor of Psychiatry at the Albert Einstein College of Medicine. She is also immediate past-president of the American Family Therapy Academy. Her previous books include *Rituals for Our Times* (with Janine Roberts, Ed.D.) and the professional book *Secrets in Families and Family Therapy*, which she edited. The mother of two grown children, she lives with her husband in Westchester, where she practices family therapy.